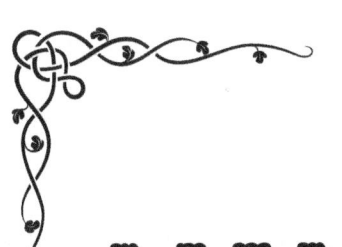

MANDALA SAFARI

Colouring Book for Adults Therapy and Antistress

Coloring books are a simple and enjoyable way to improve your mental and emotional well-being. Whether you're looking to relax after a long day or boost your creativity and focus, this is a coloring book for all those occasions.

I hope you have fun!

Anne Ginger

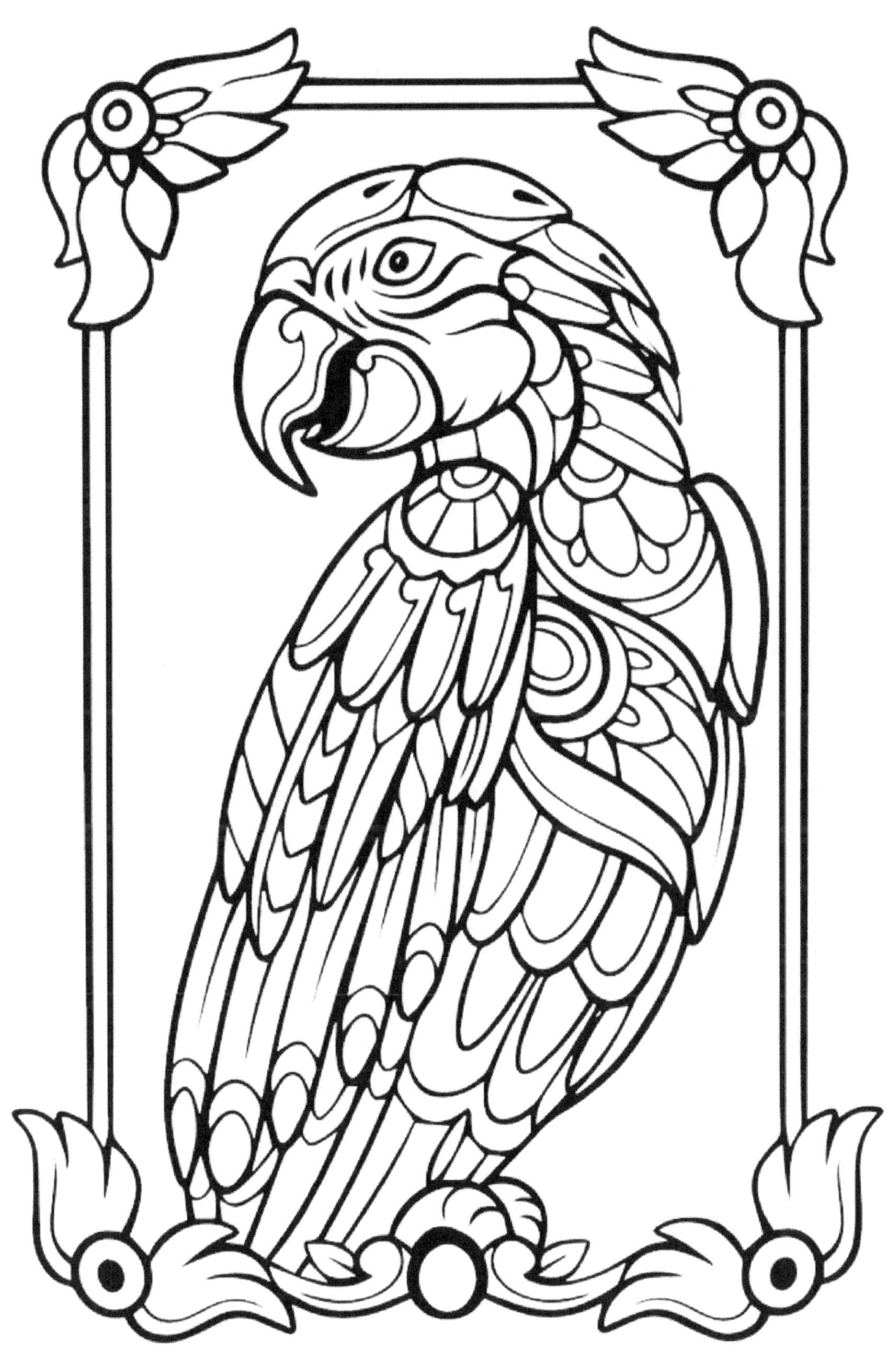

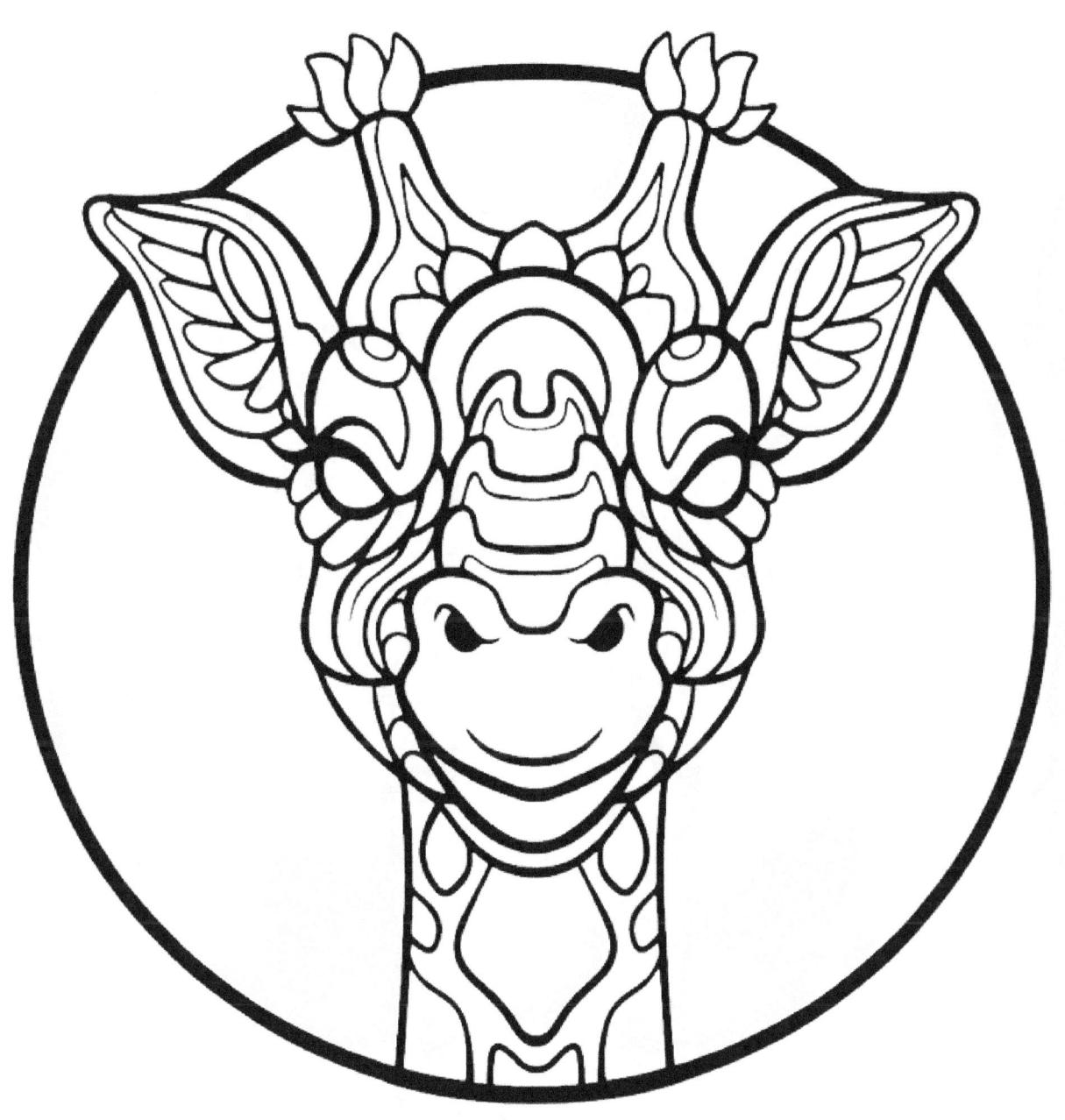

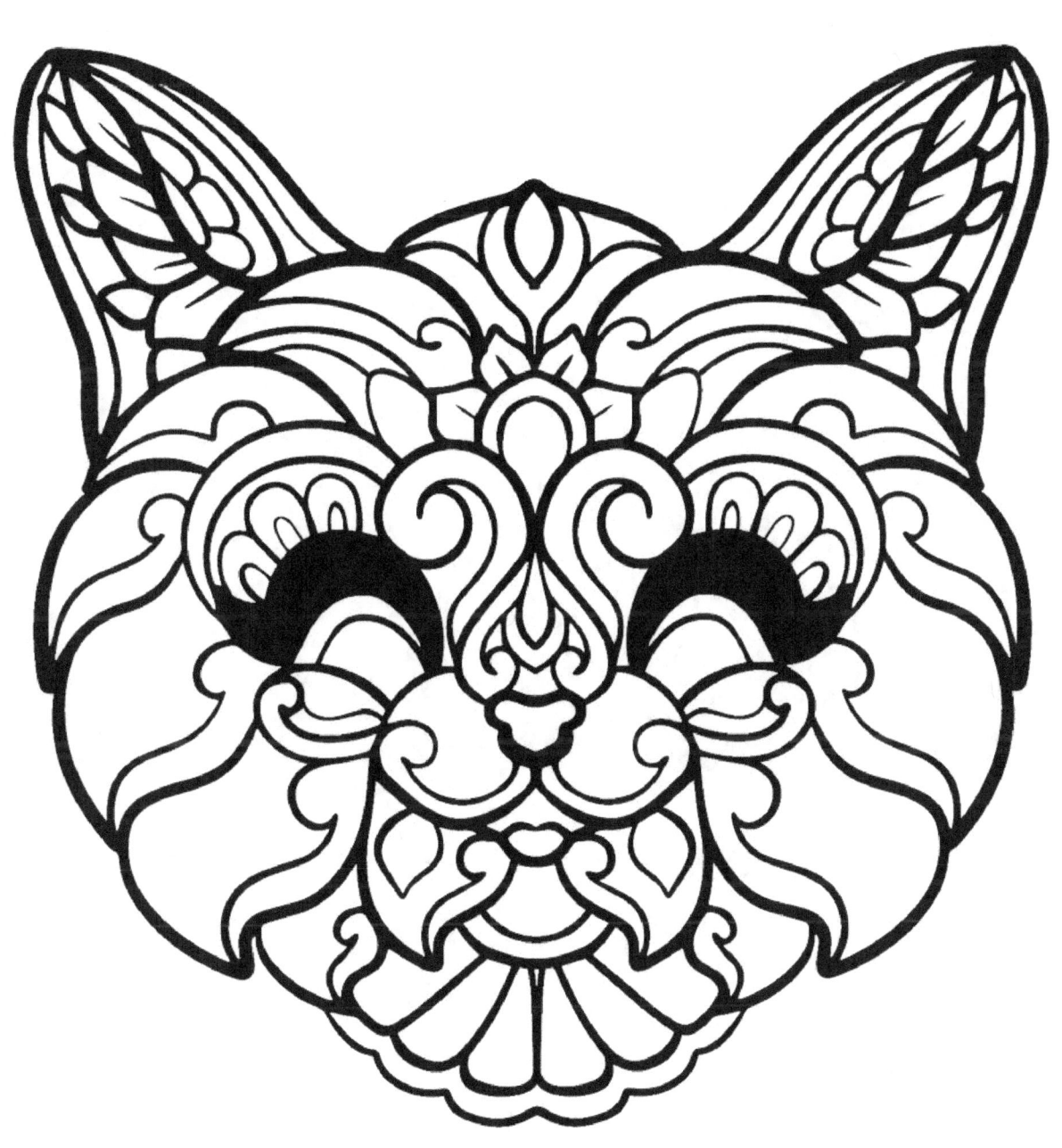

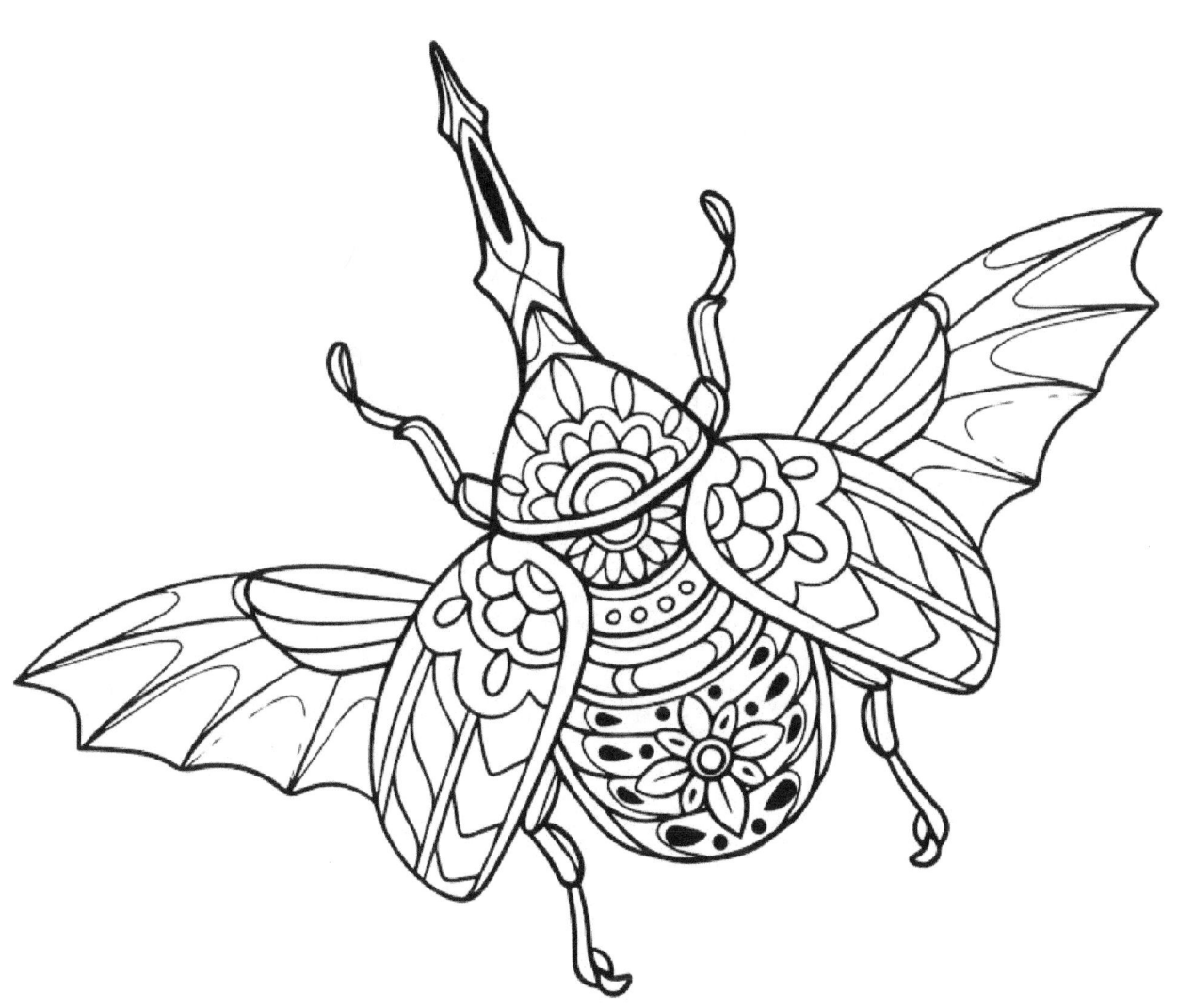

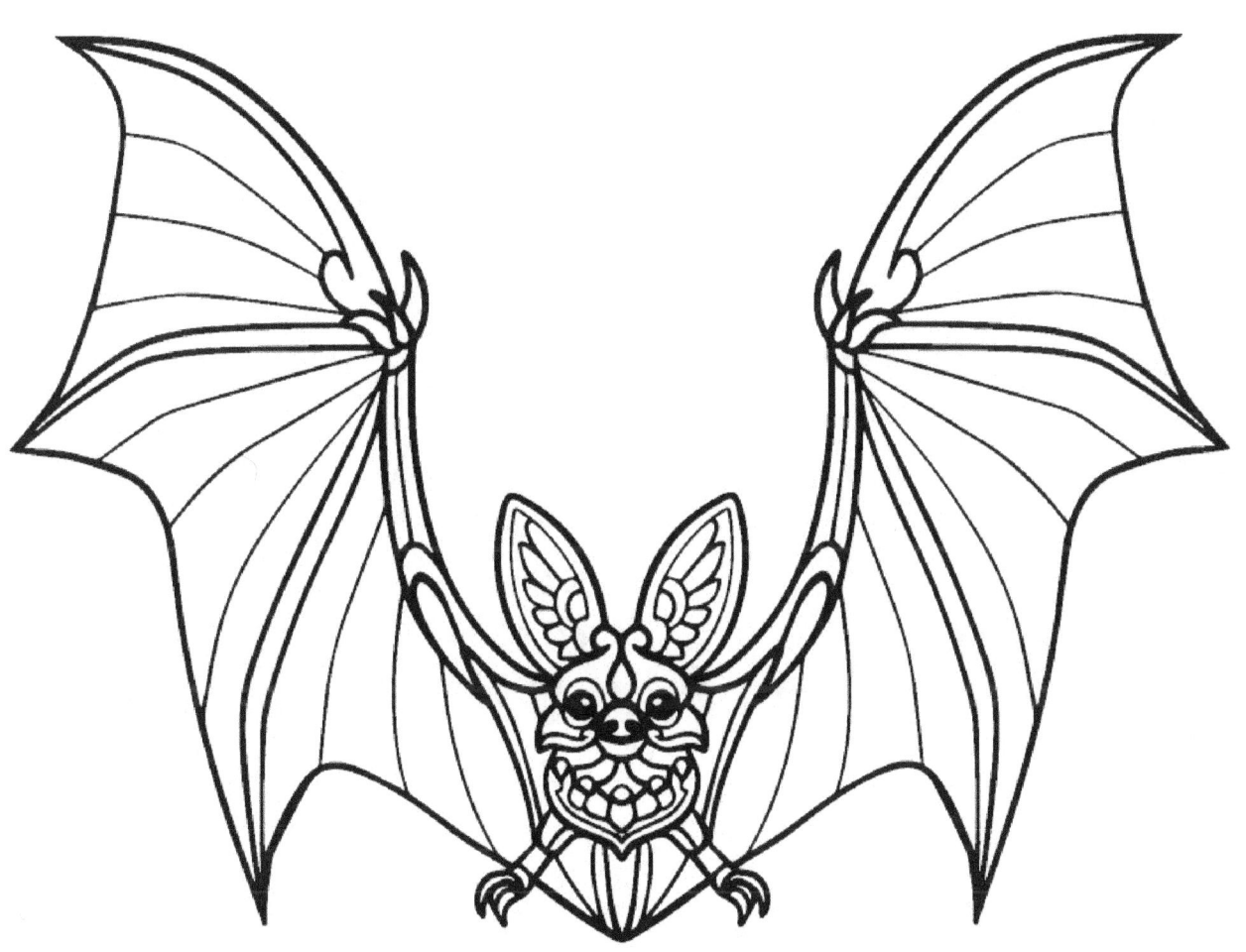

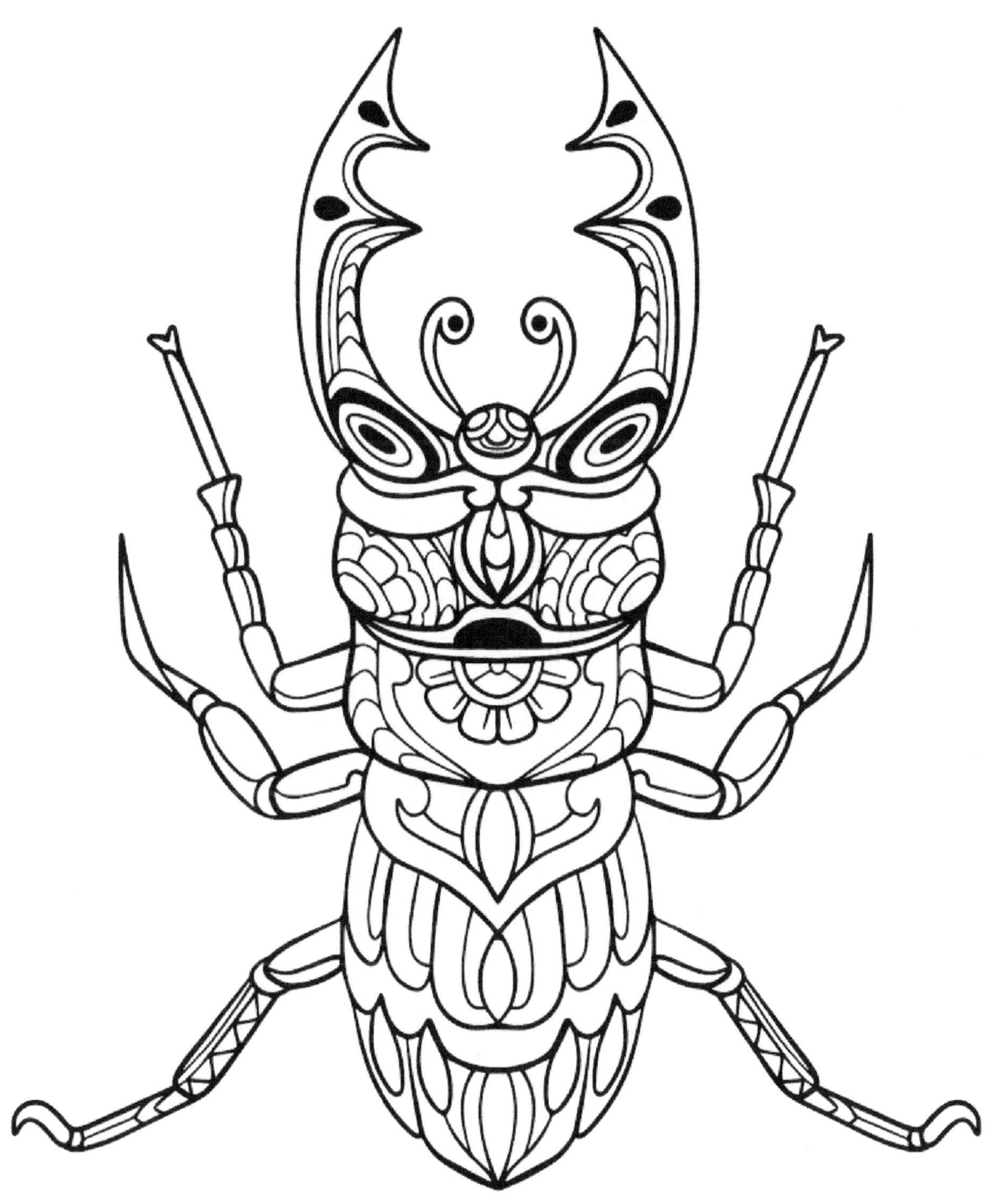

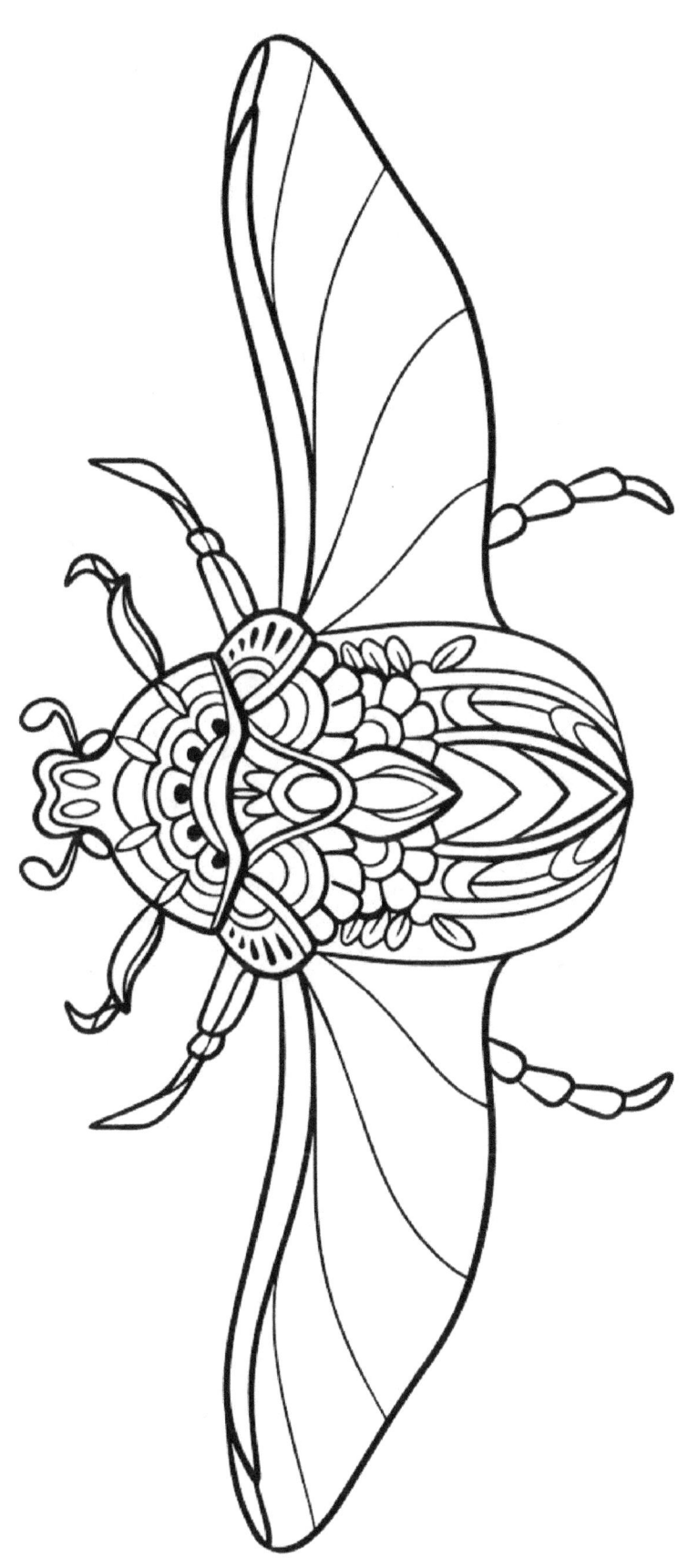

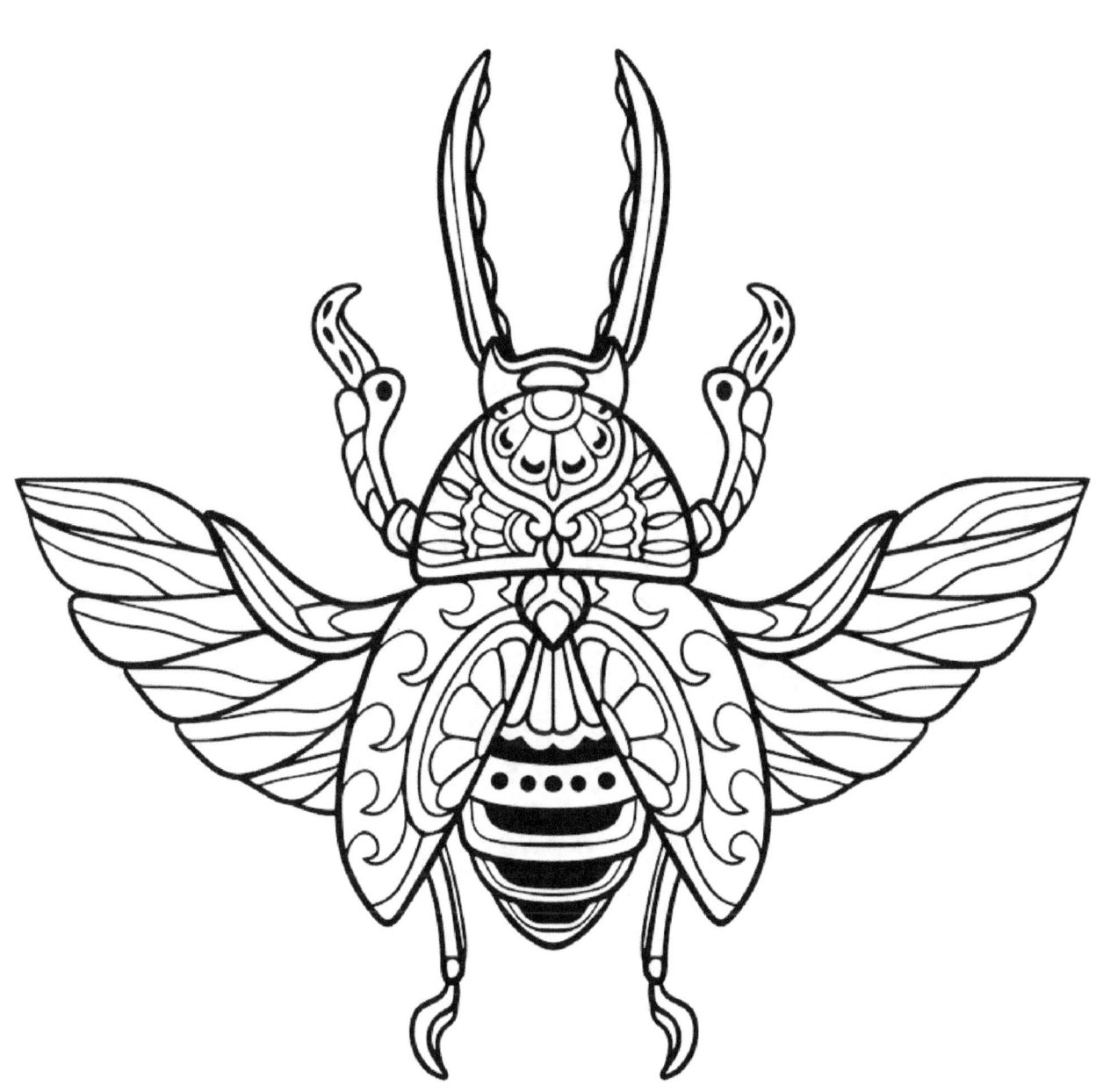

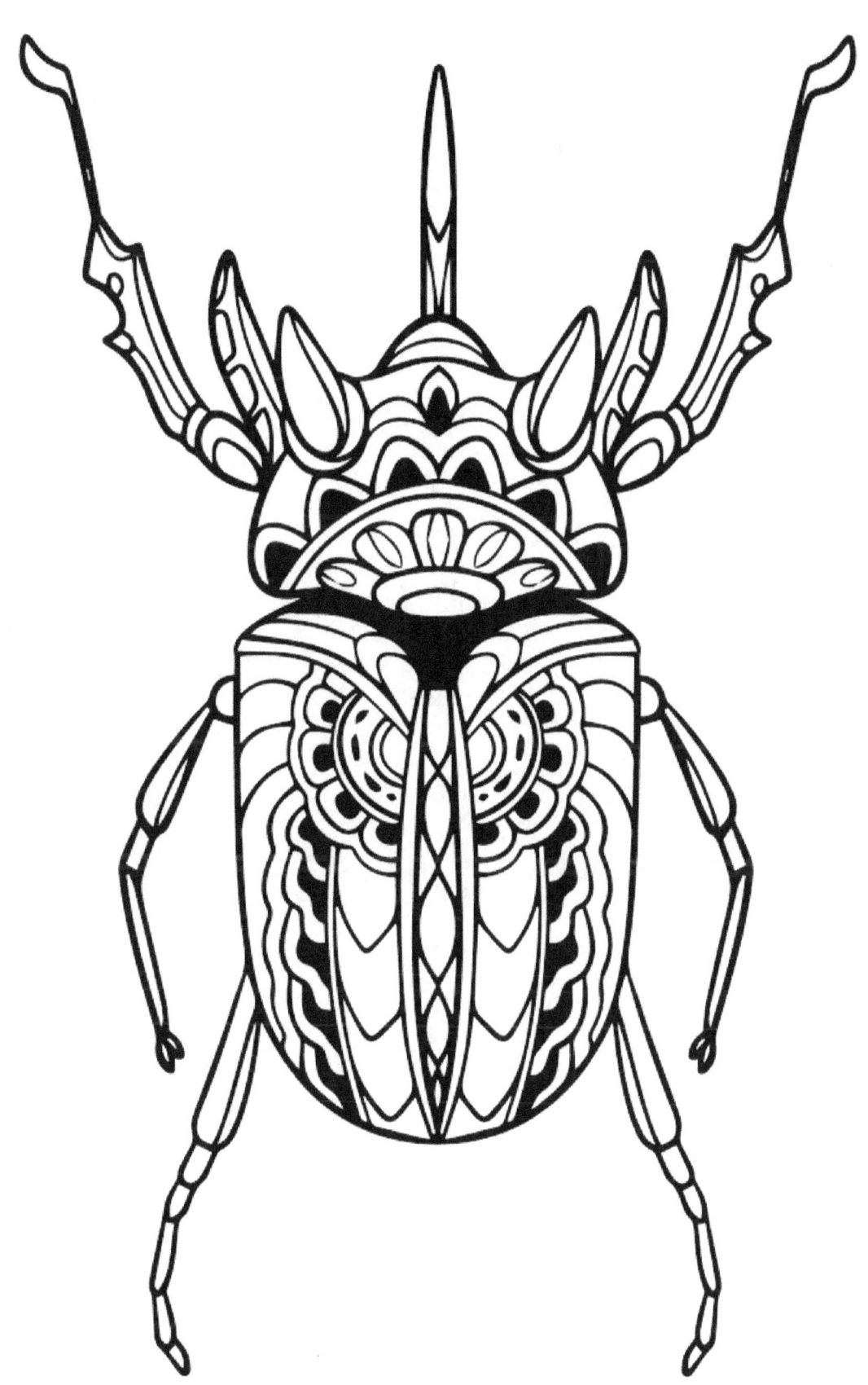

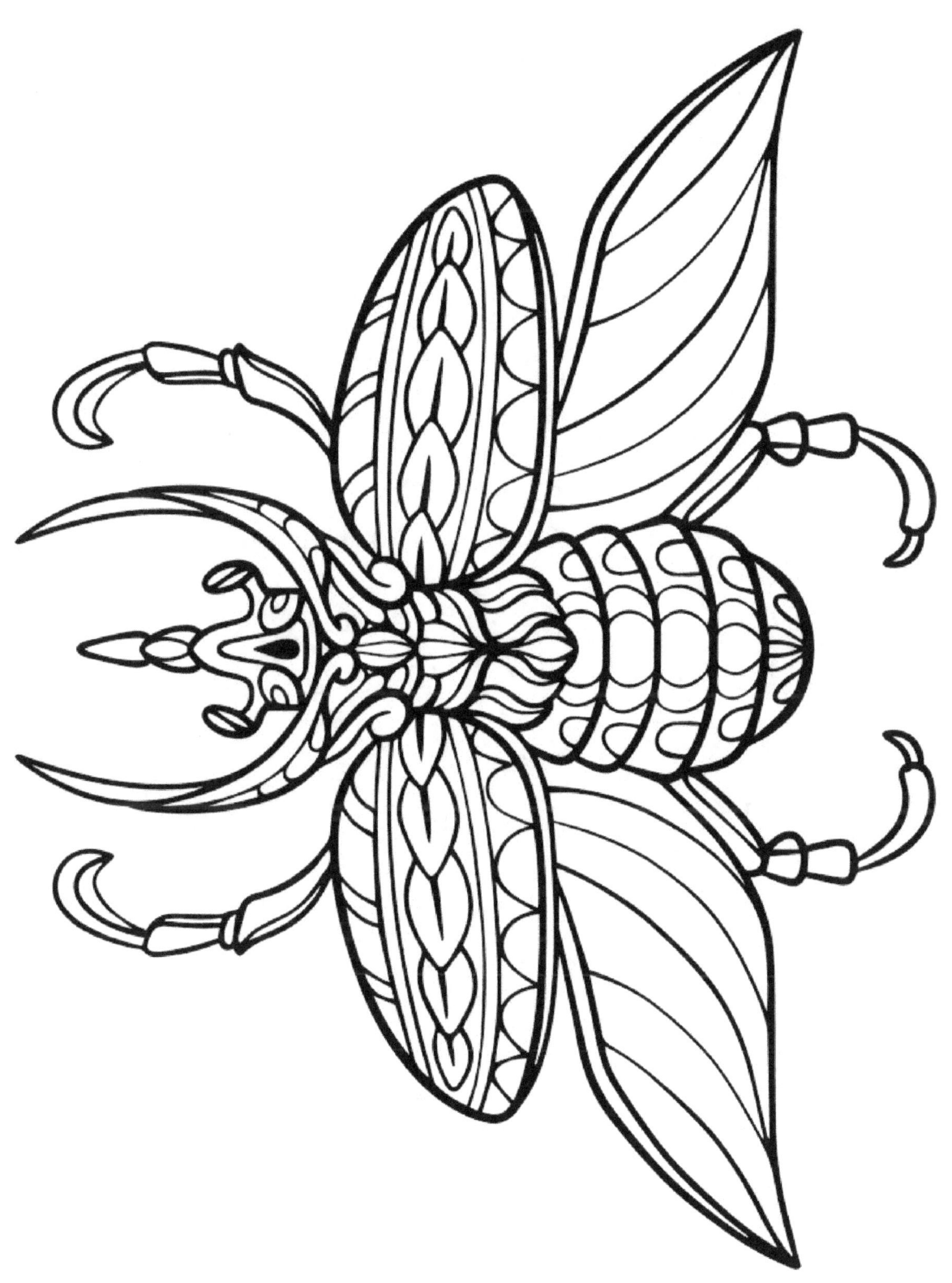

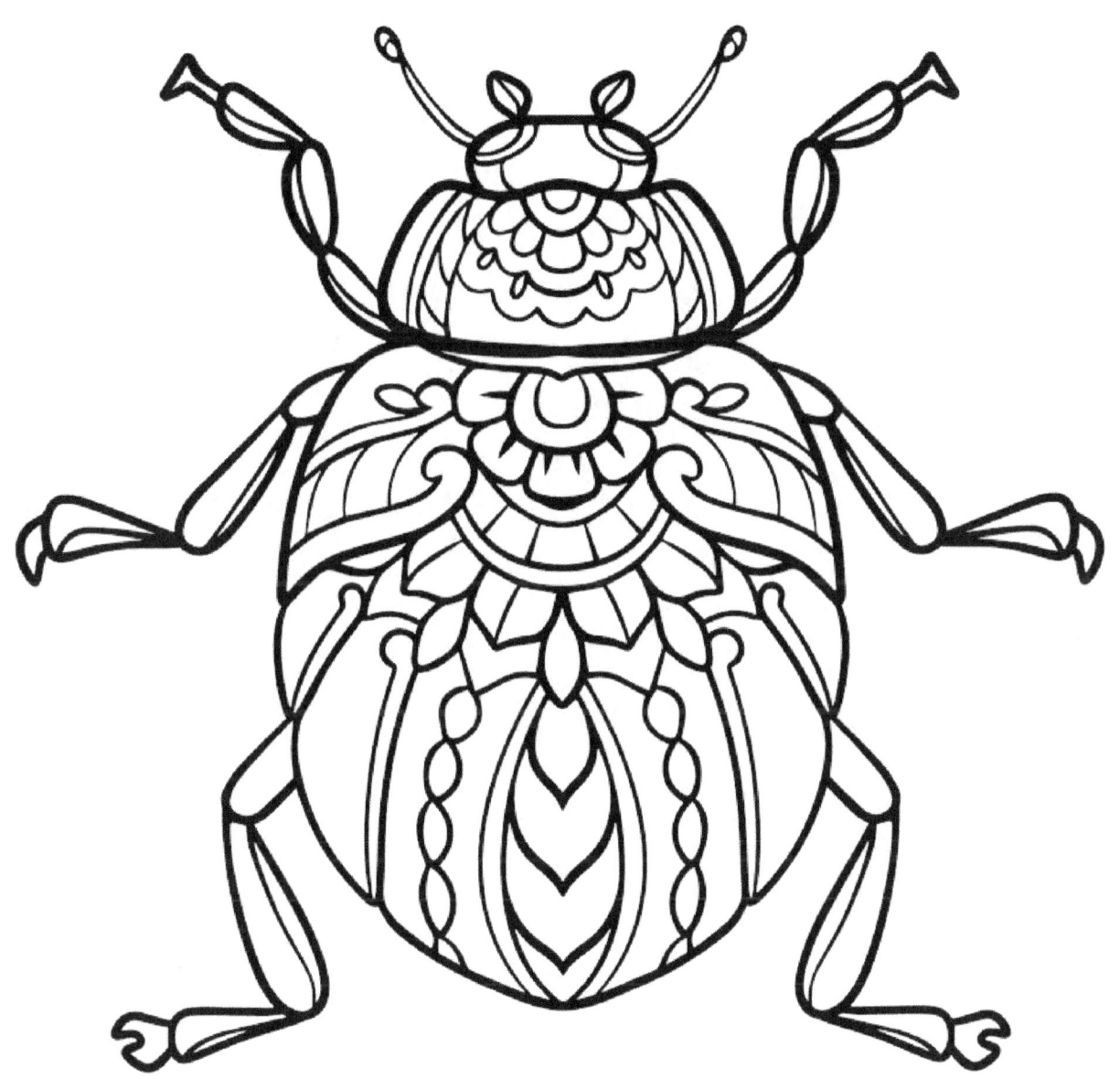

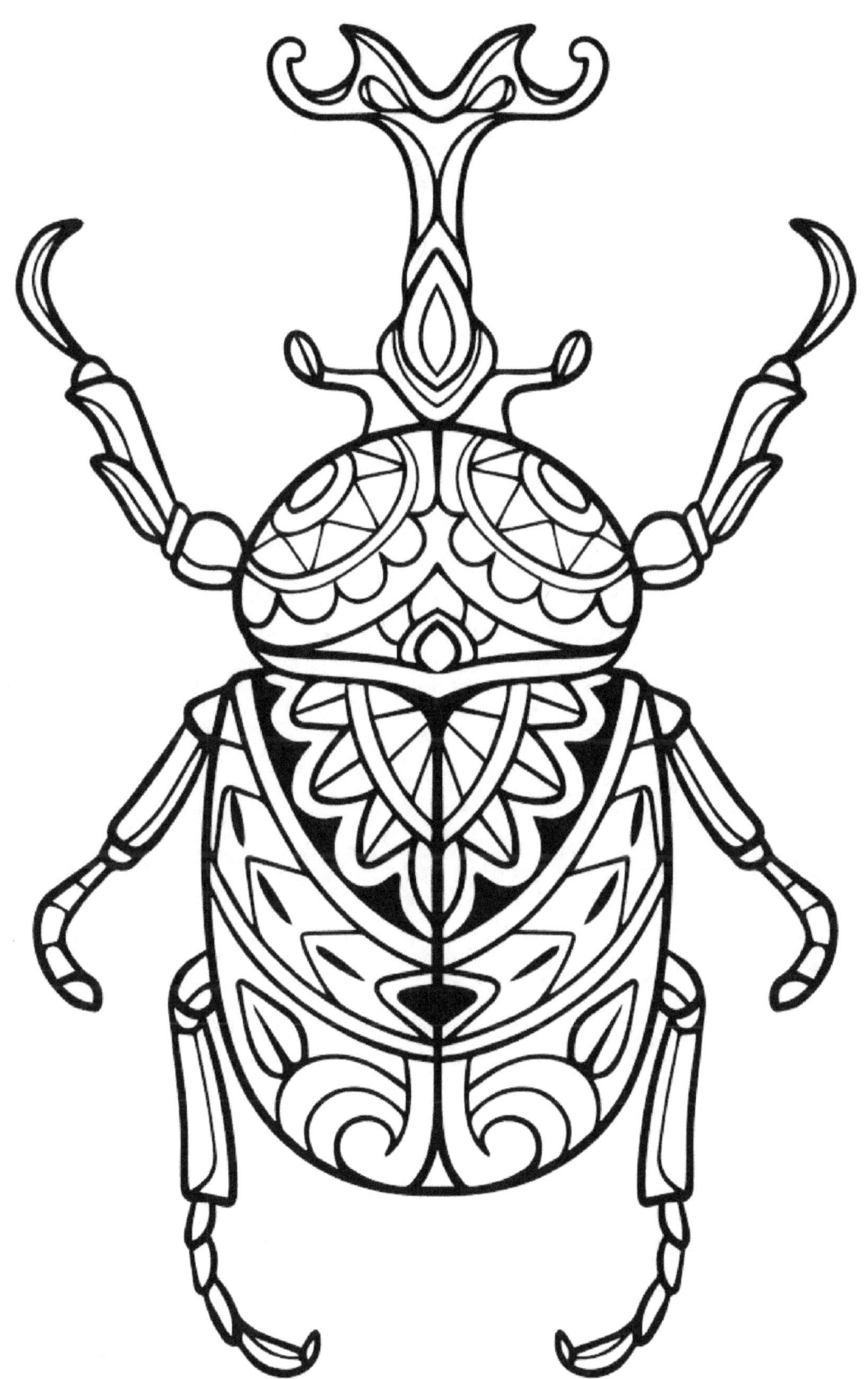

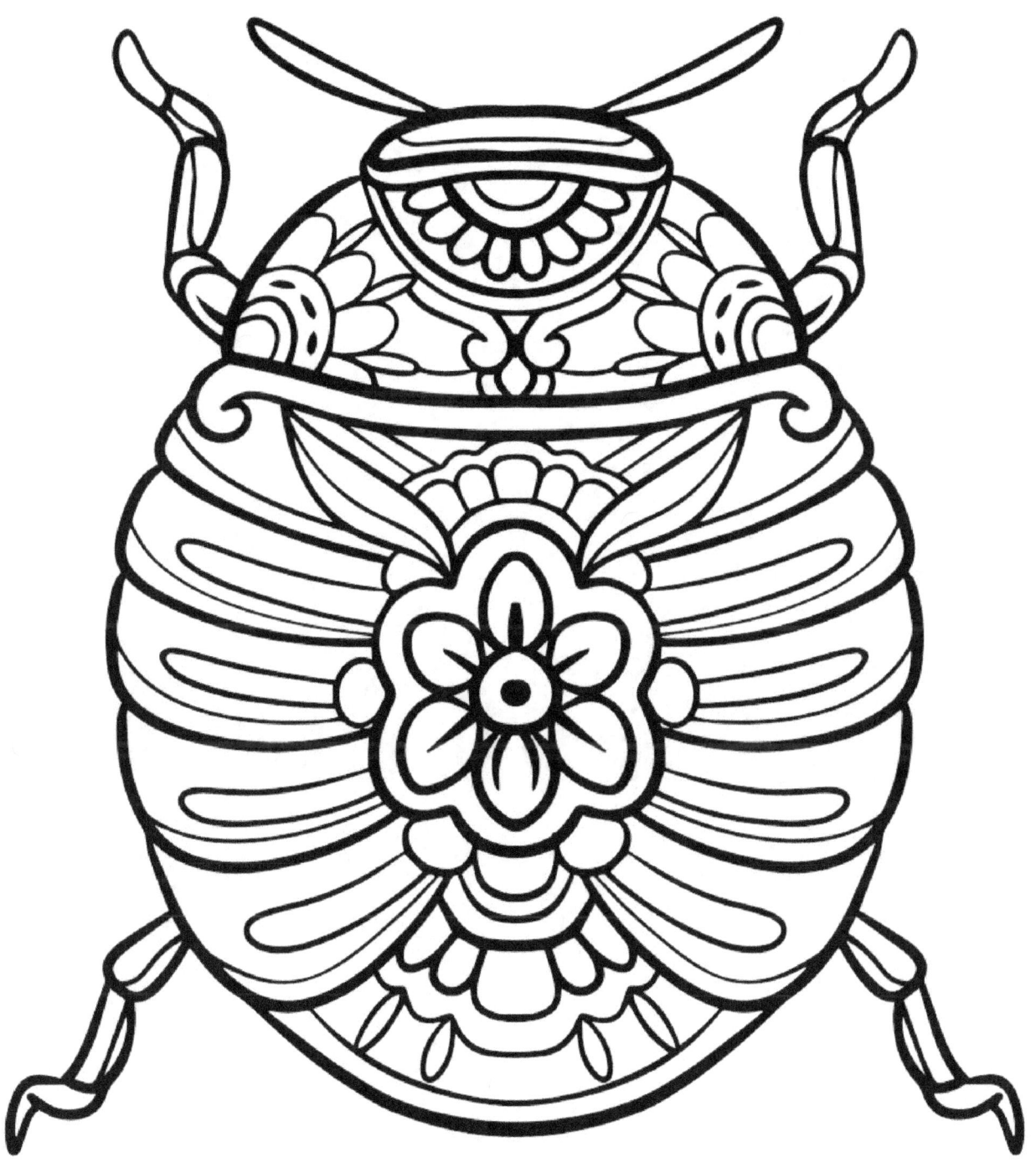

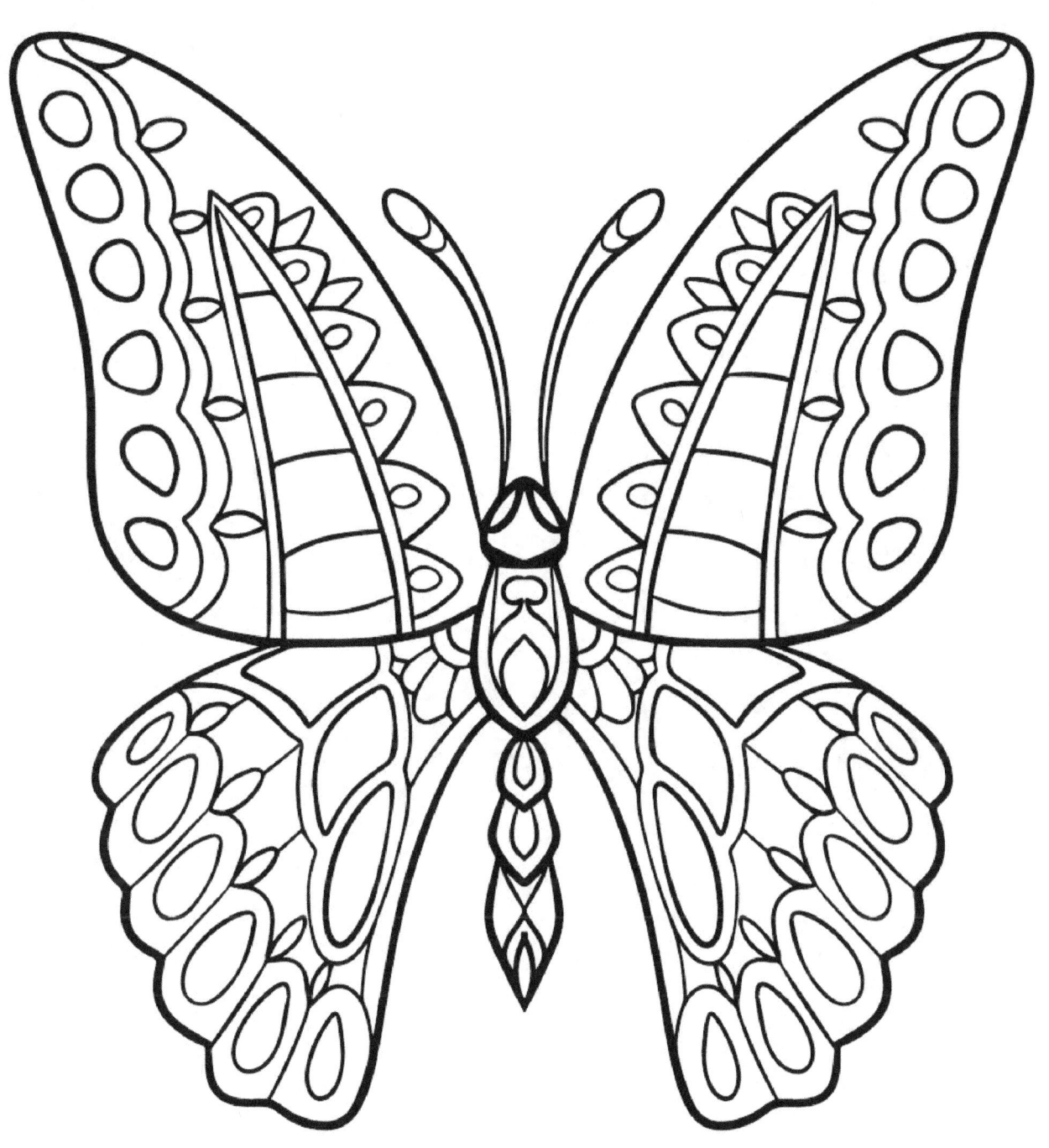

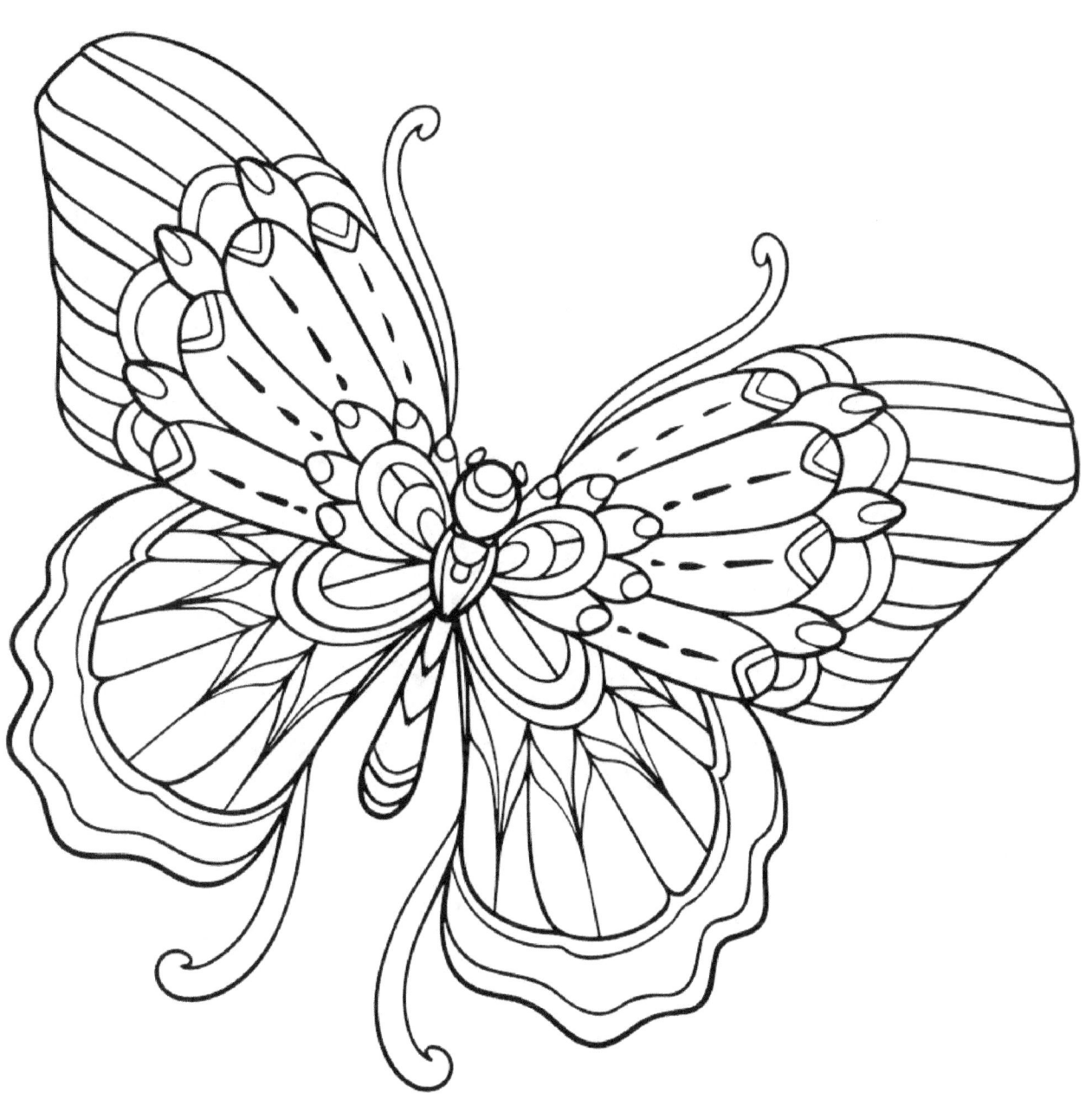

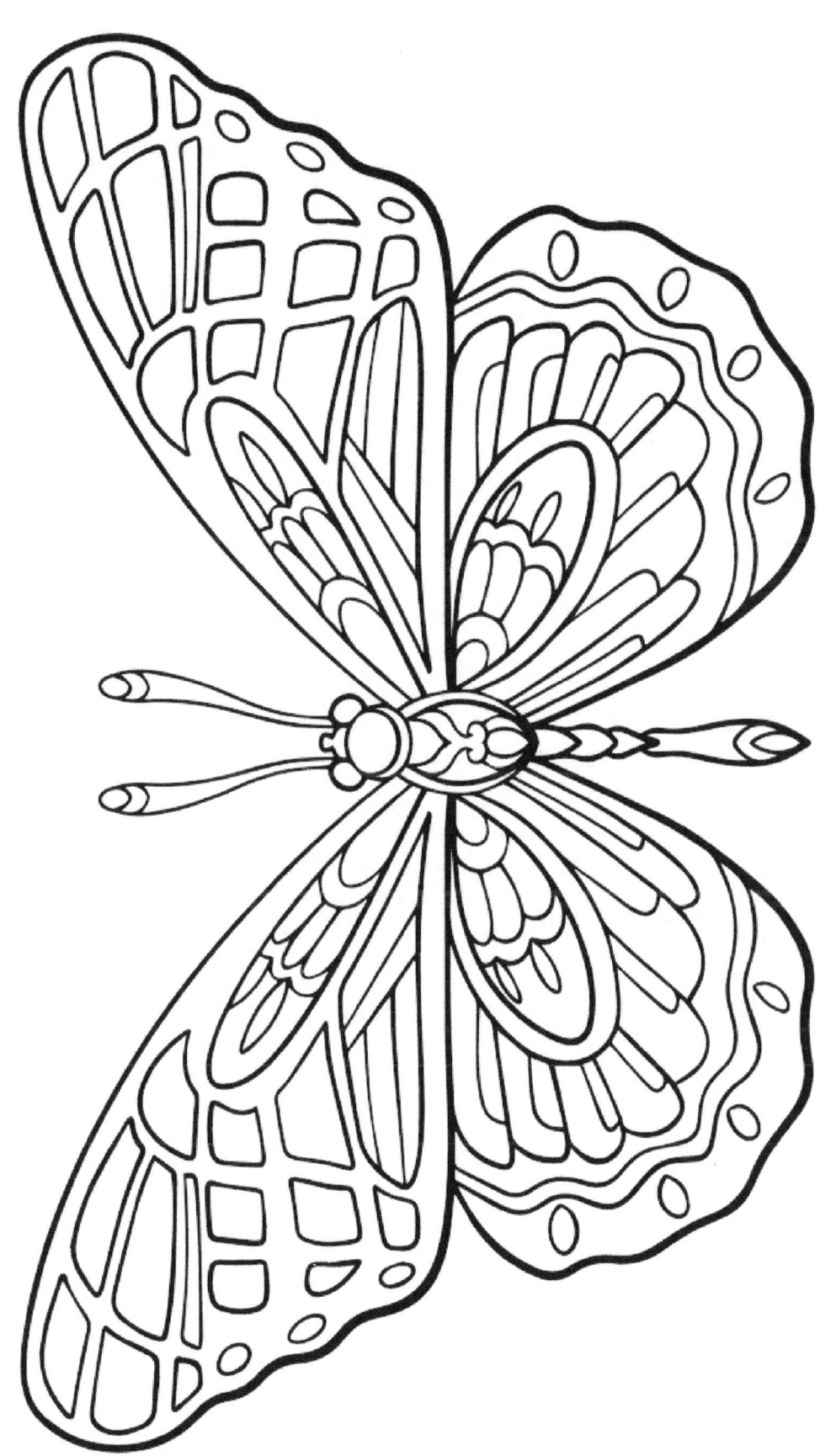

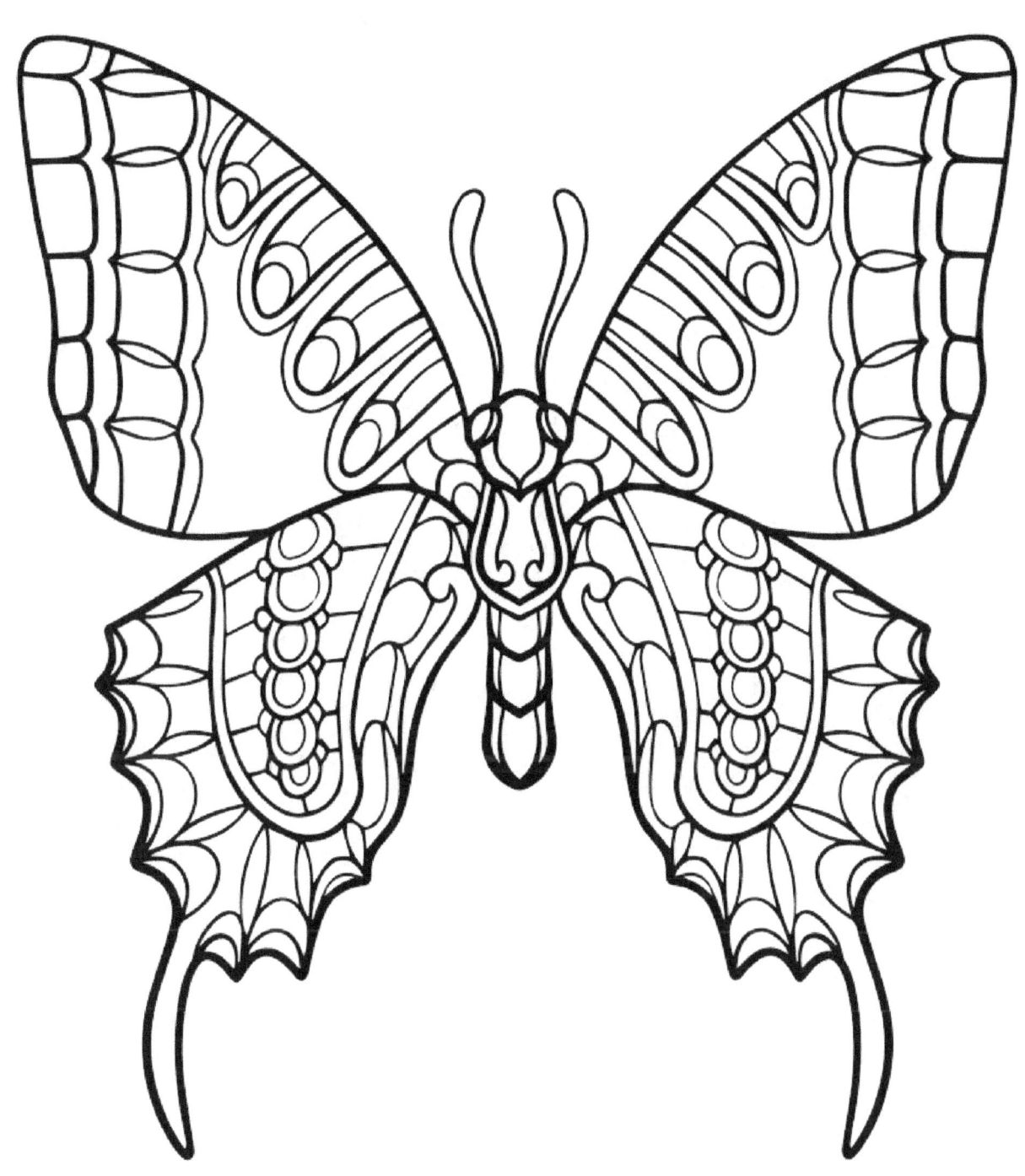

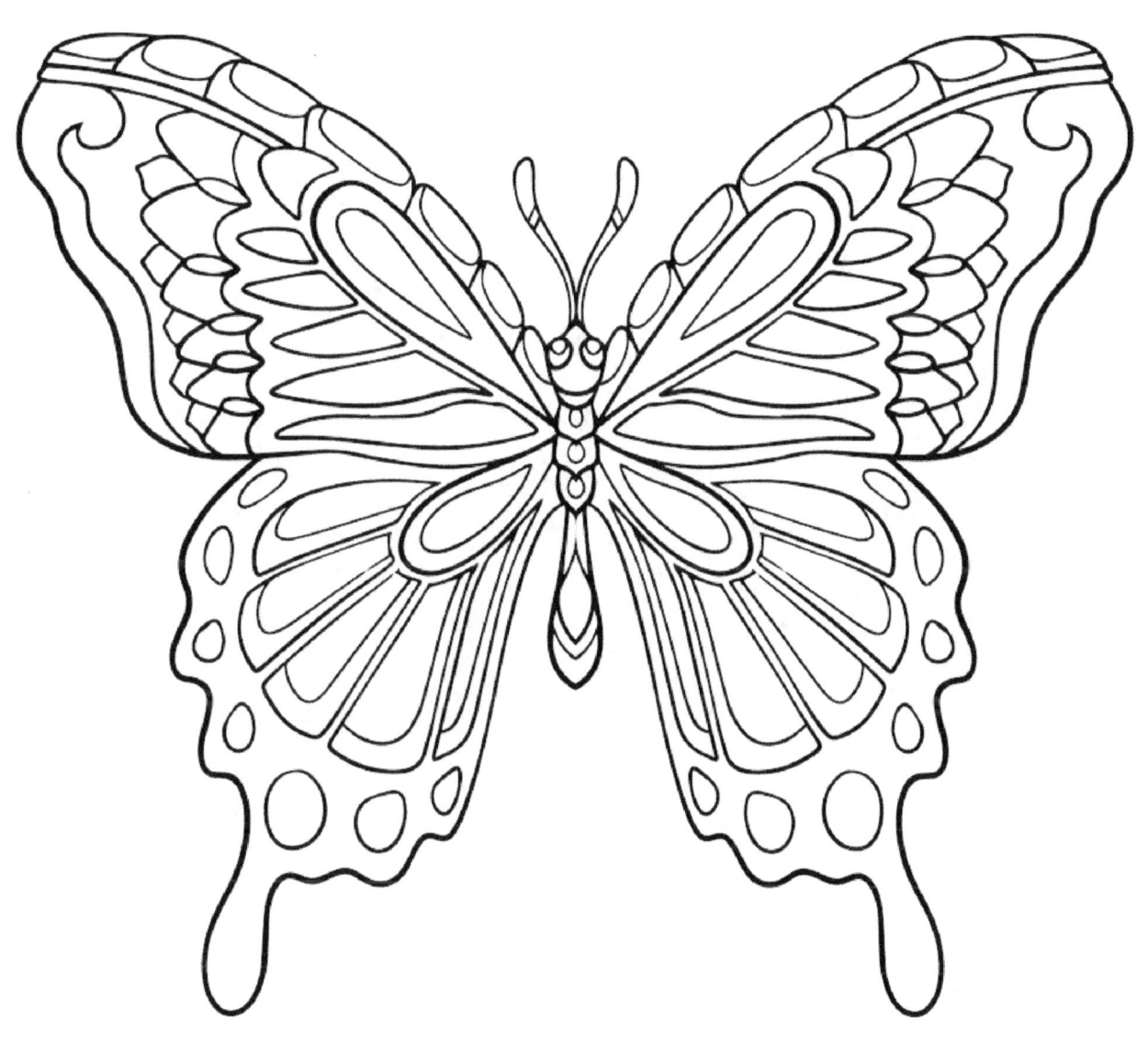

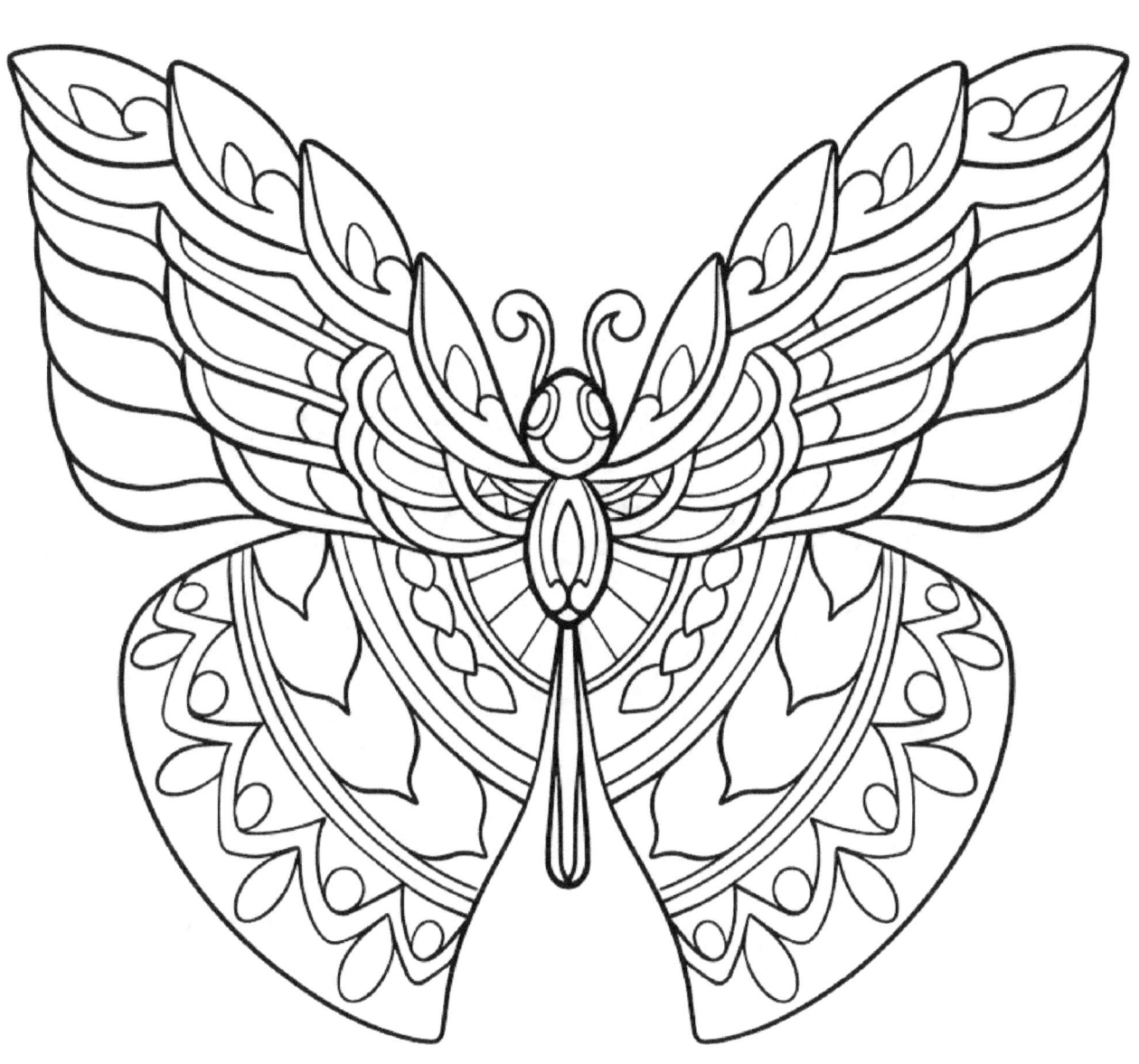

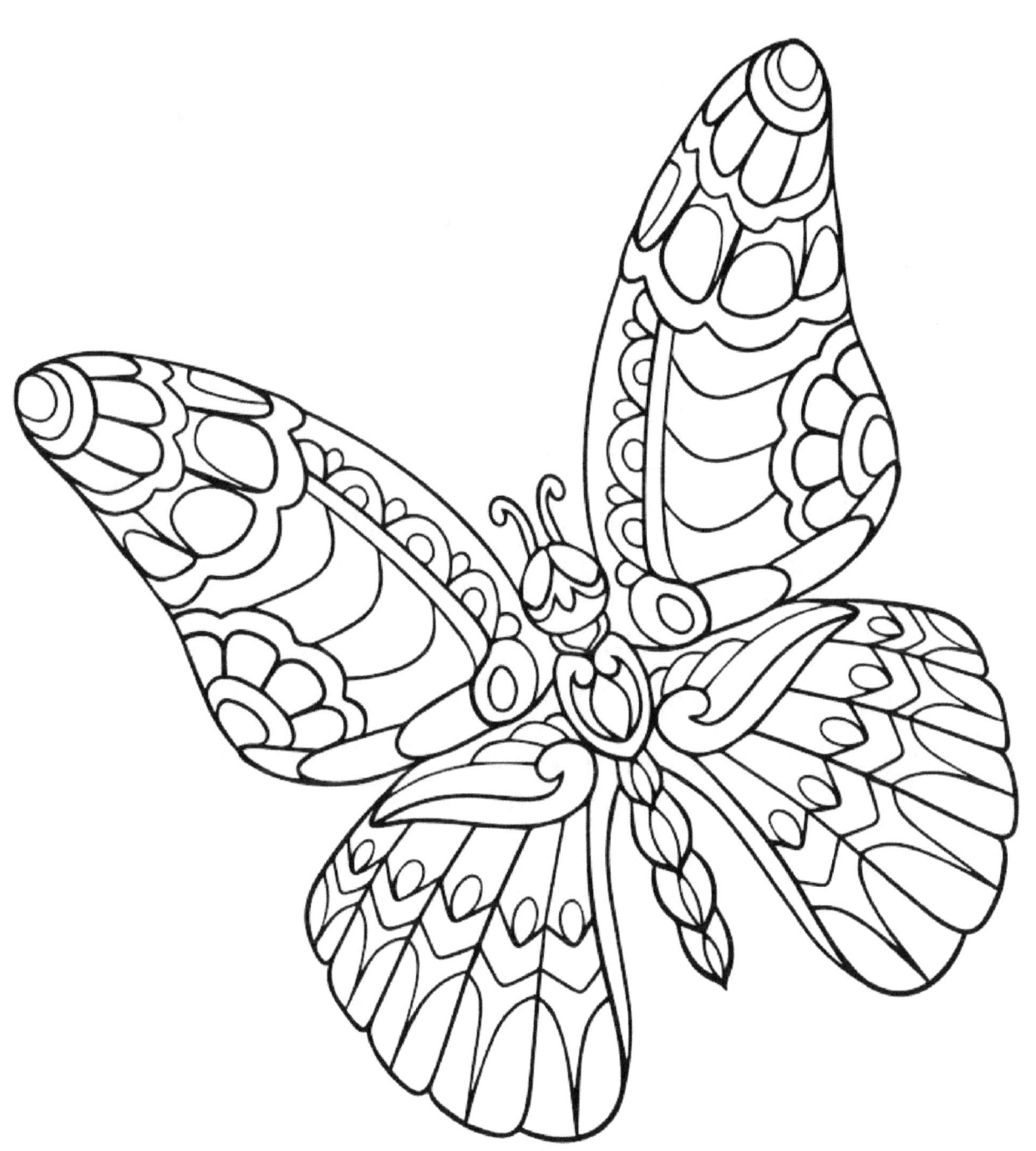

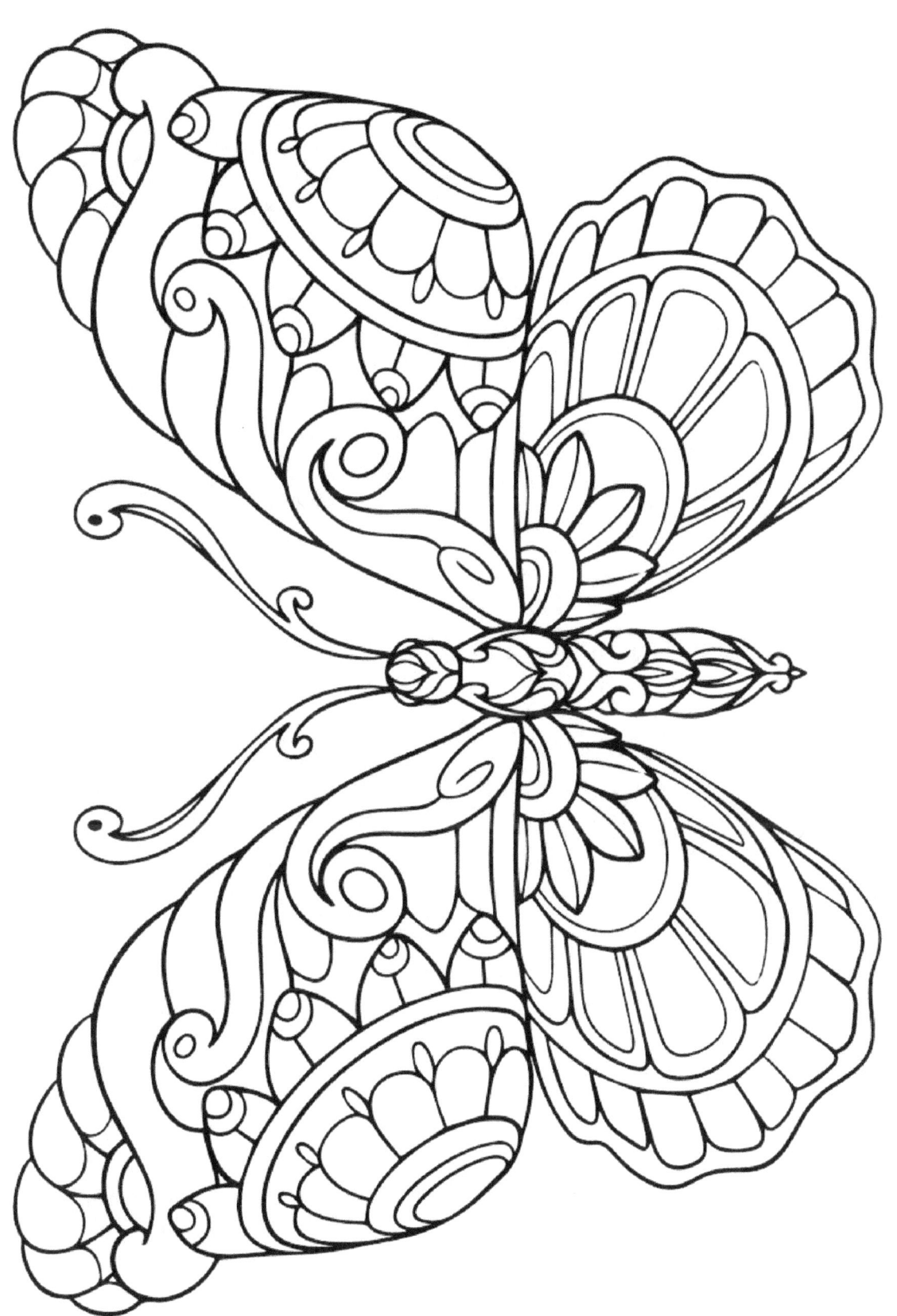

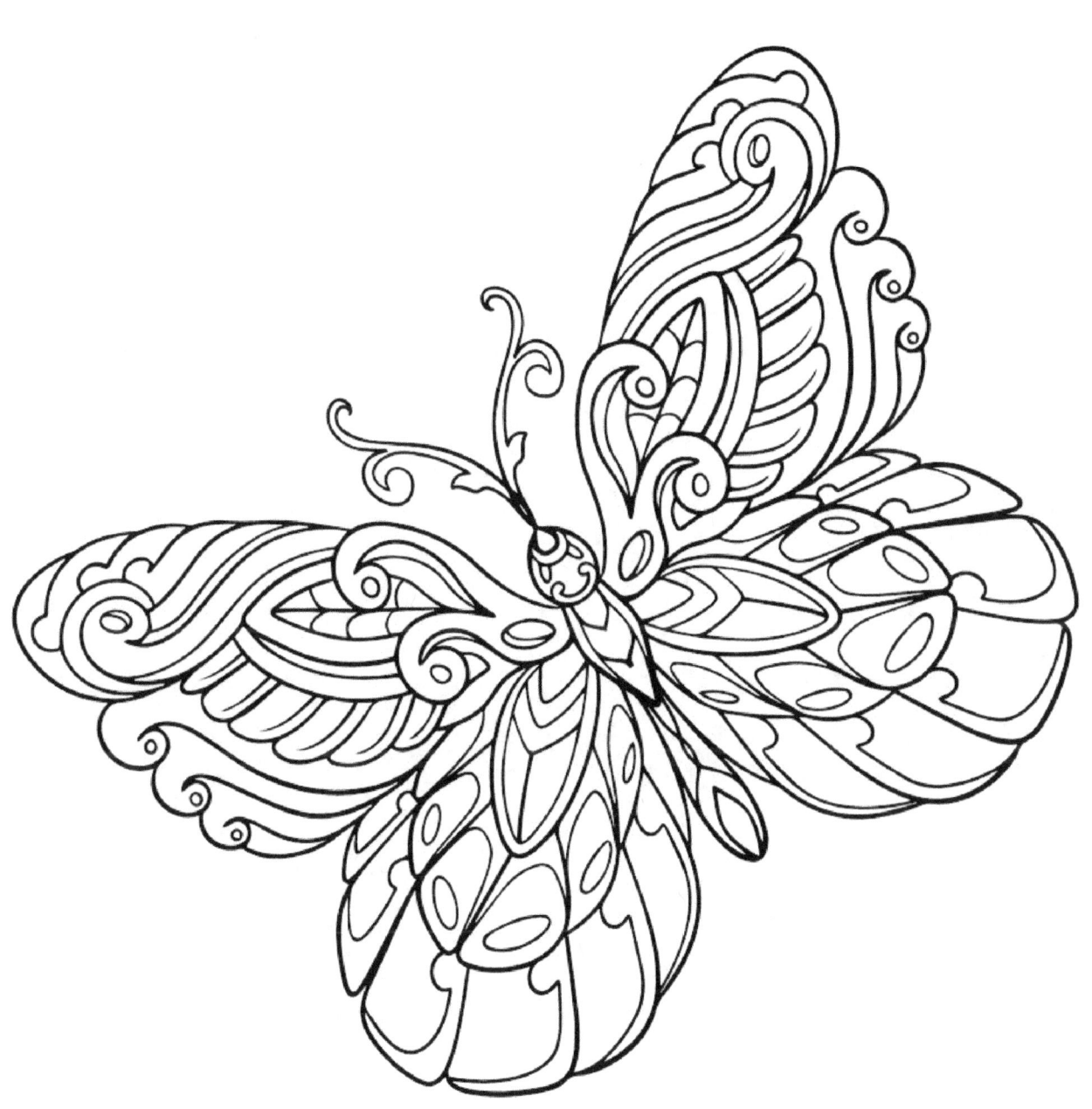

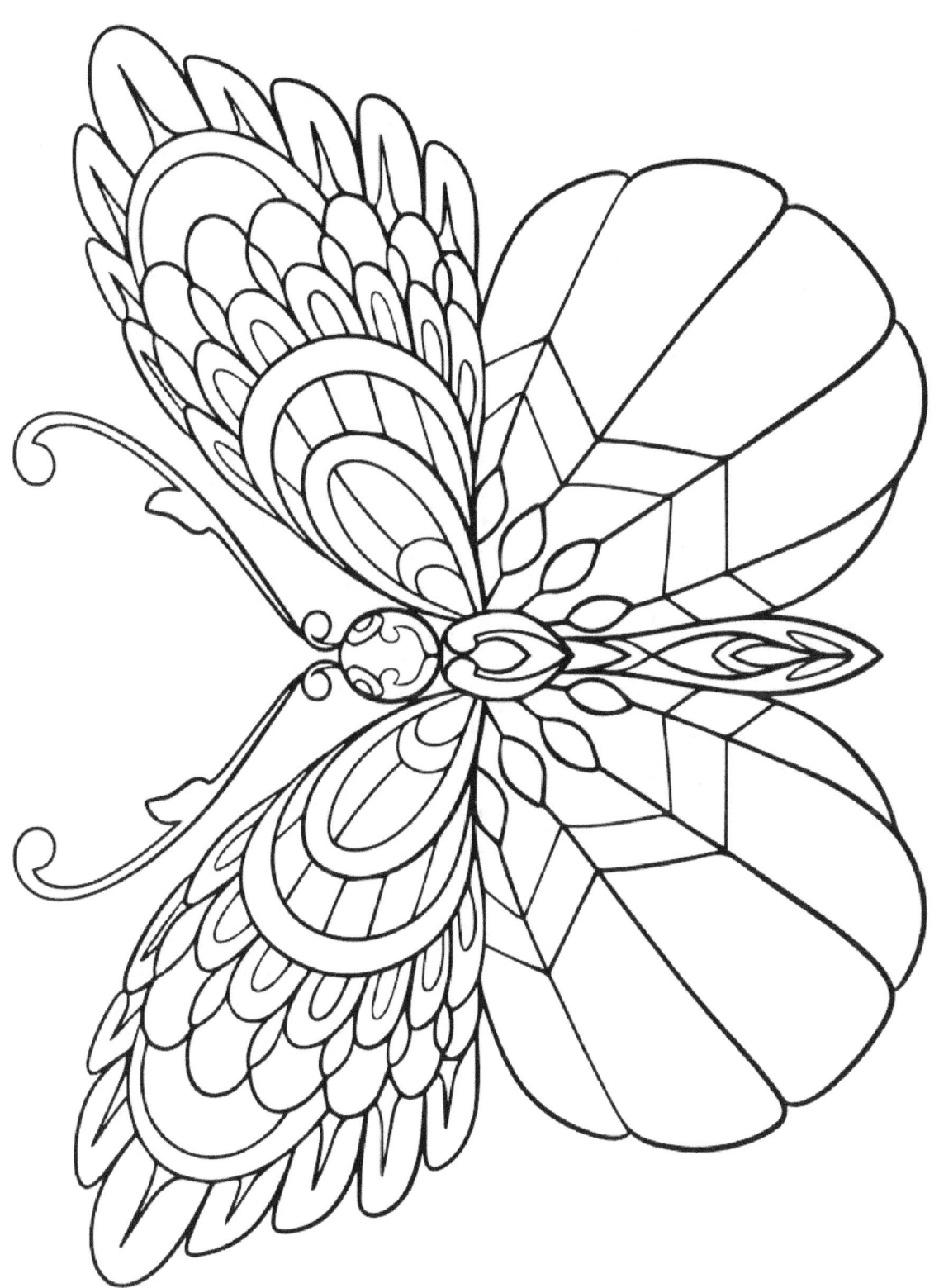

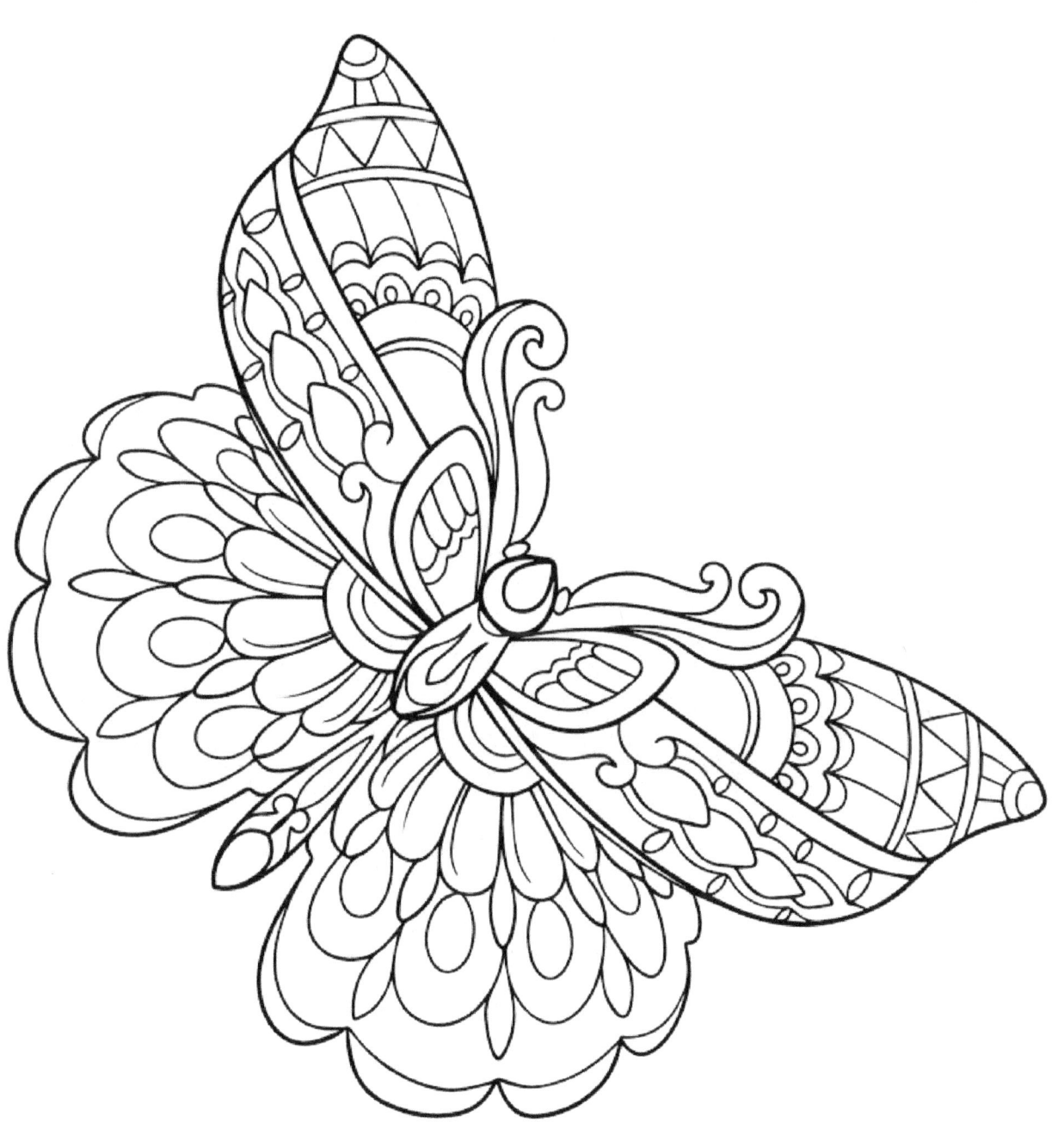

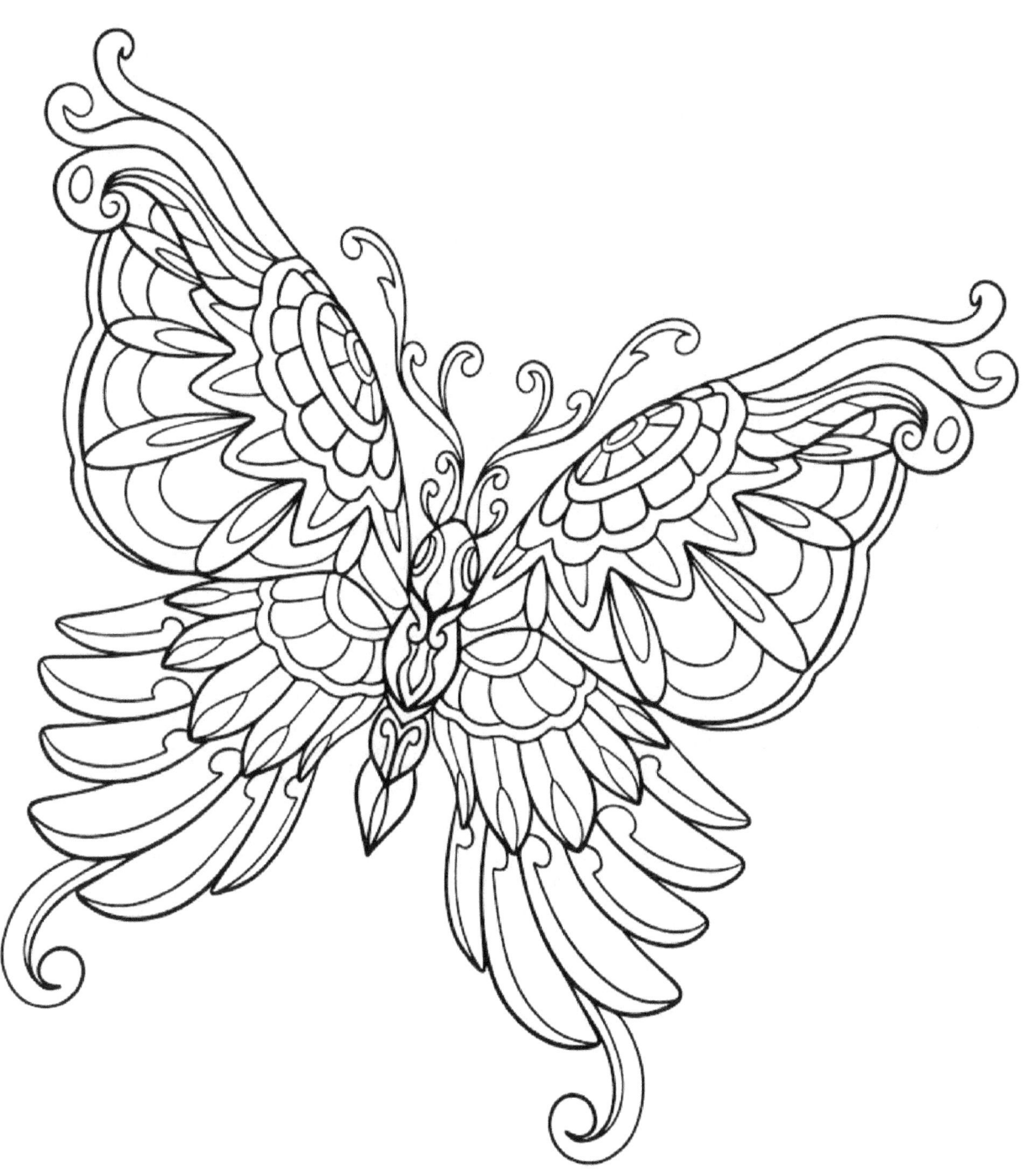

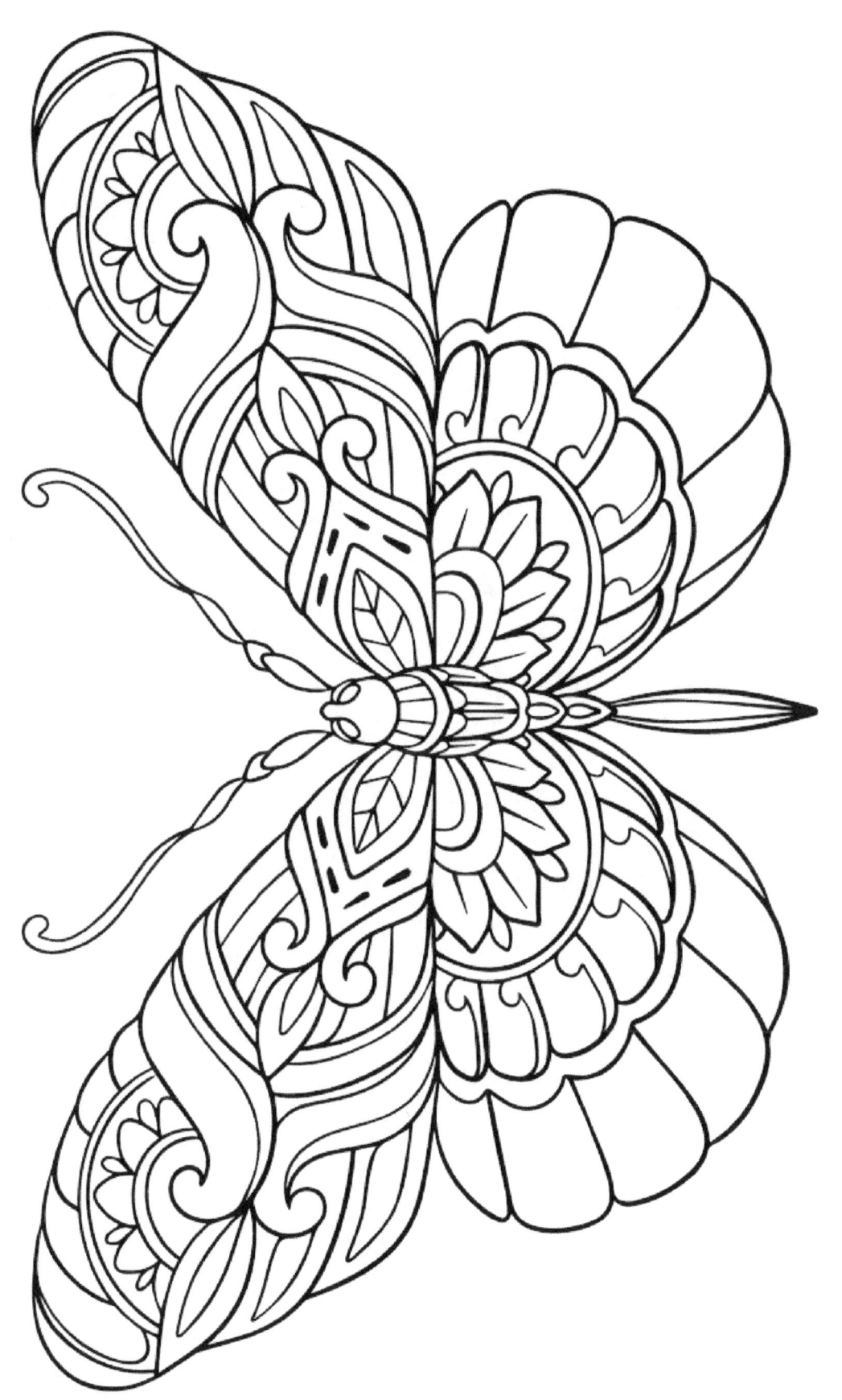

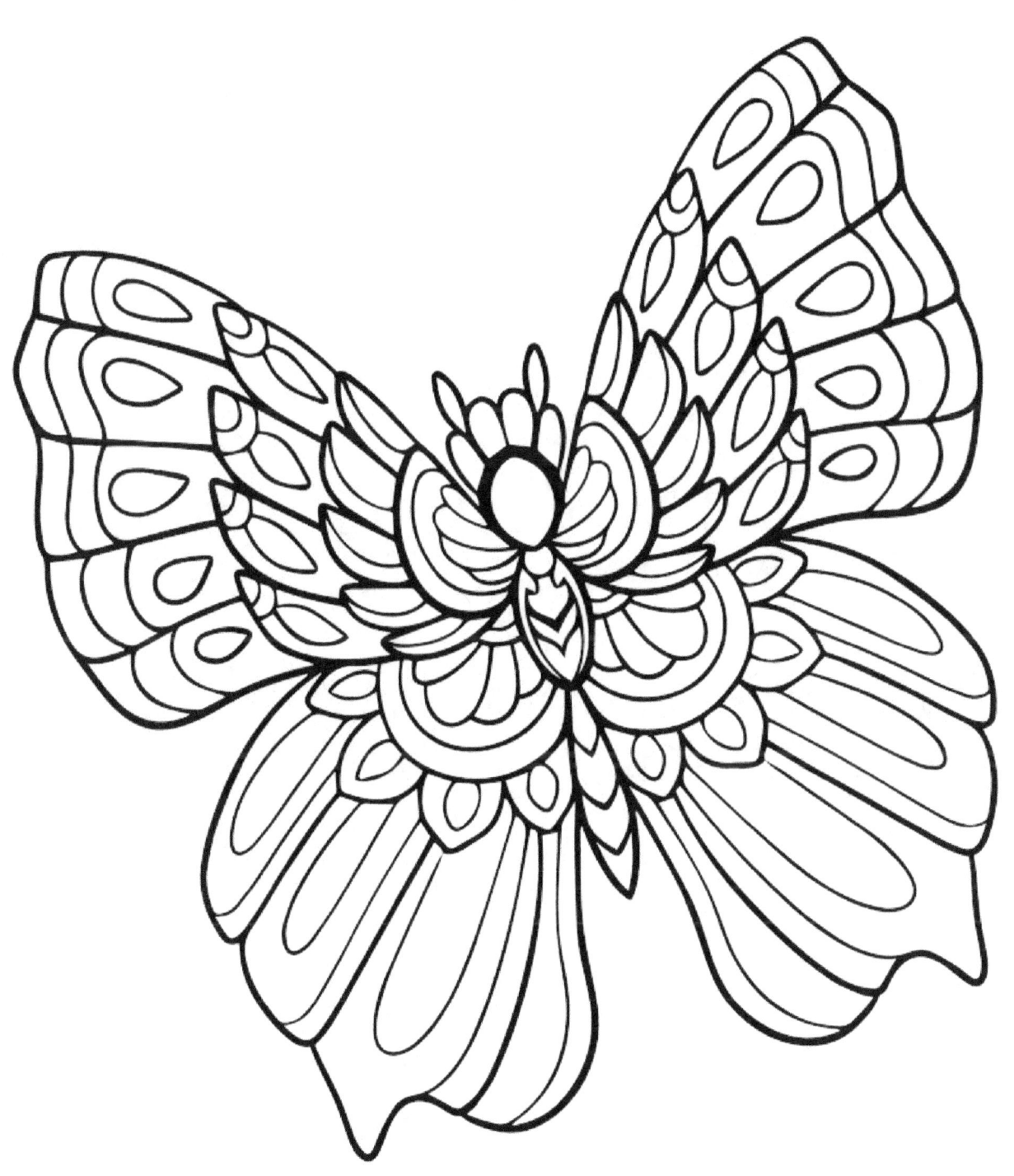

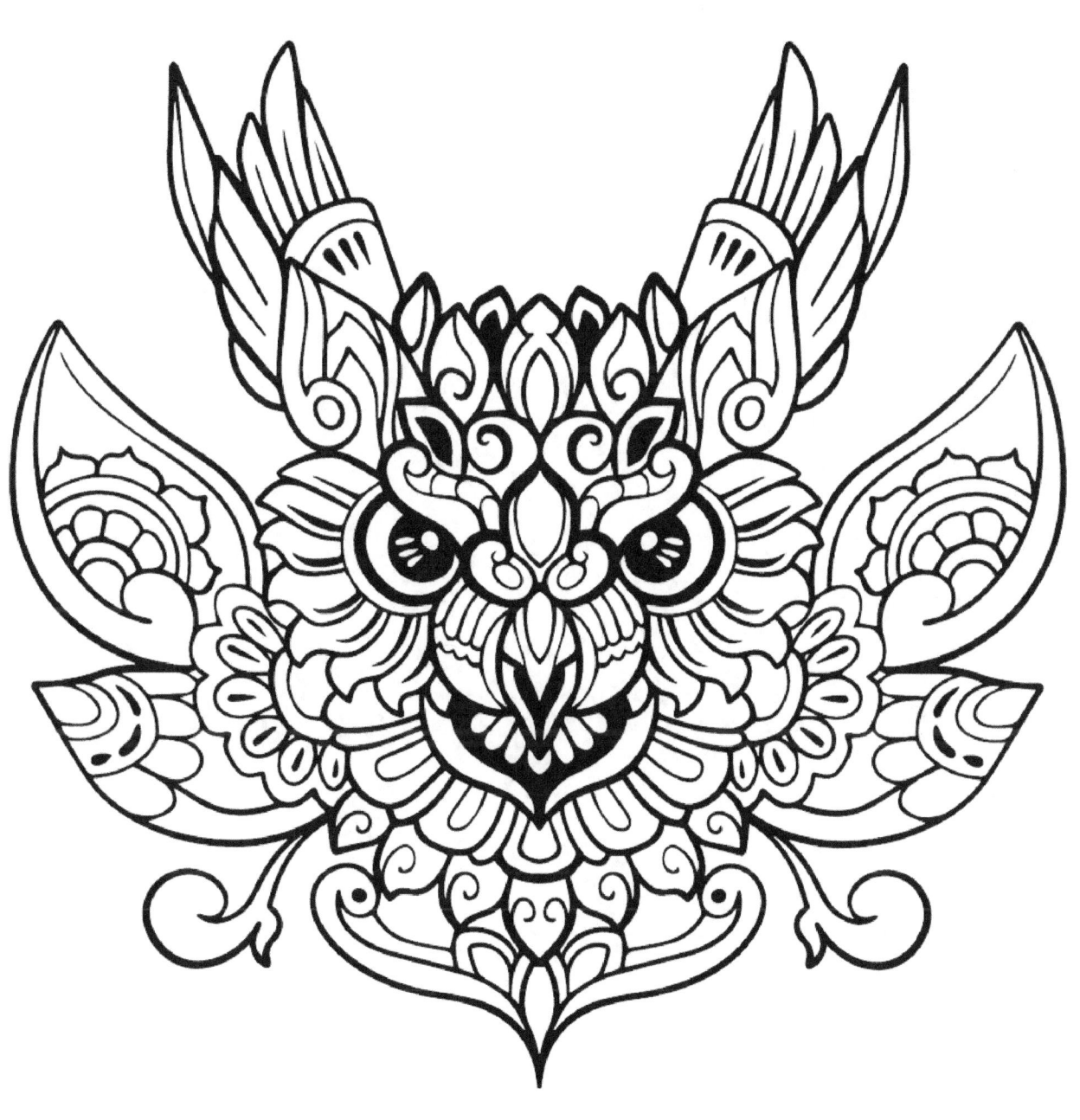

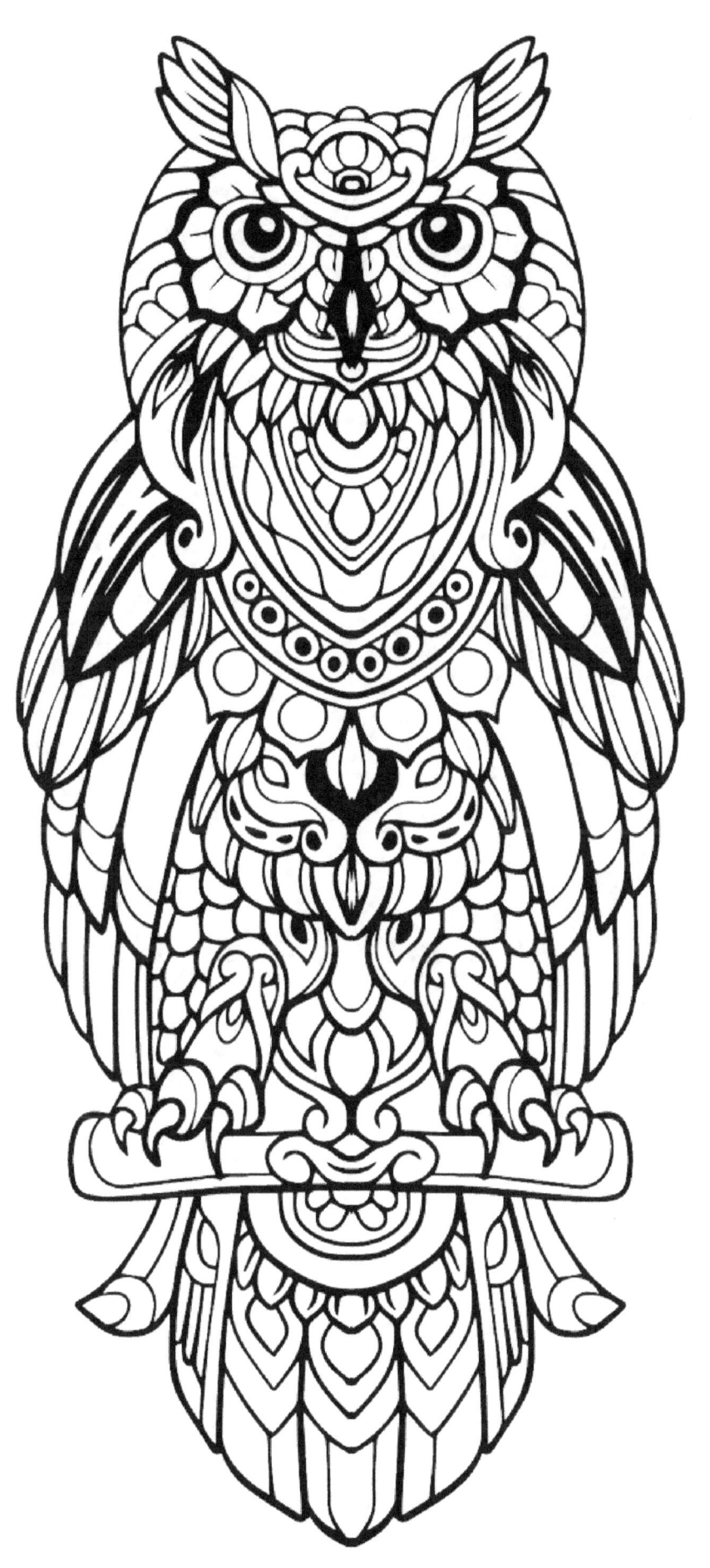

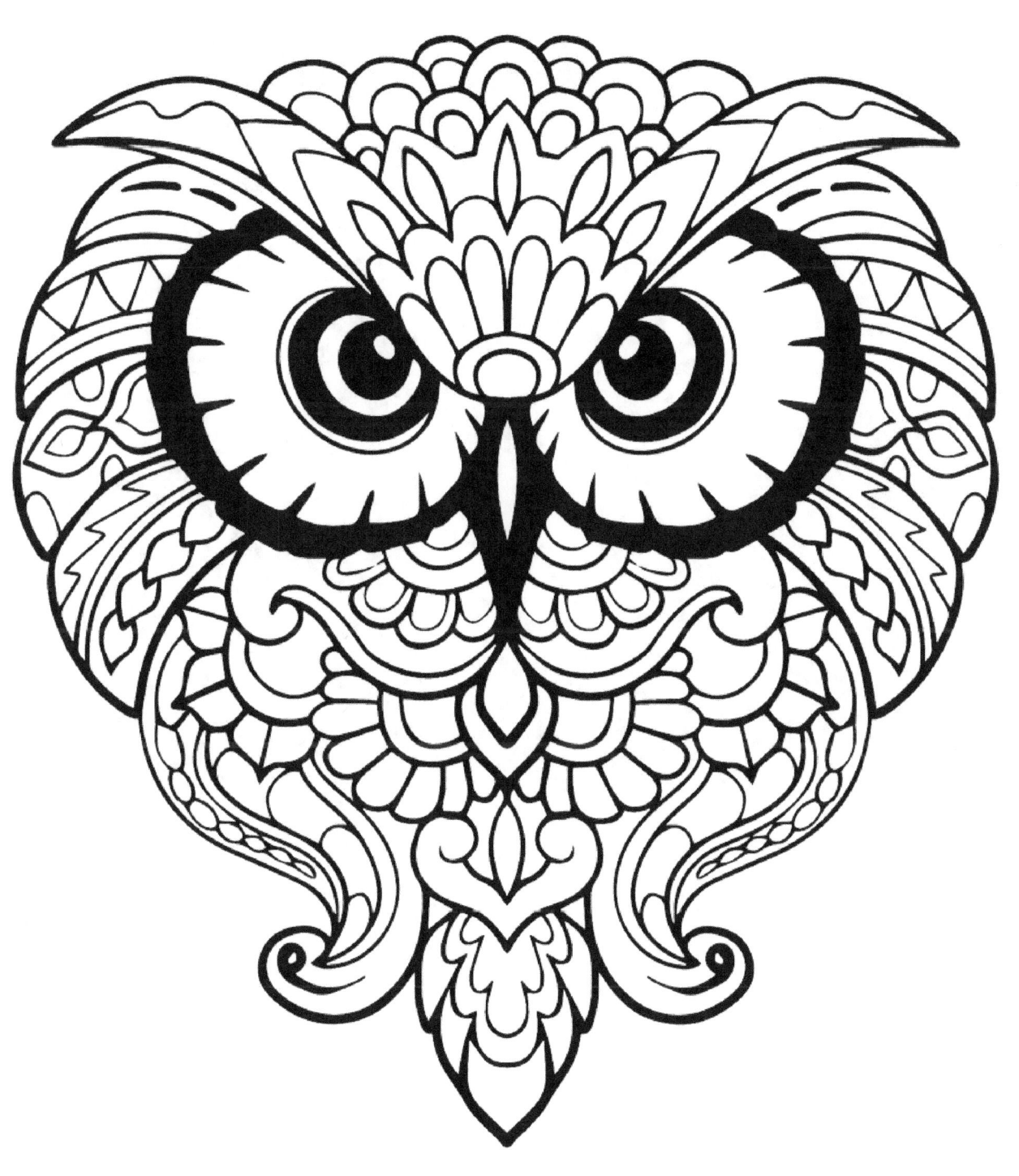

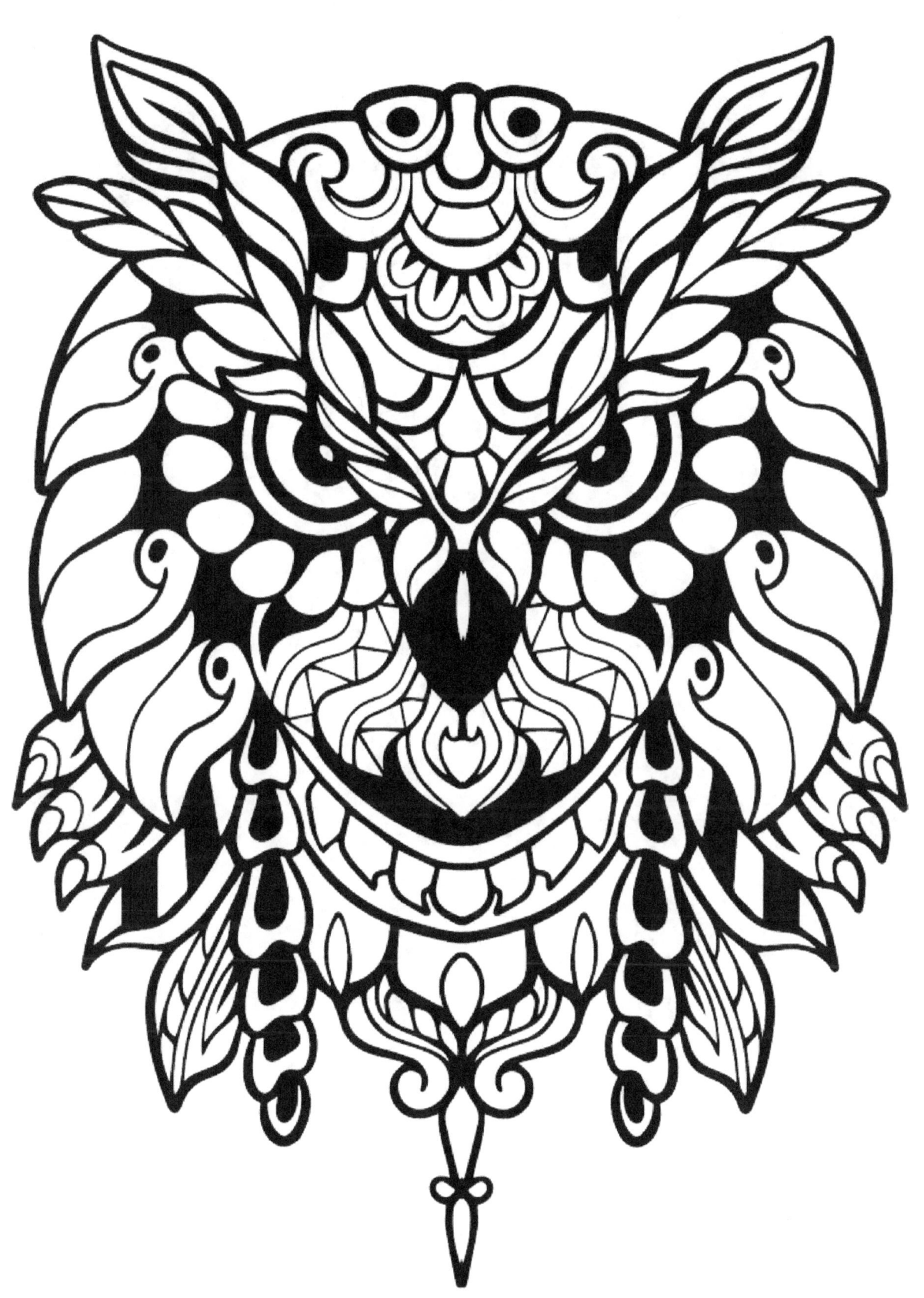

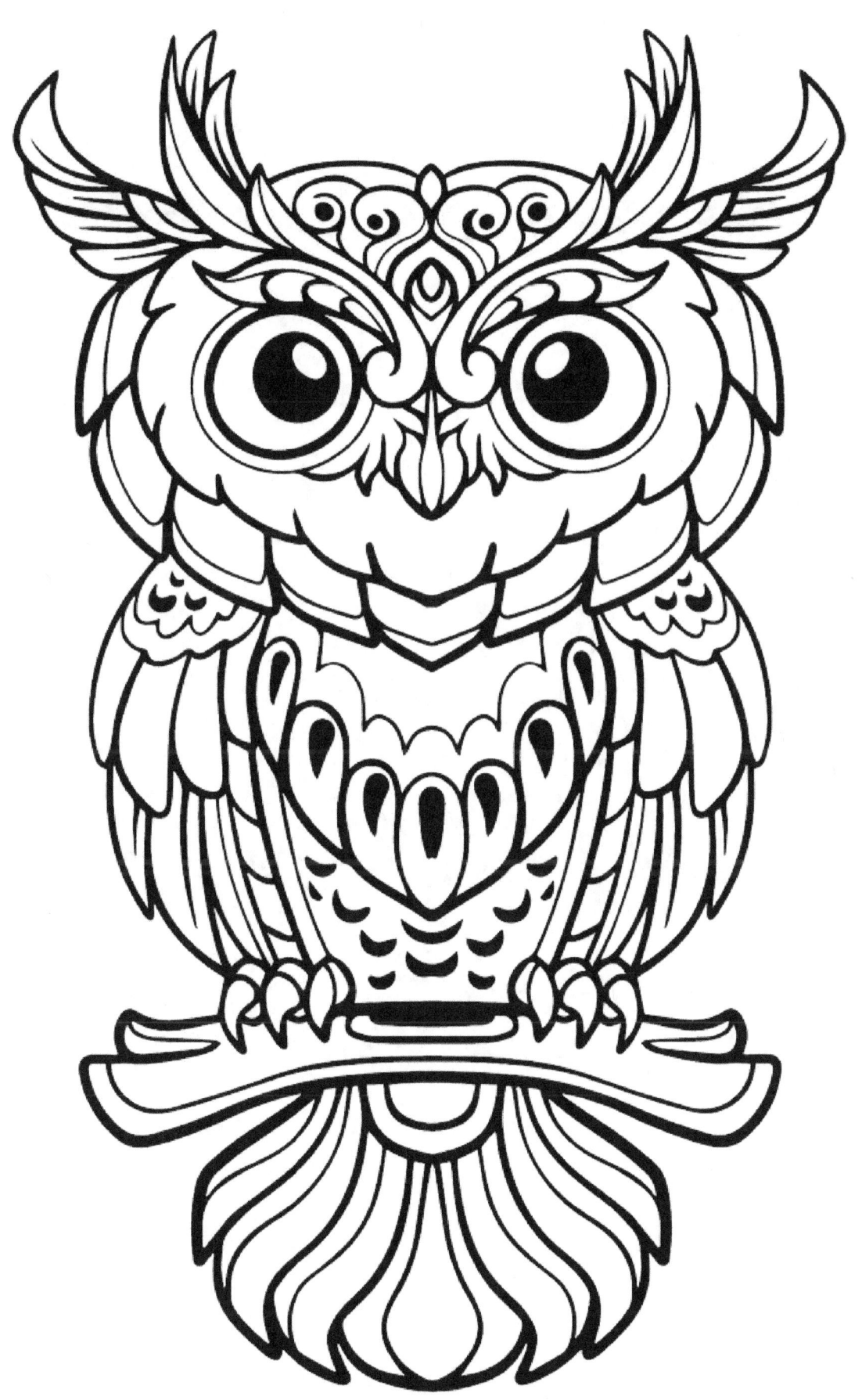

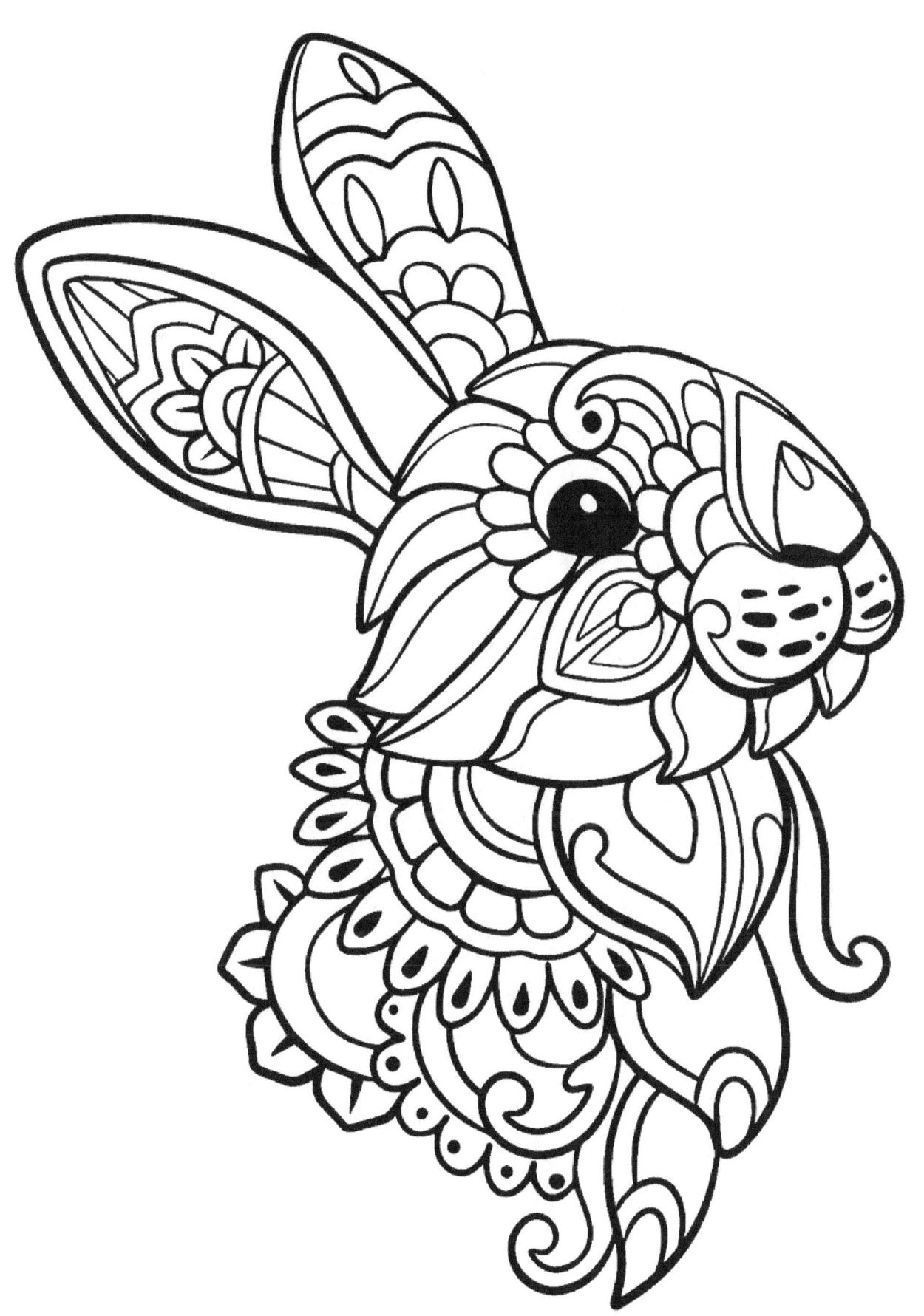

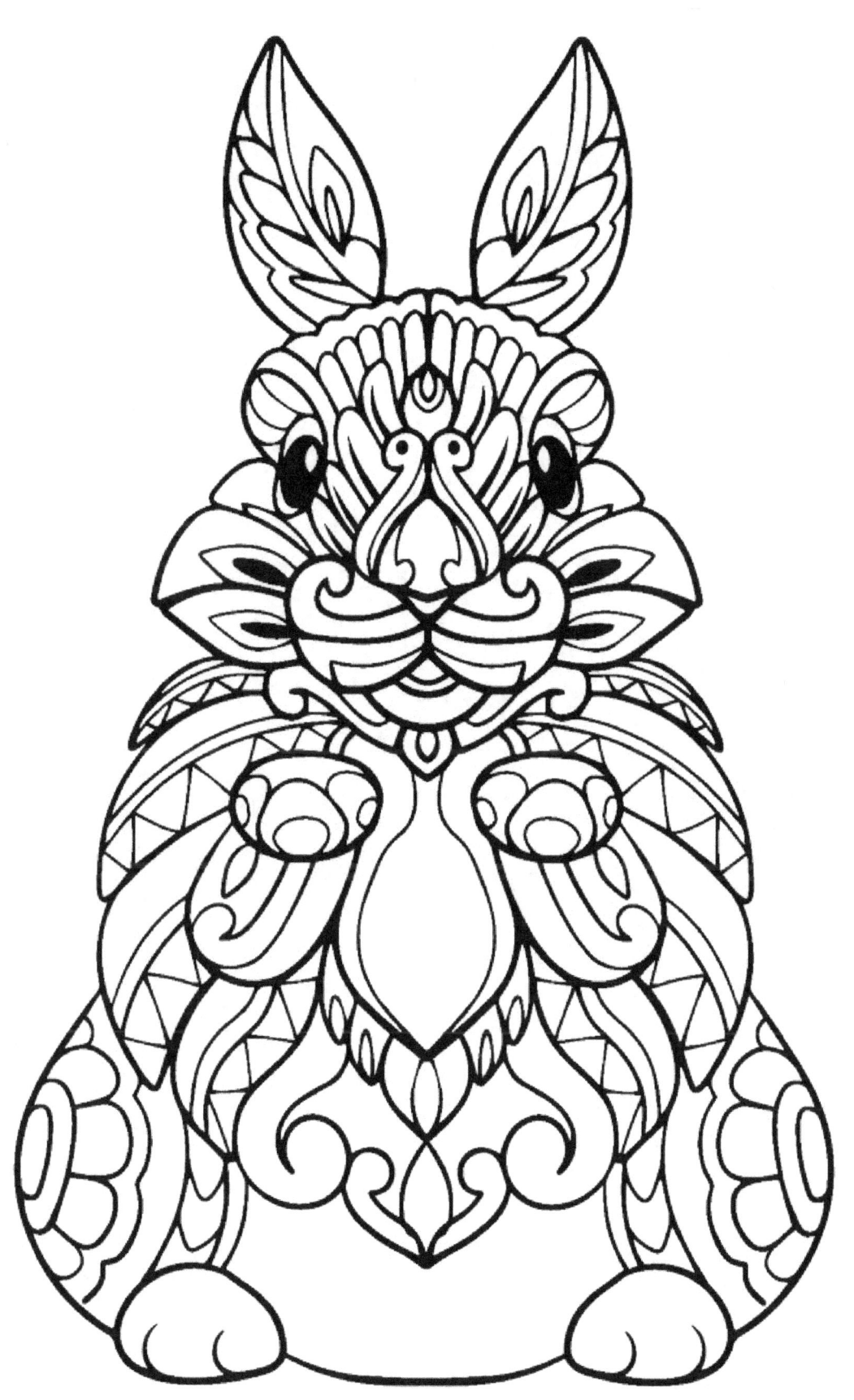

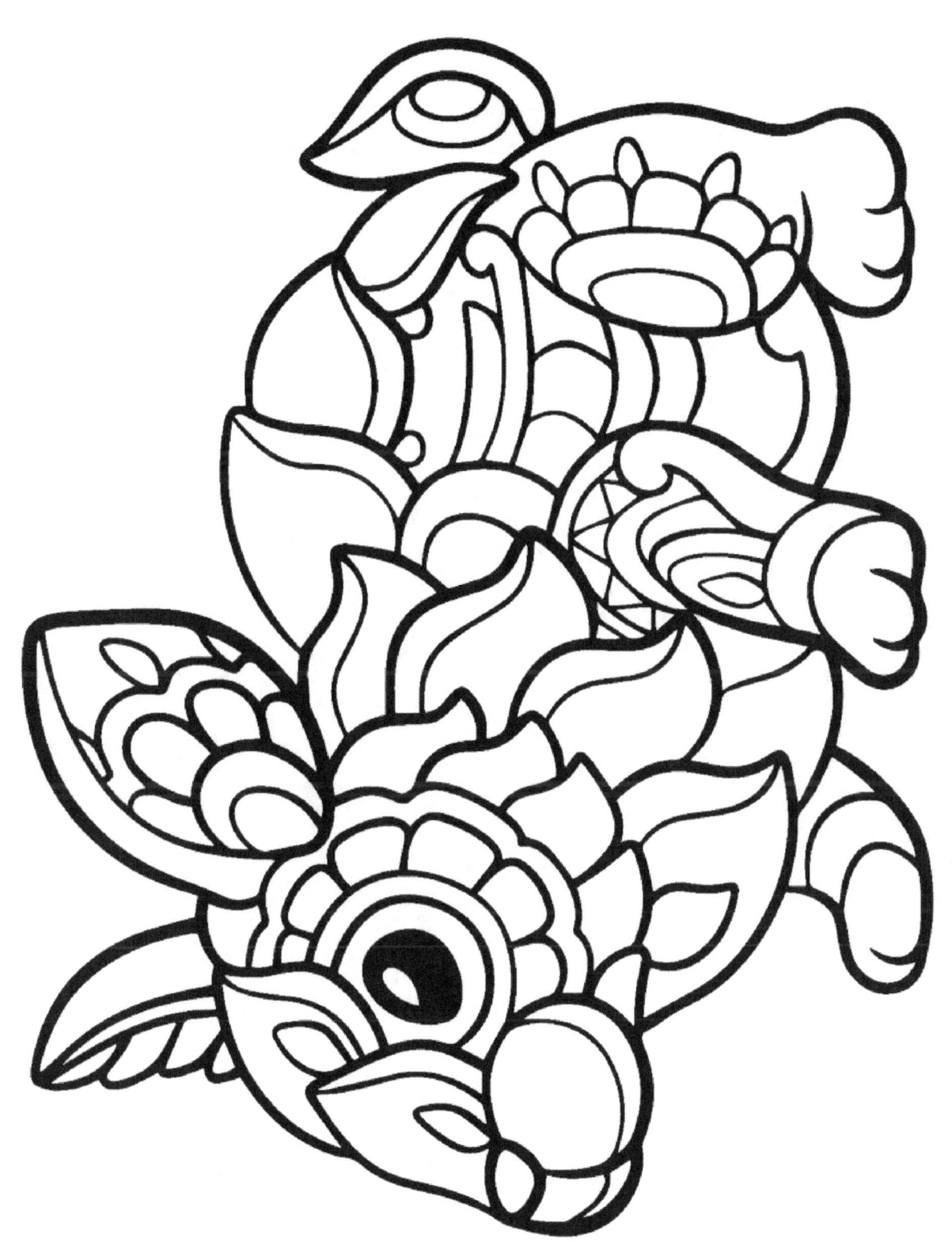

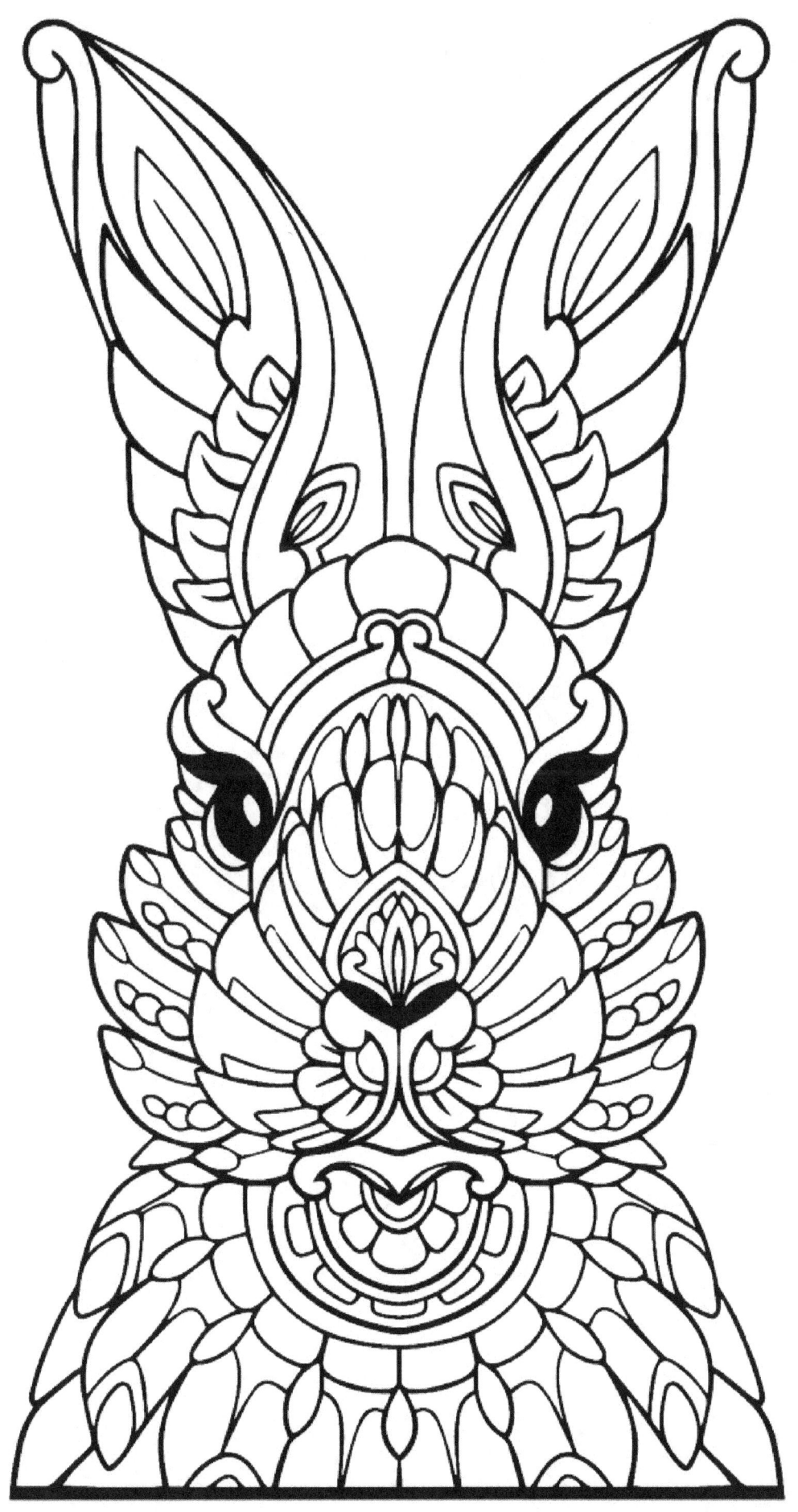

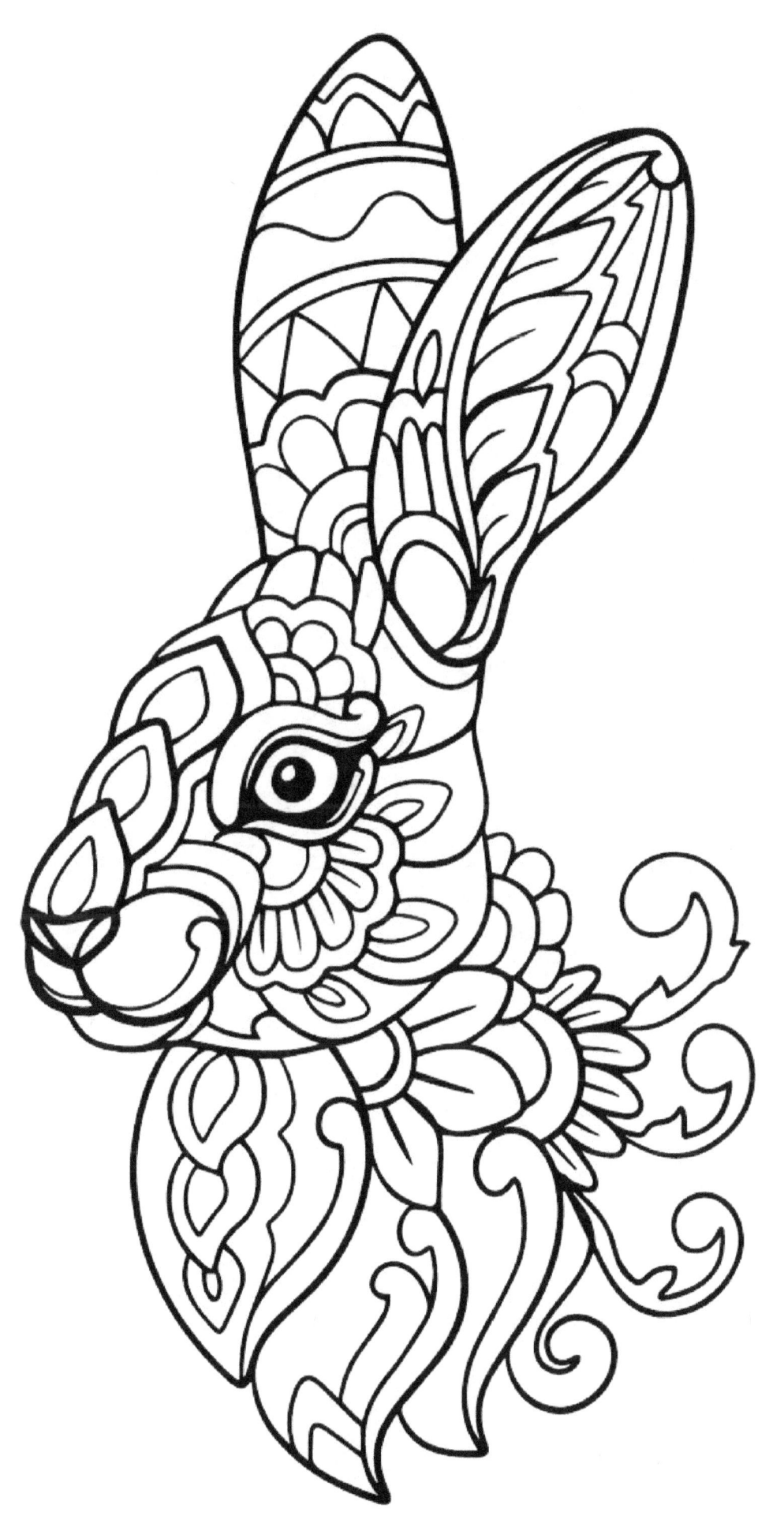

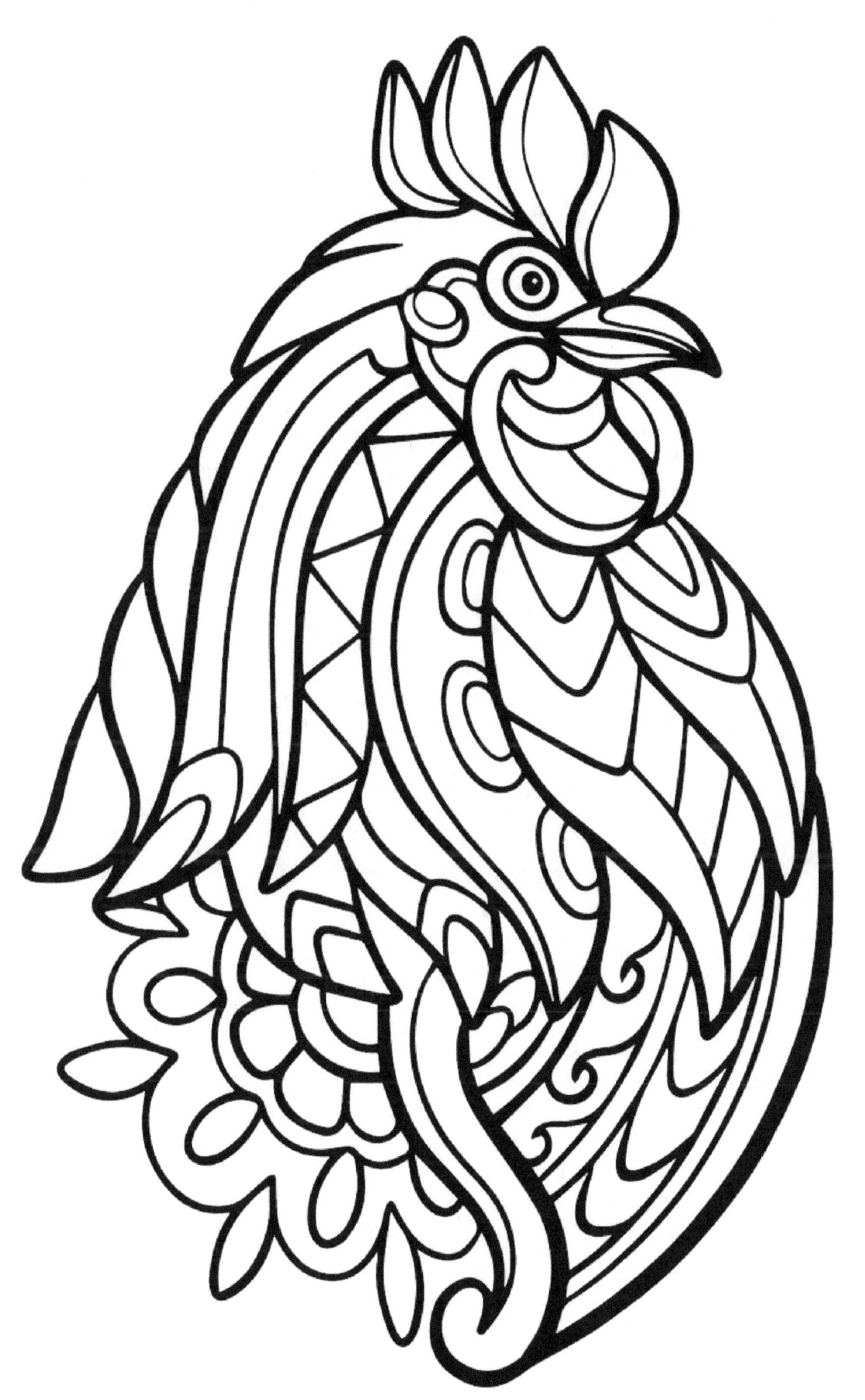

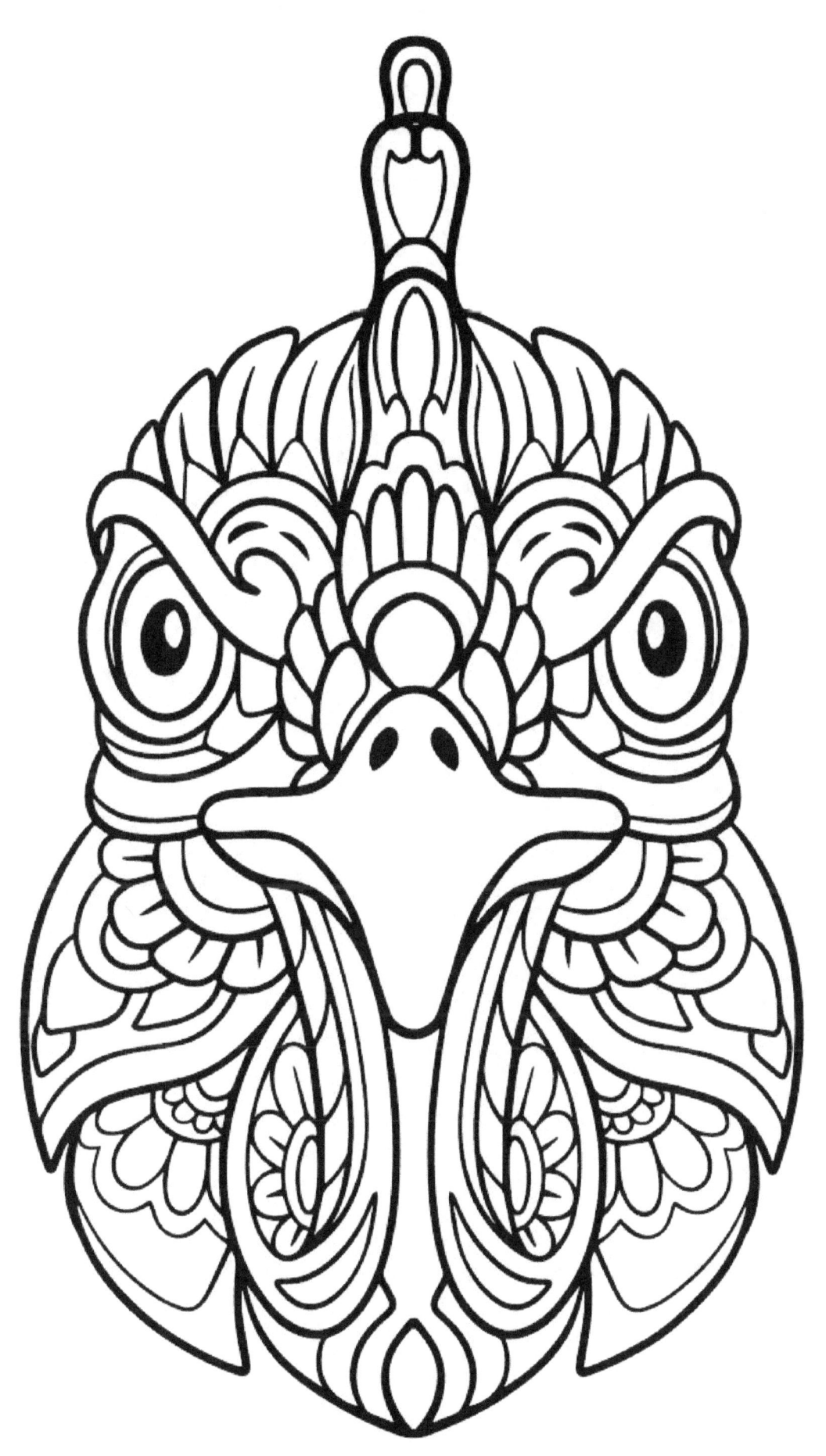

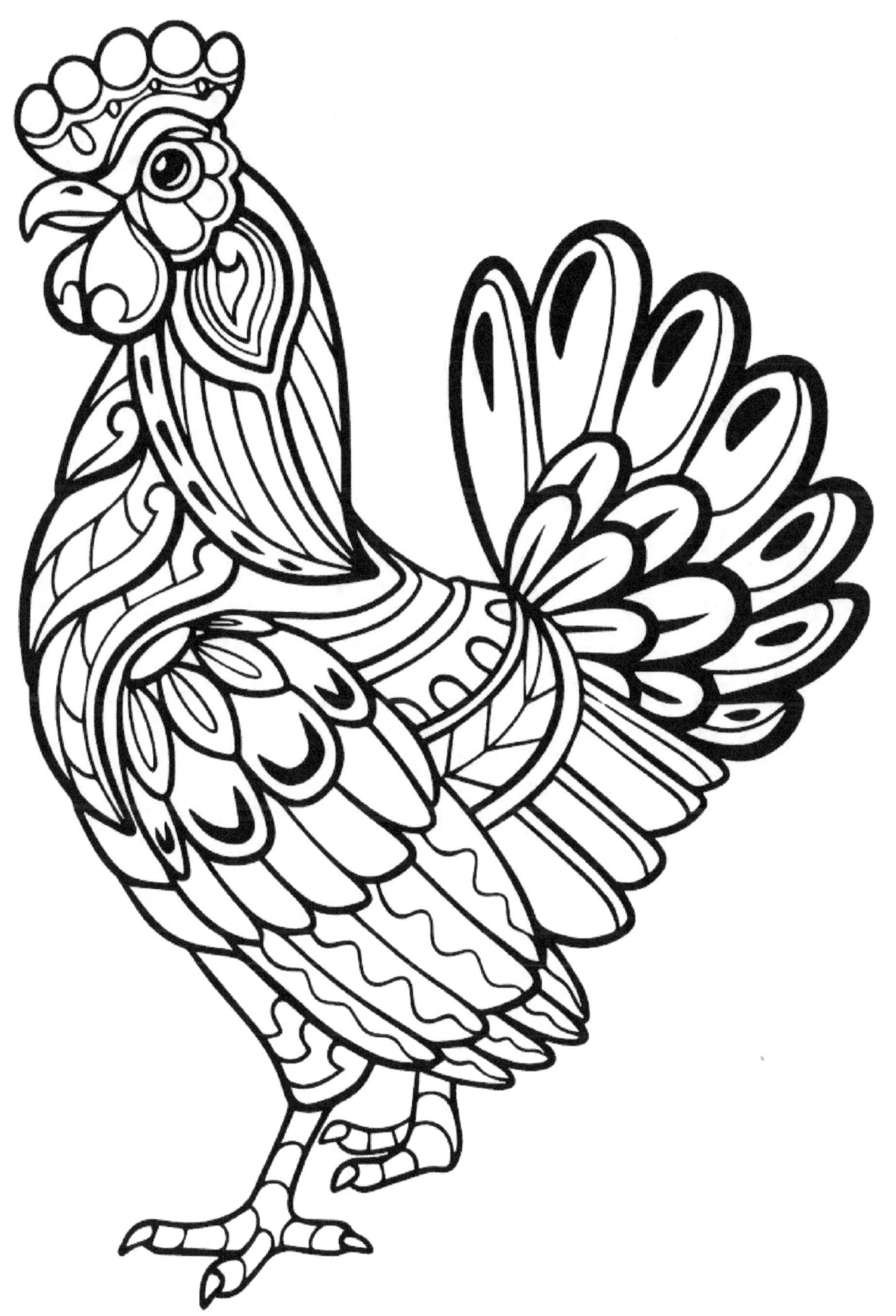

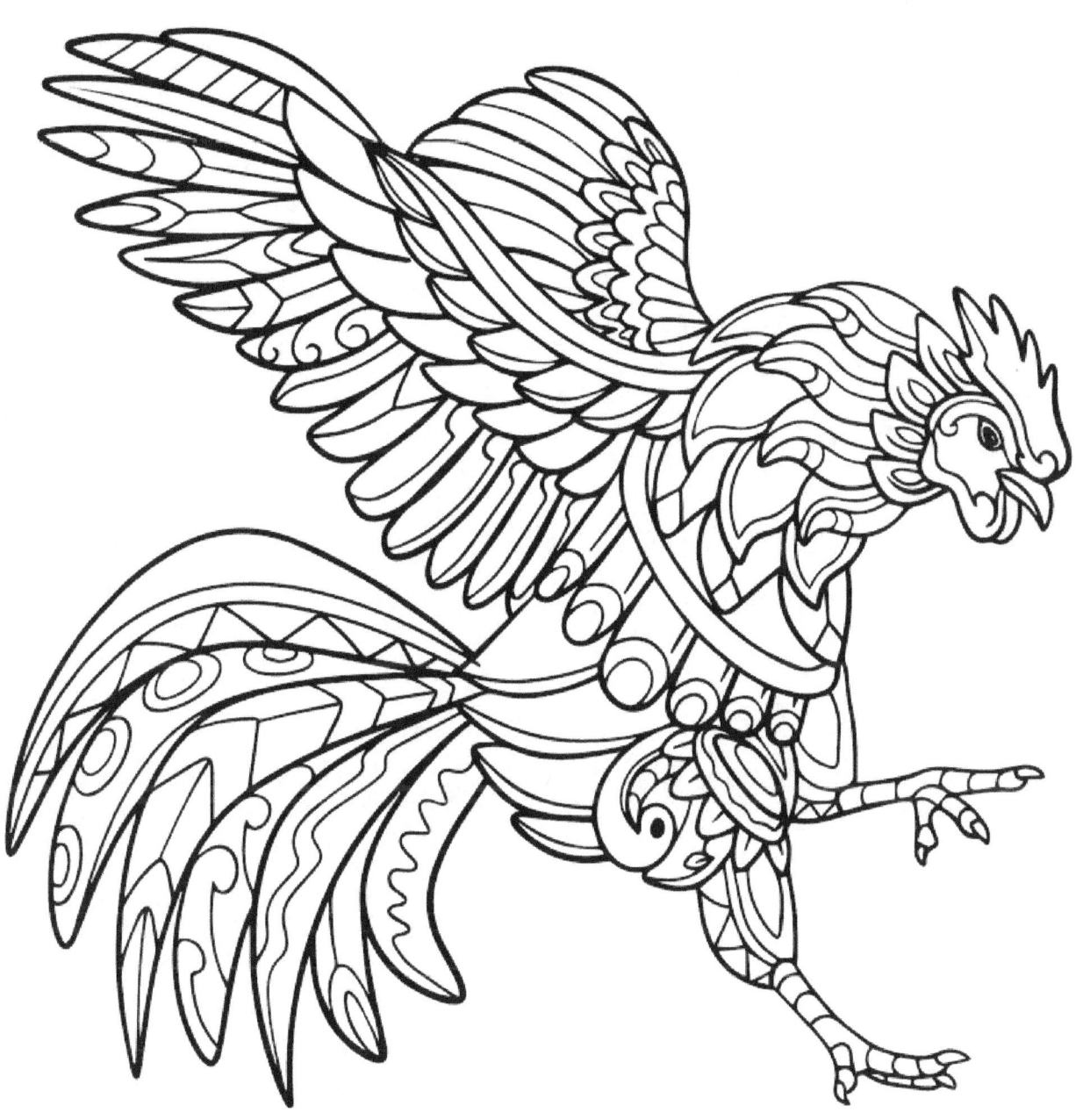

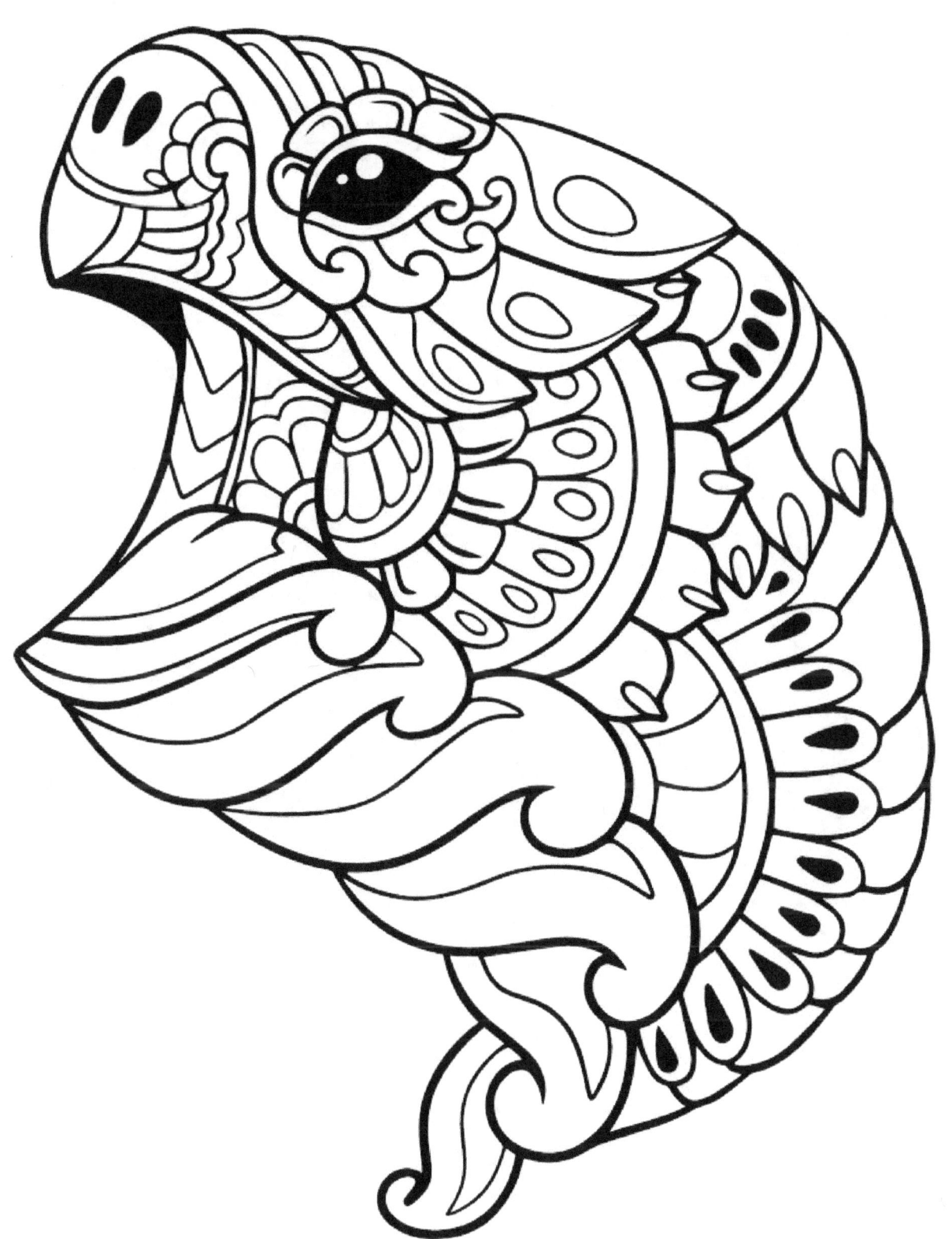

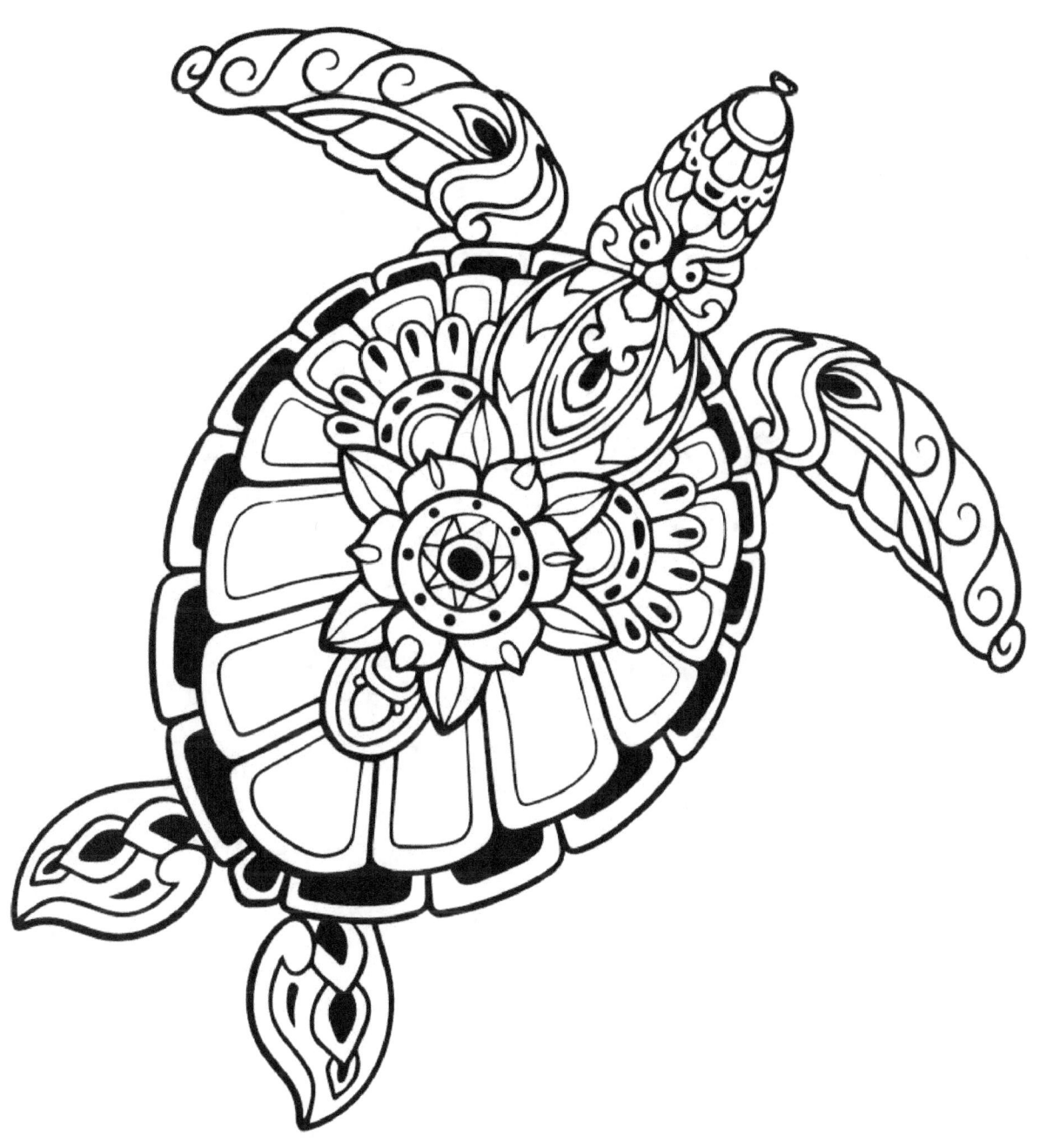

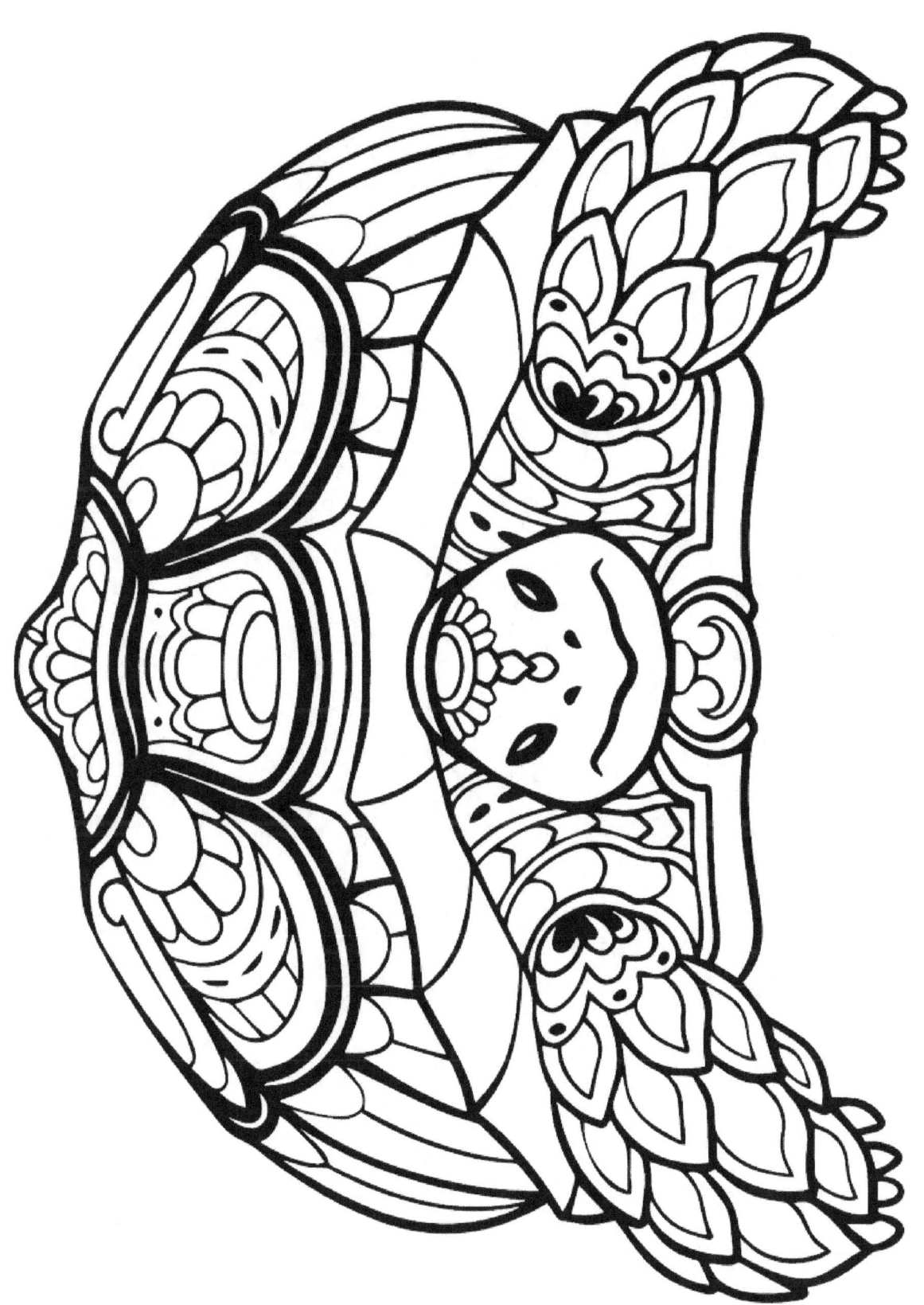

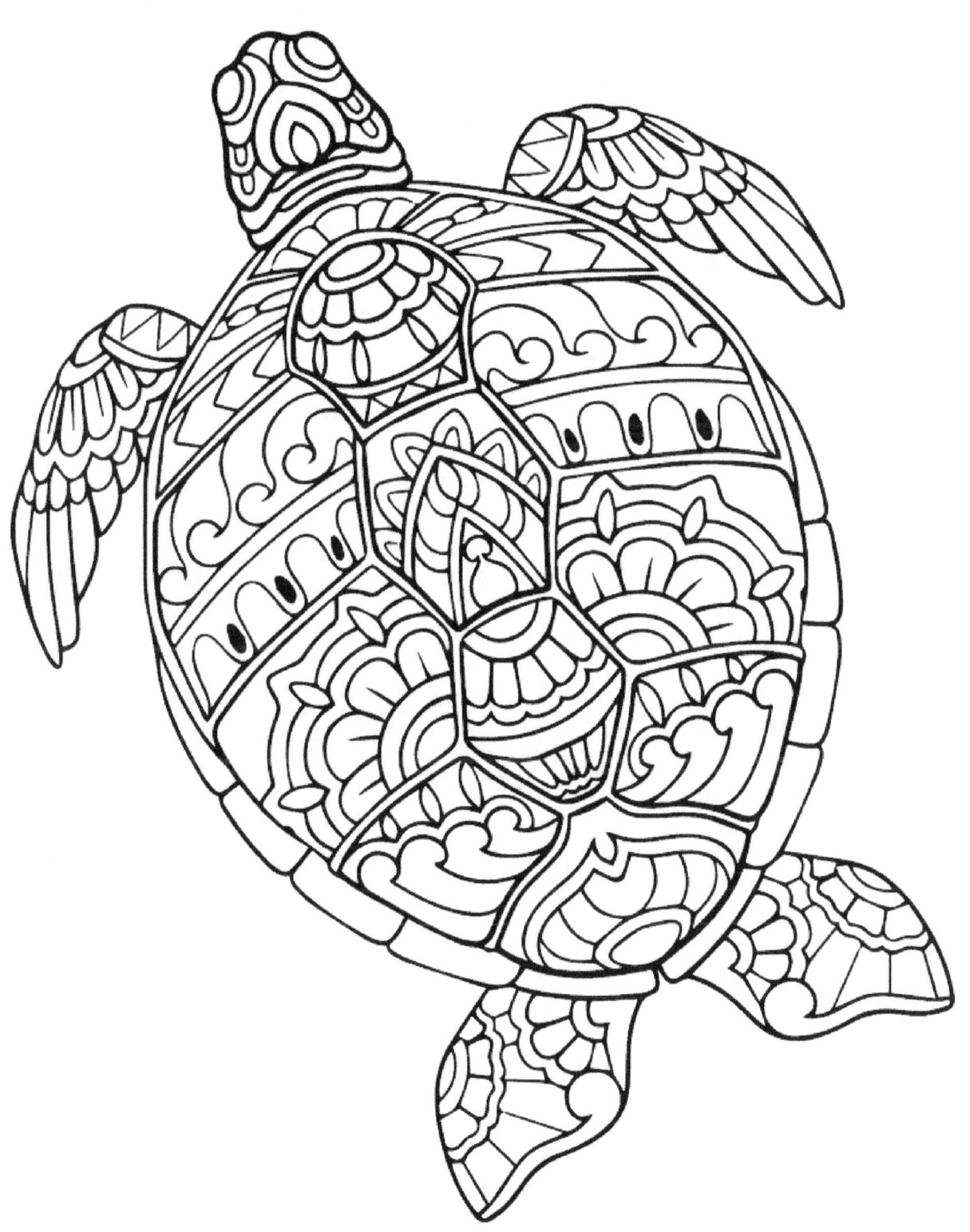

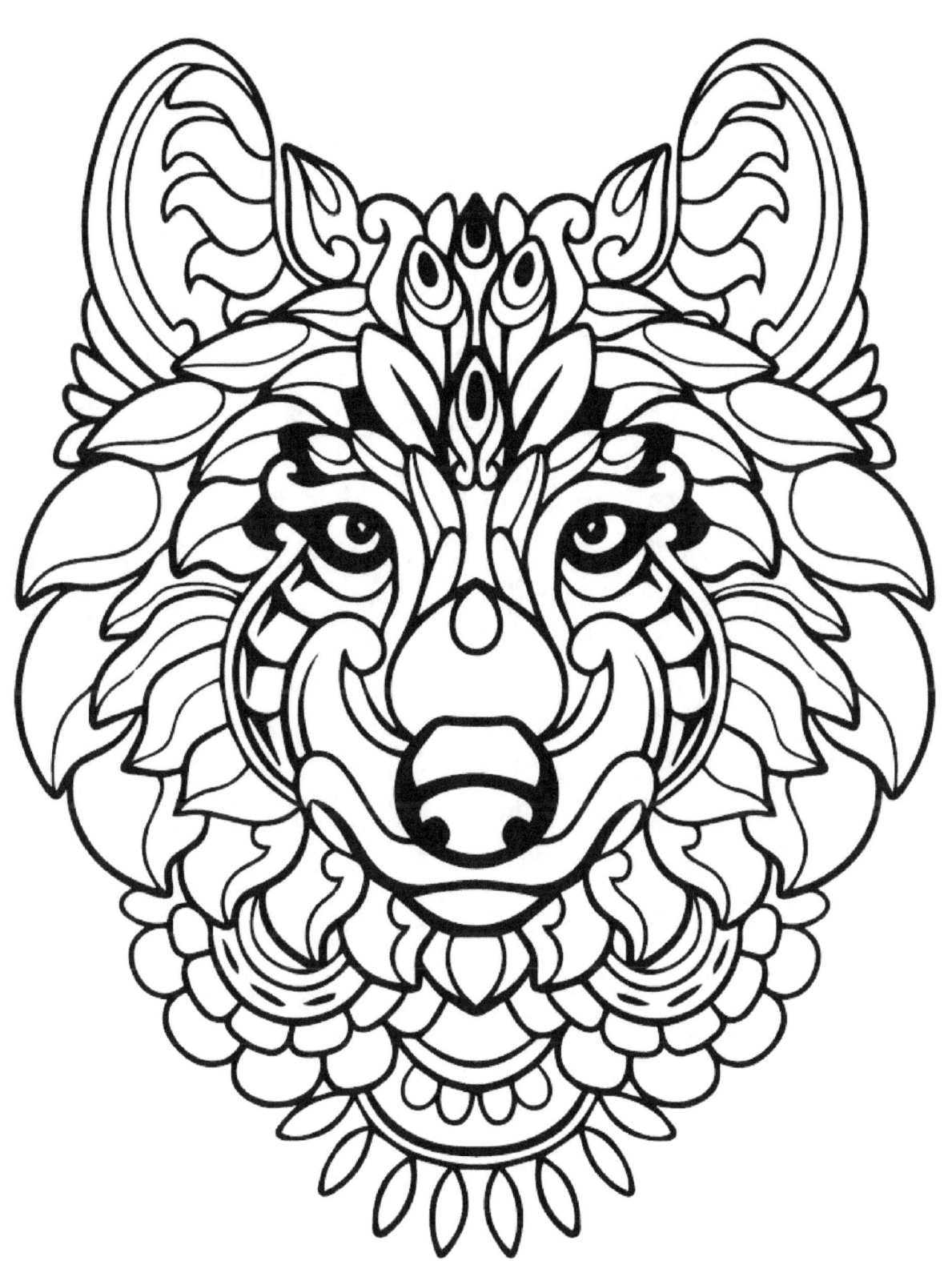

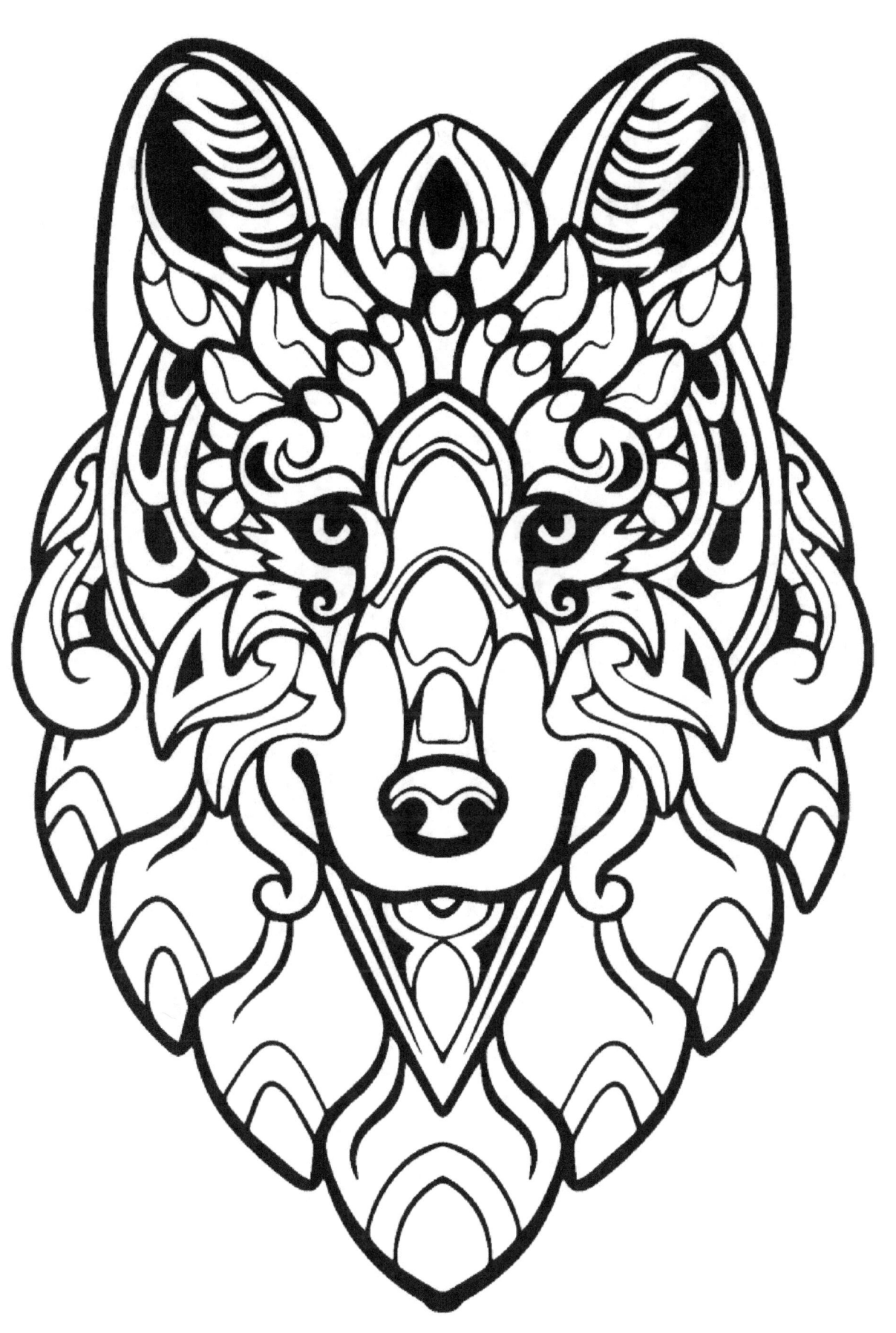

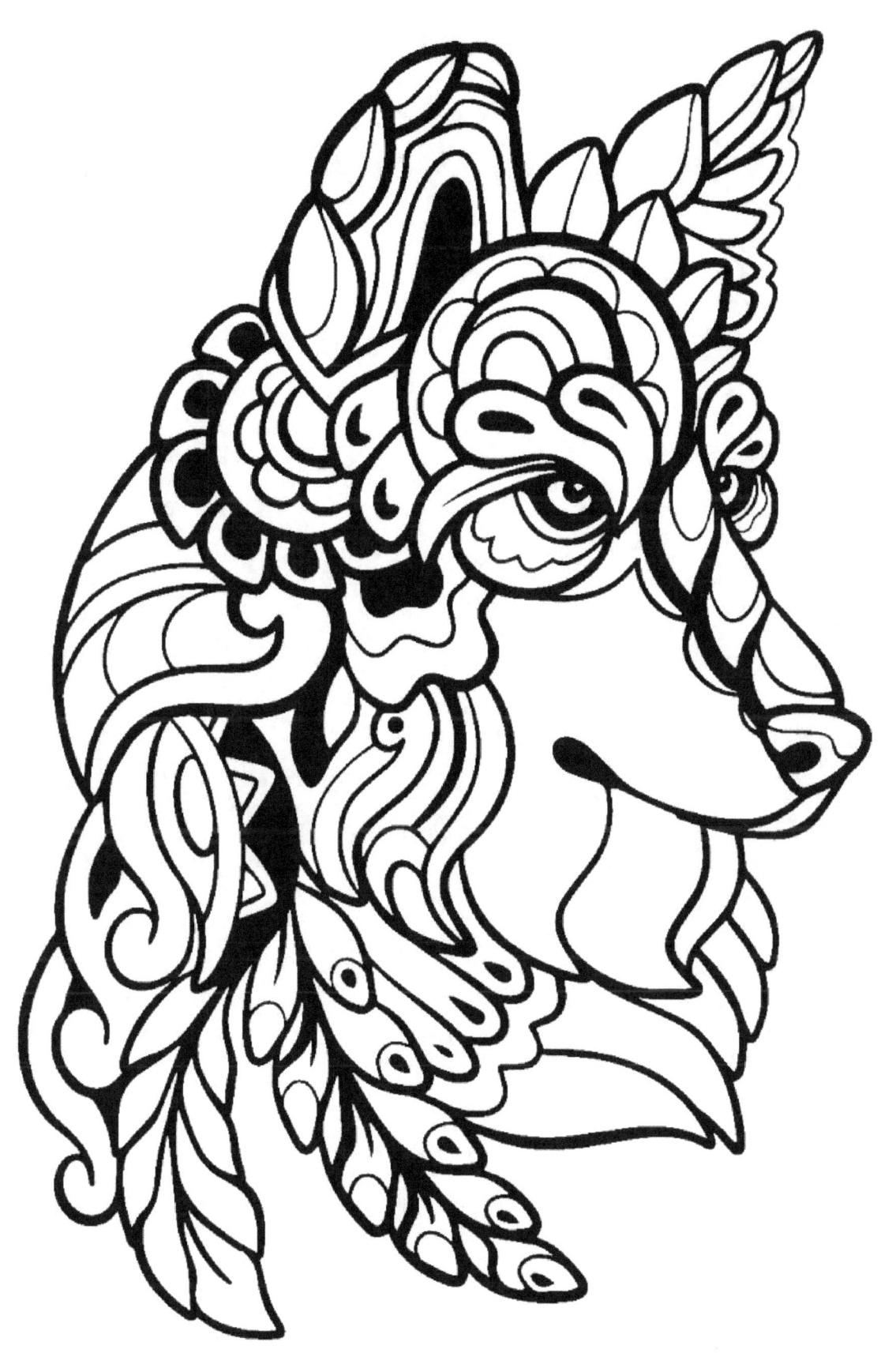

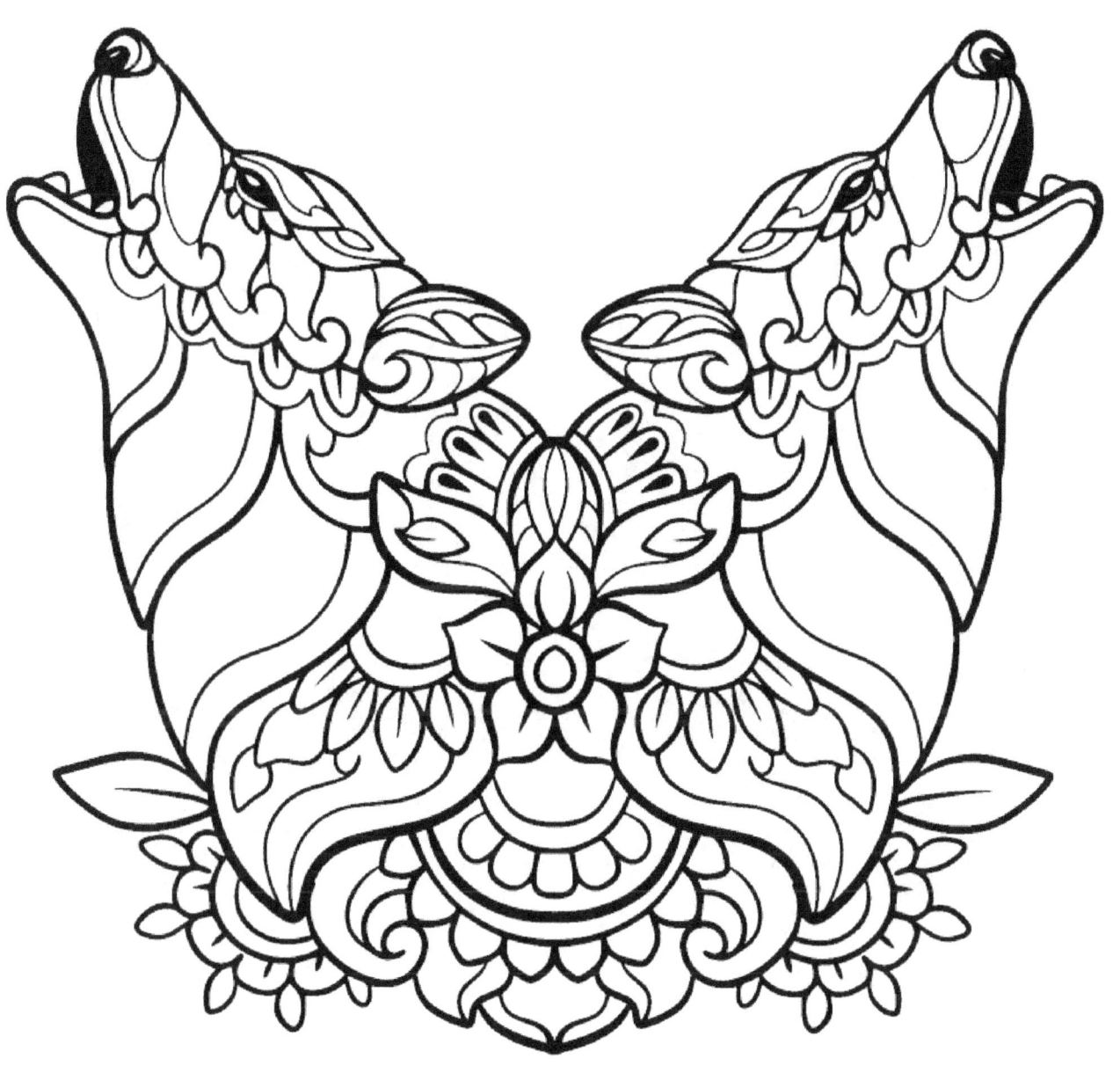

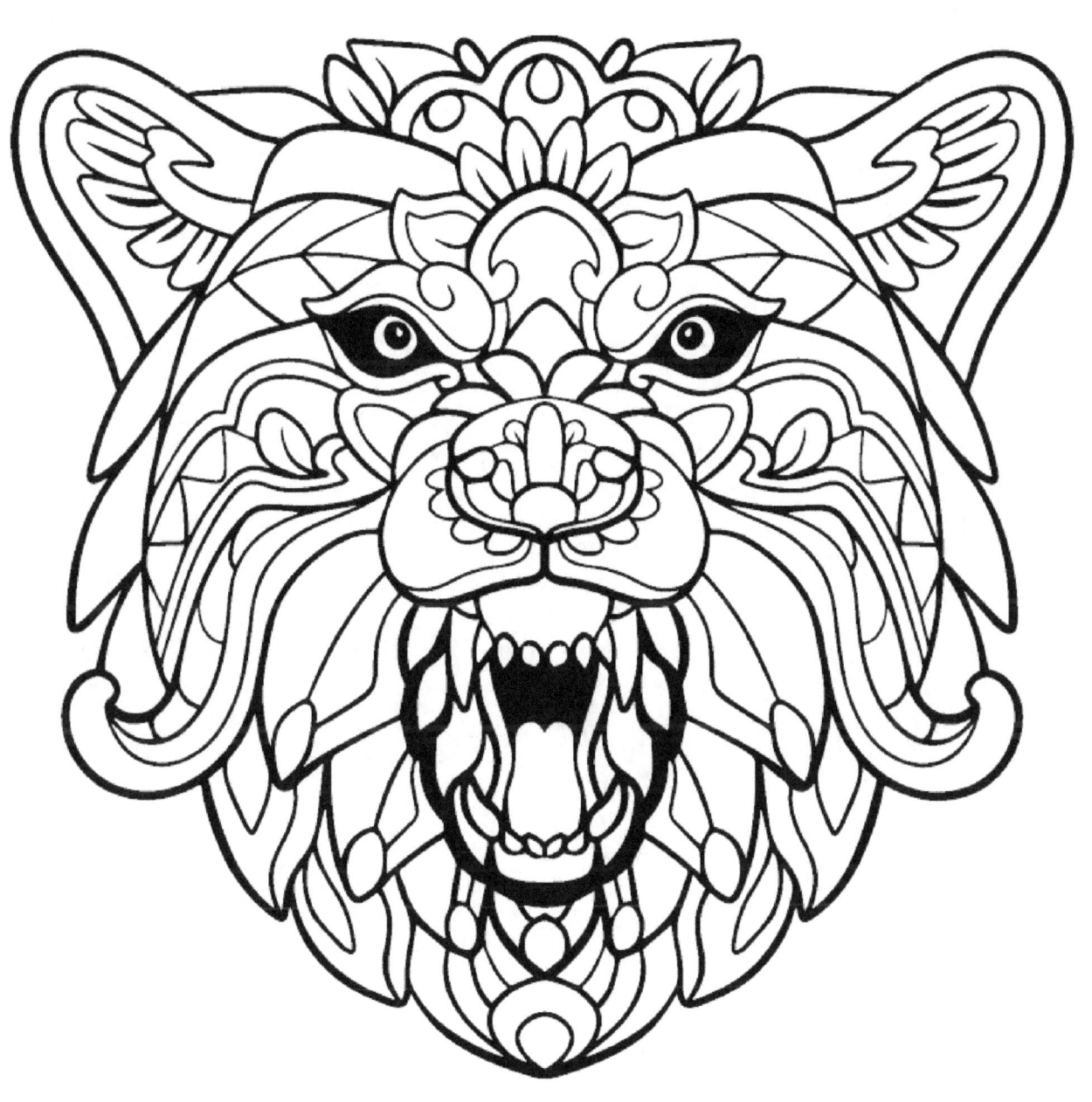

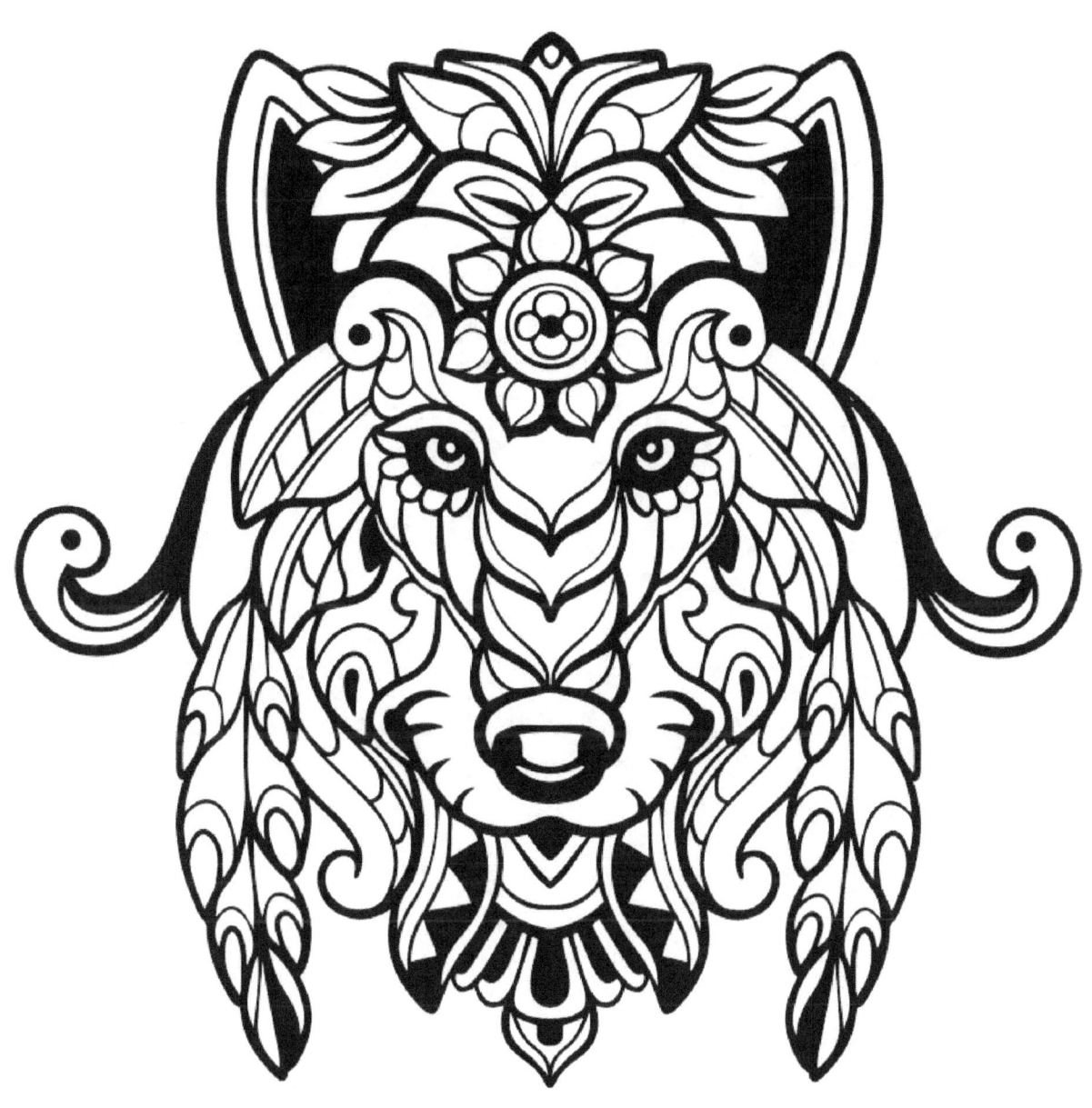

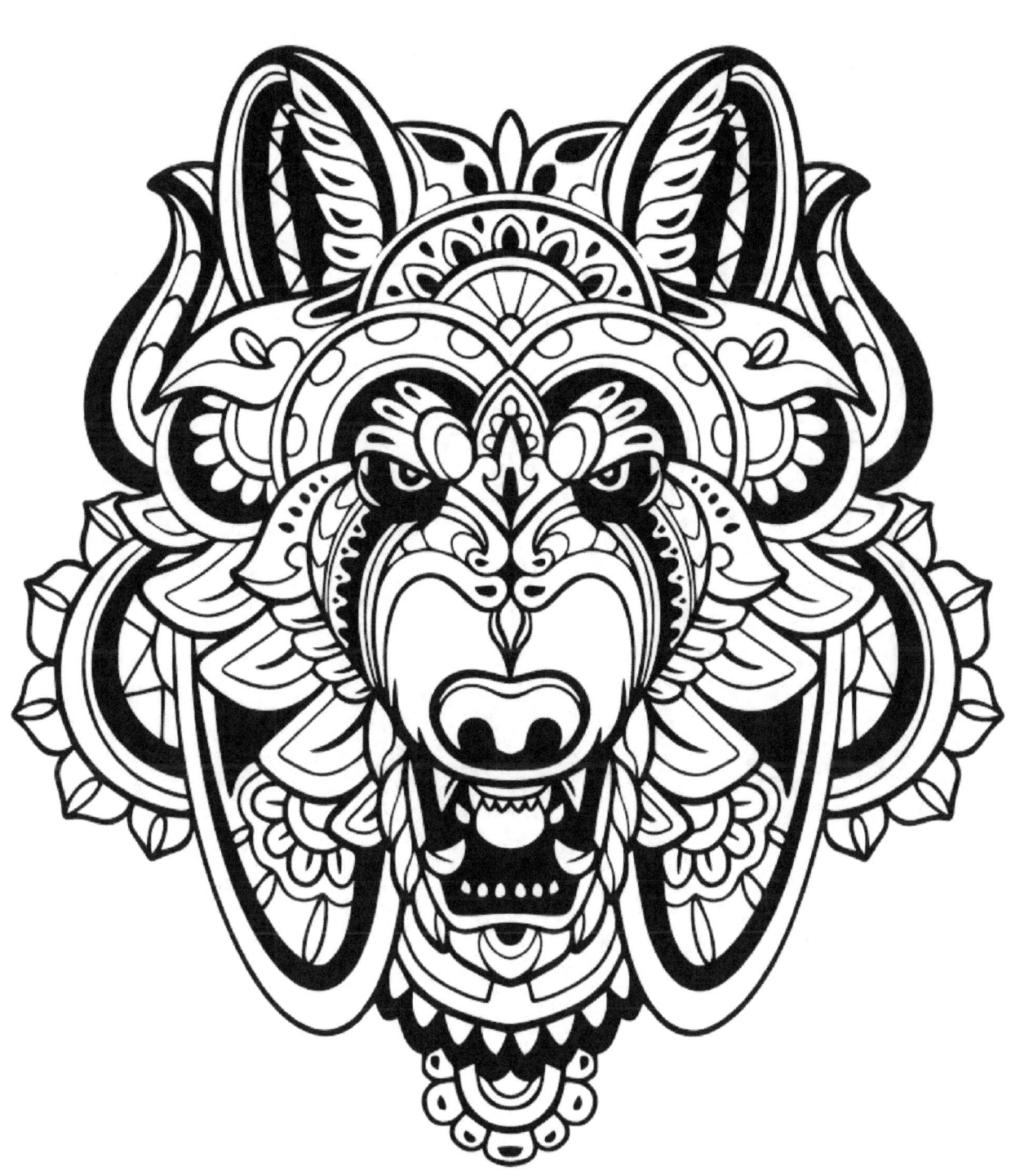

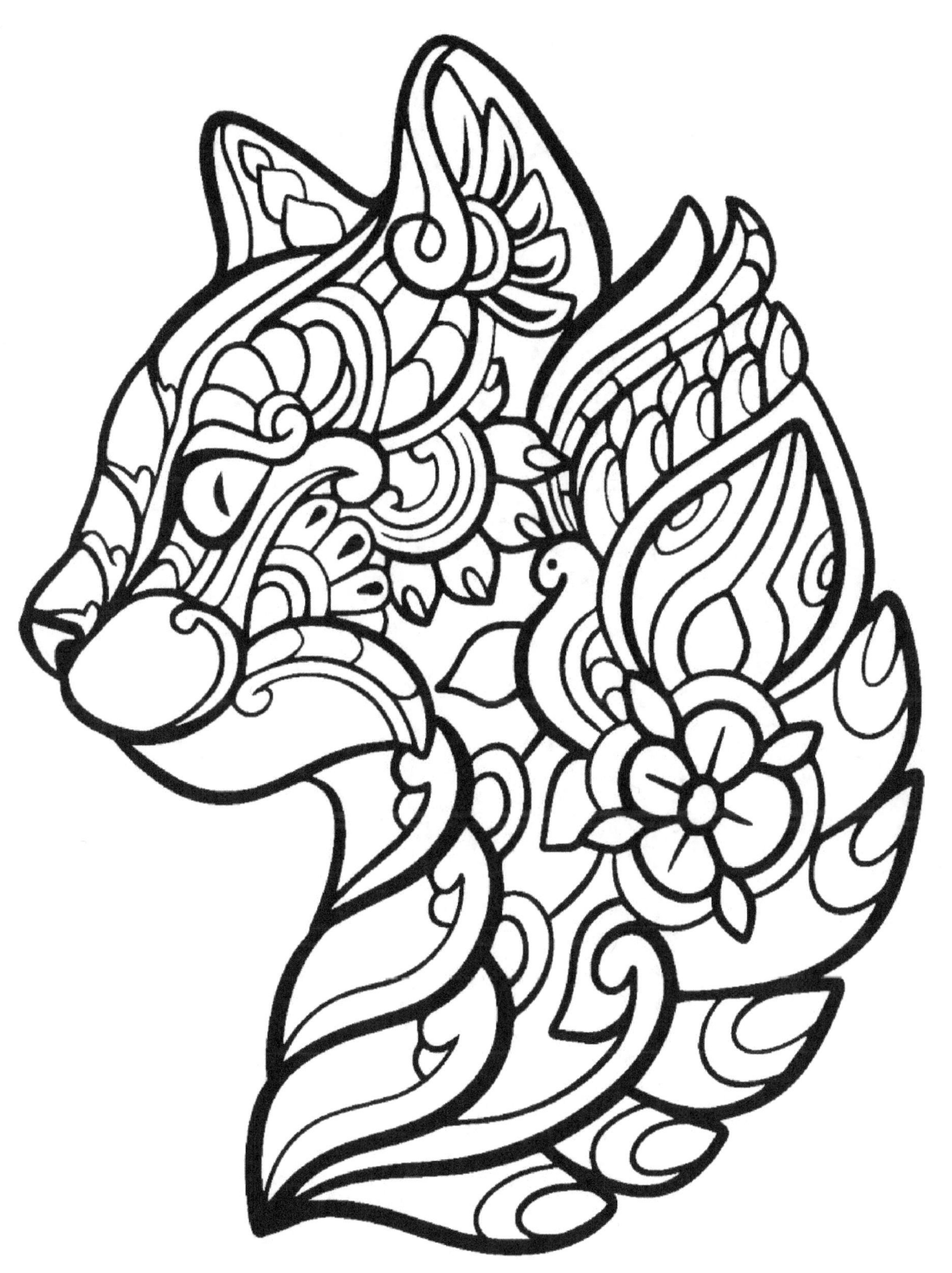

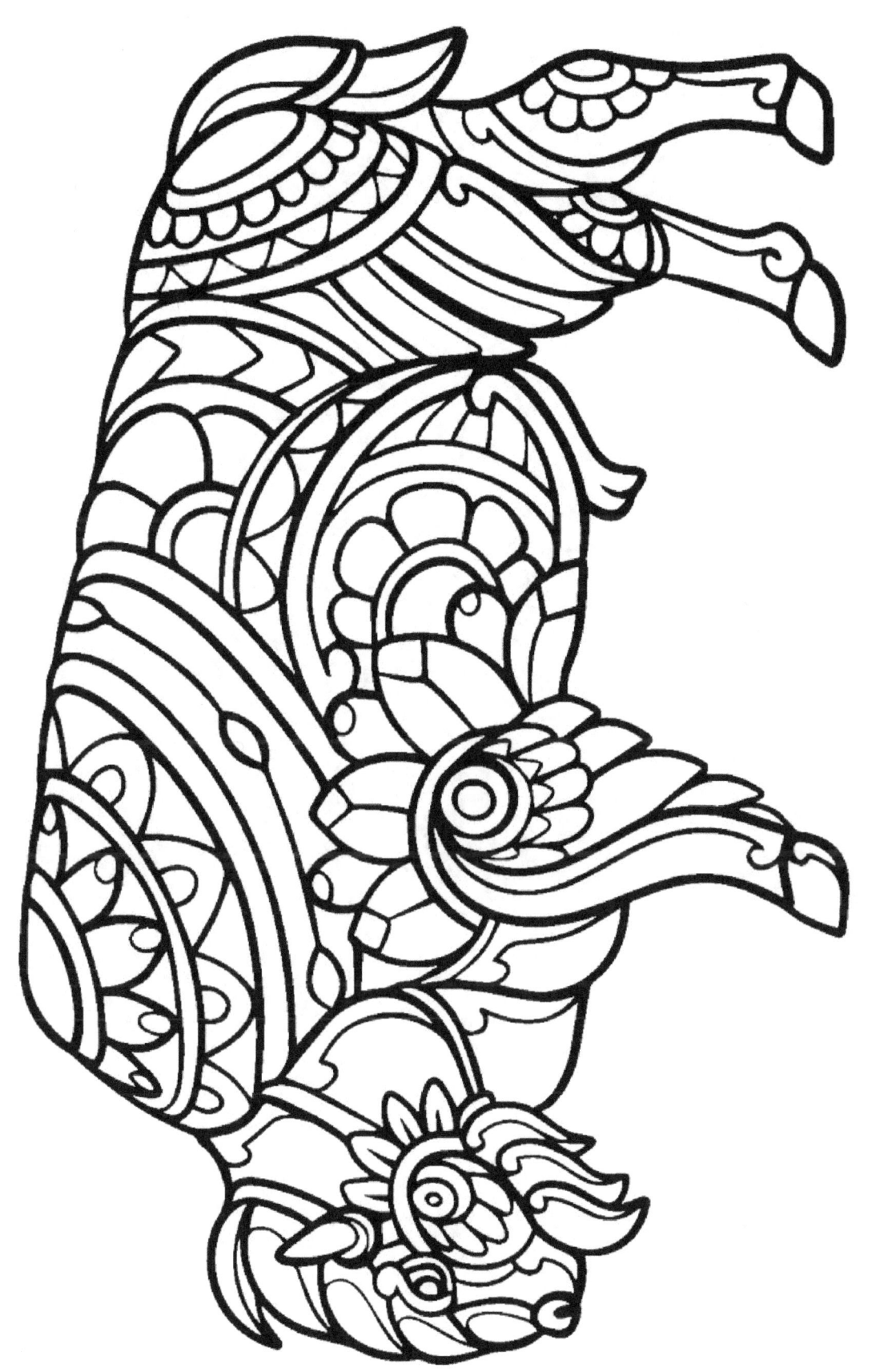

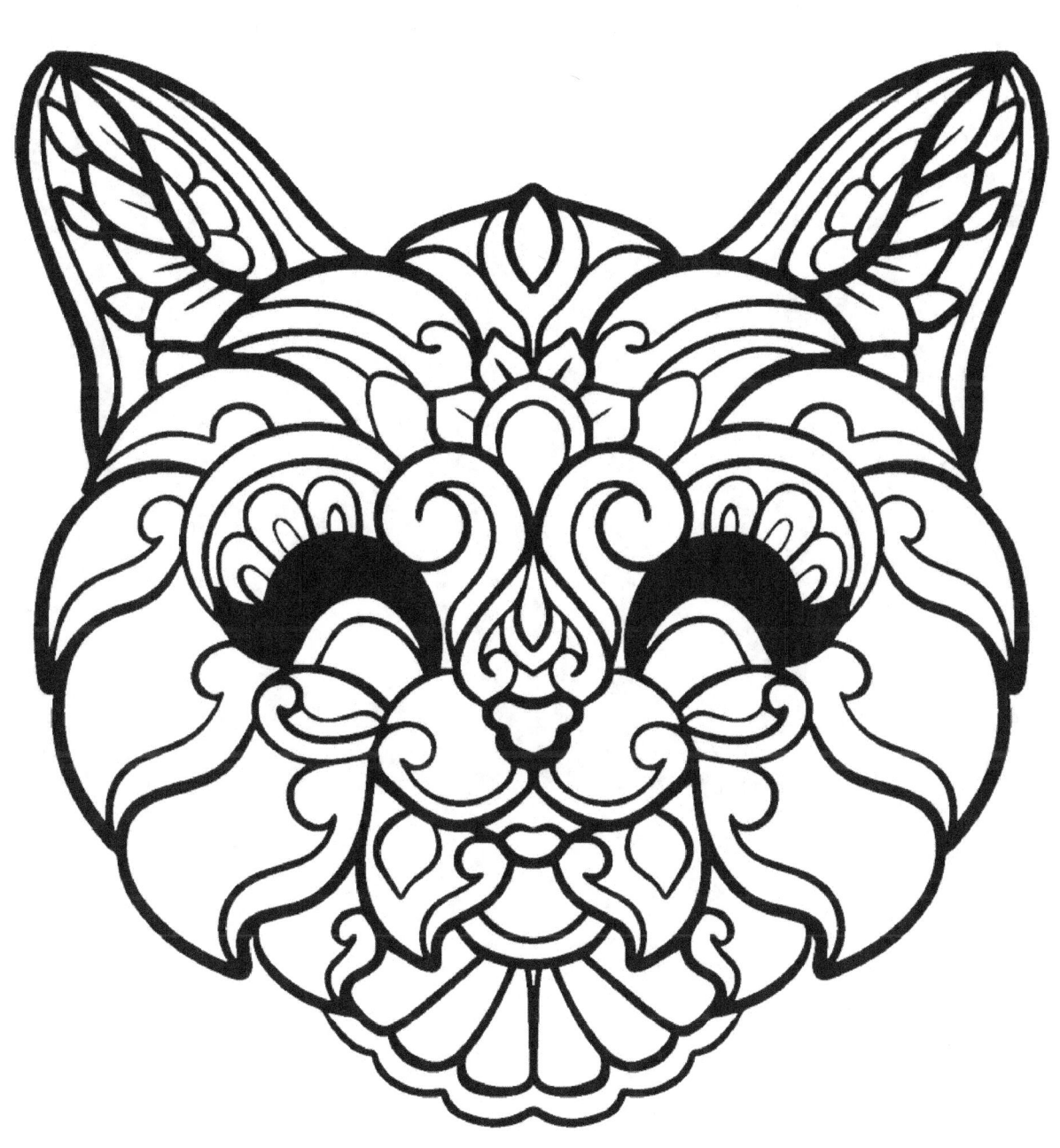

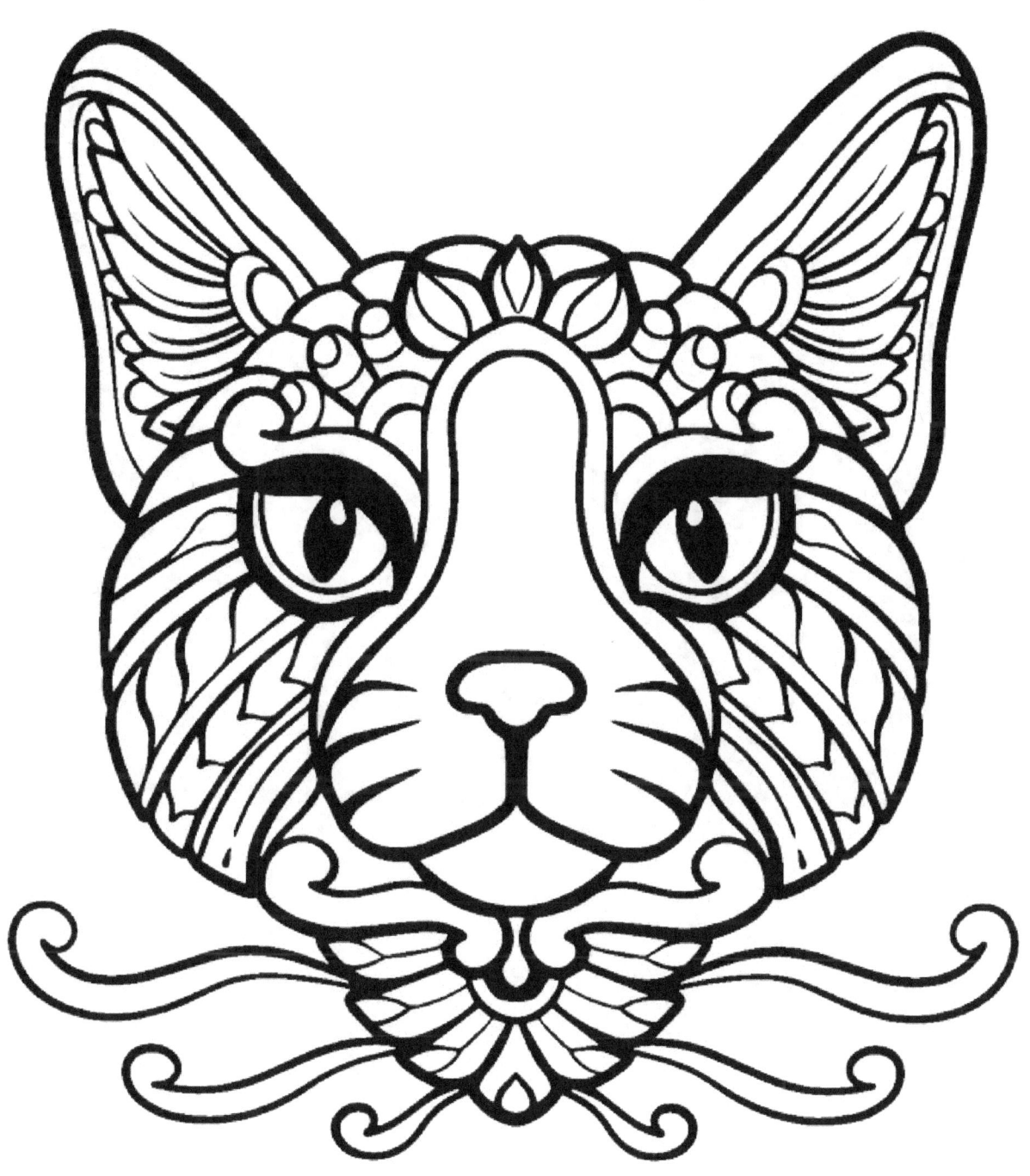

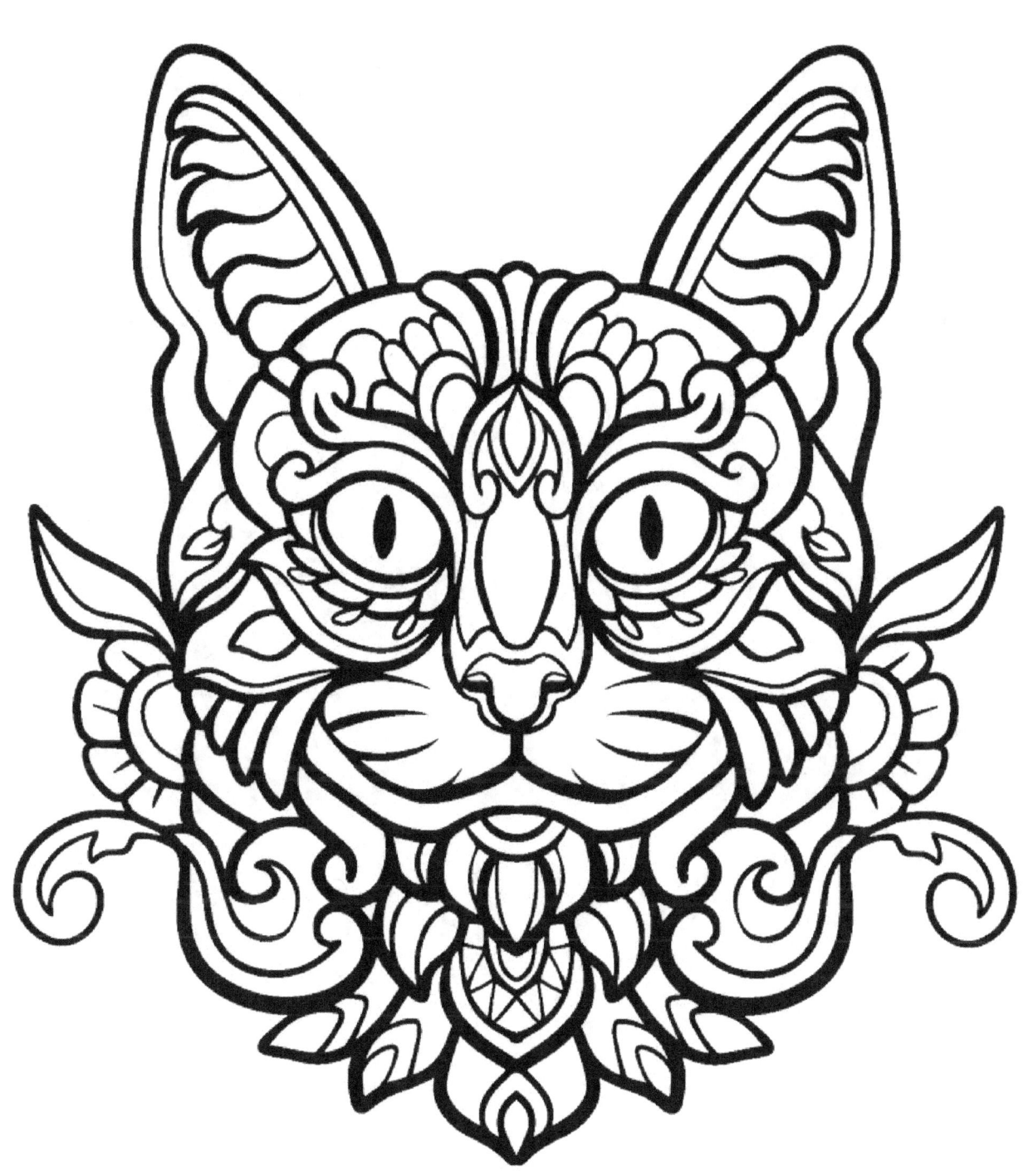

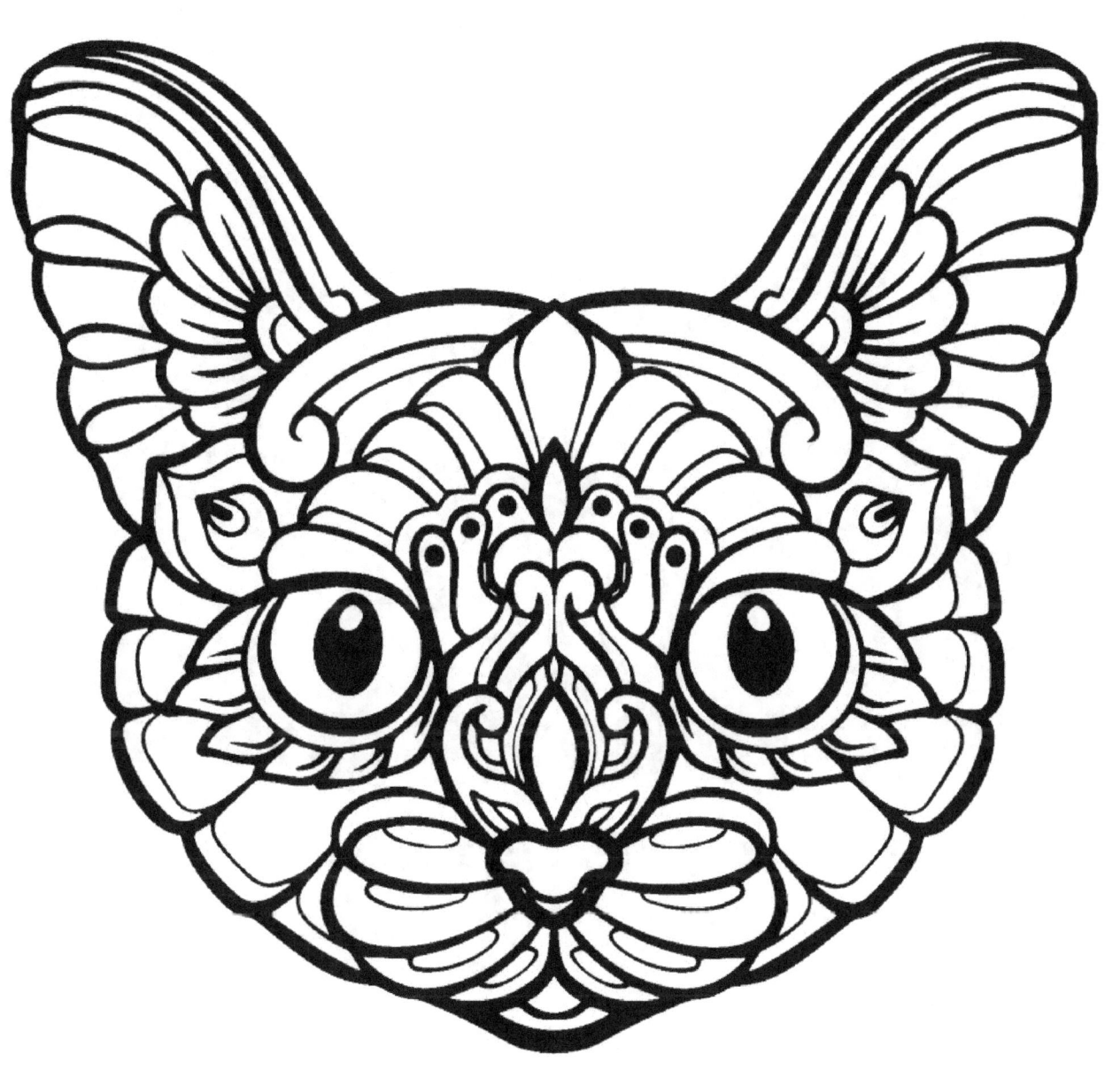

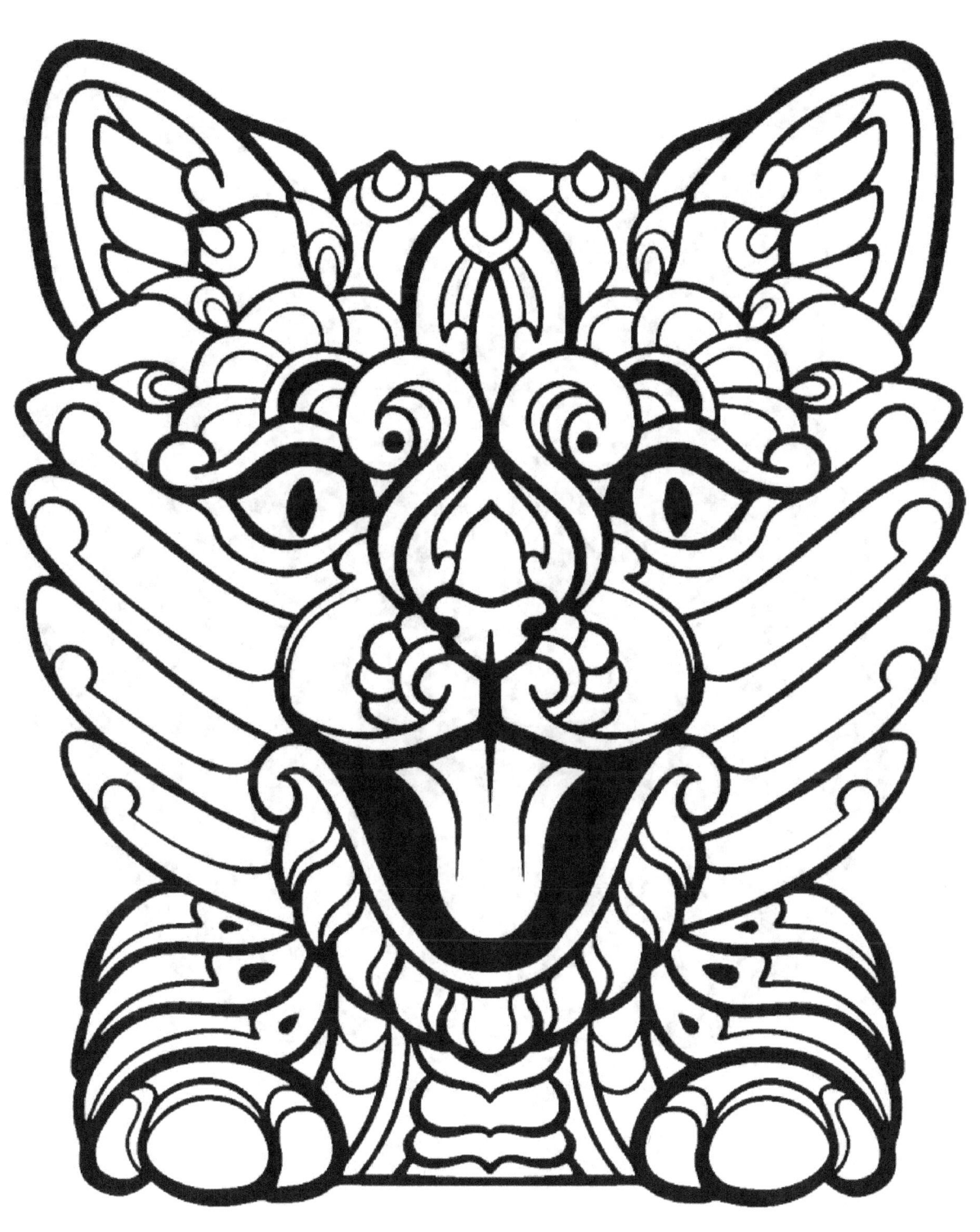

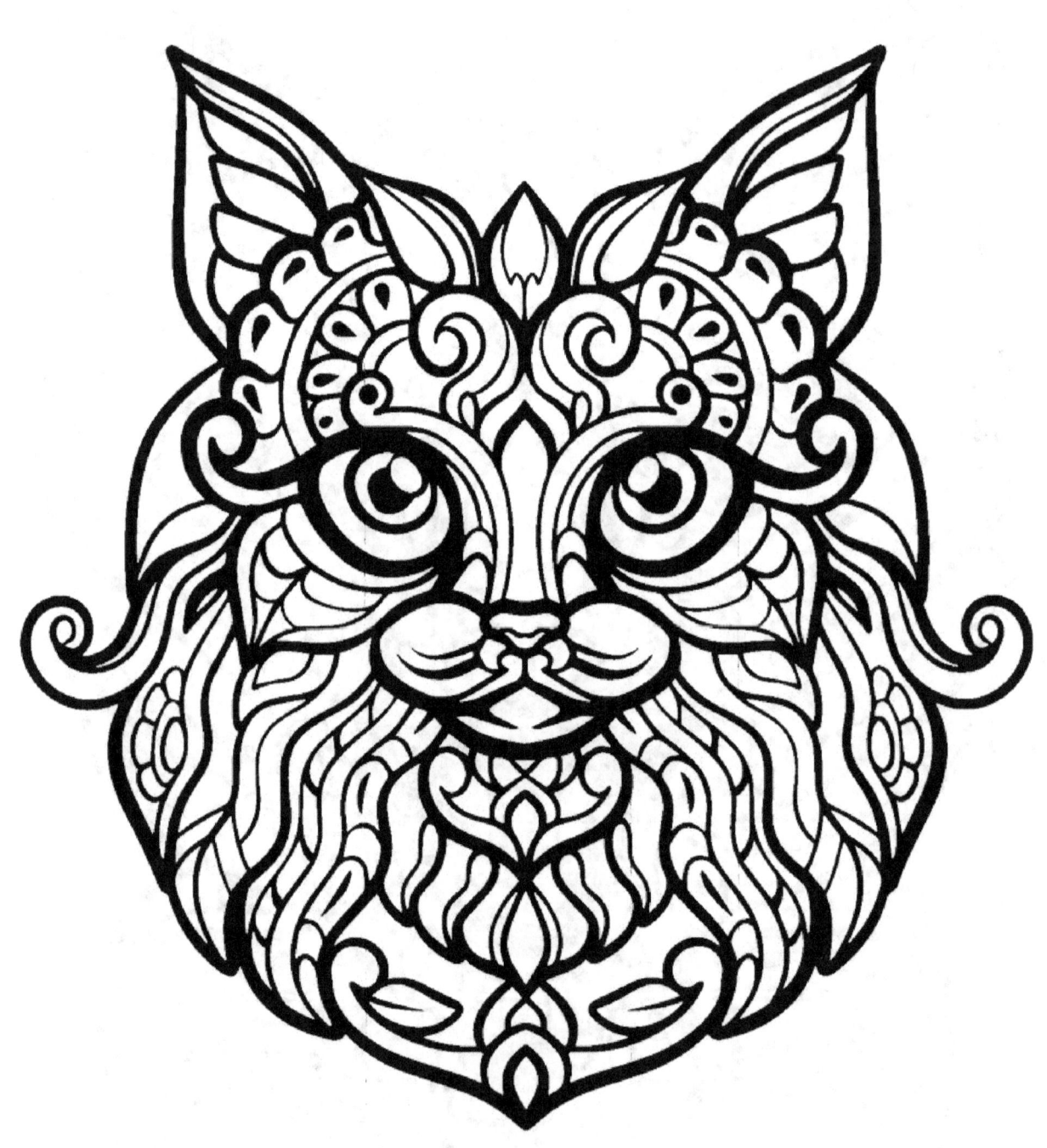

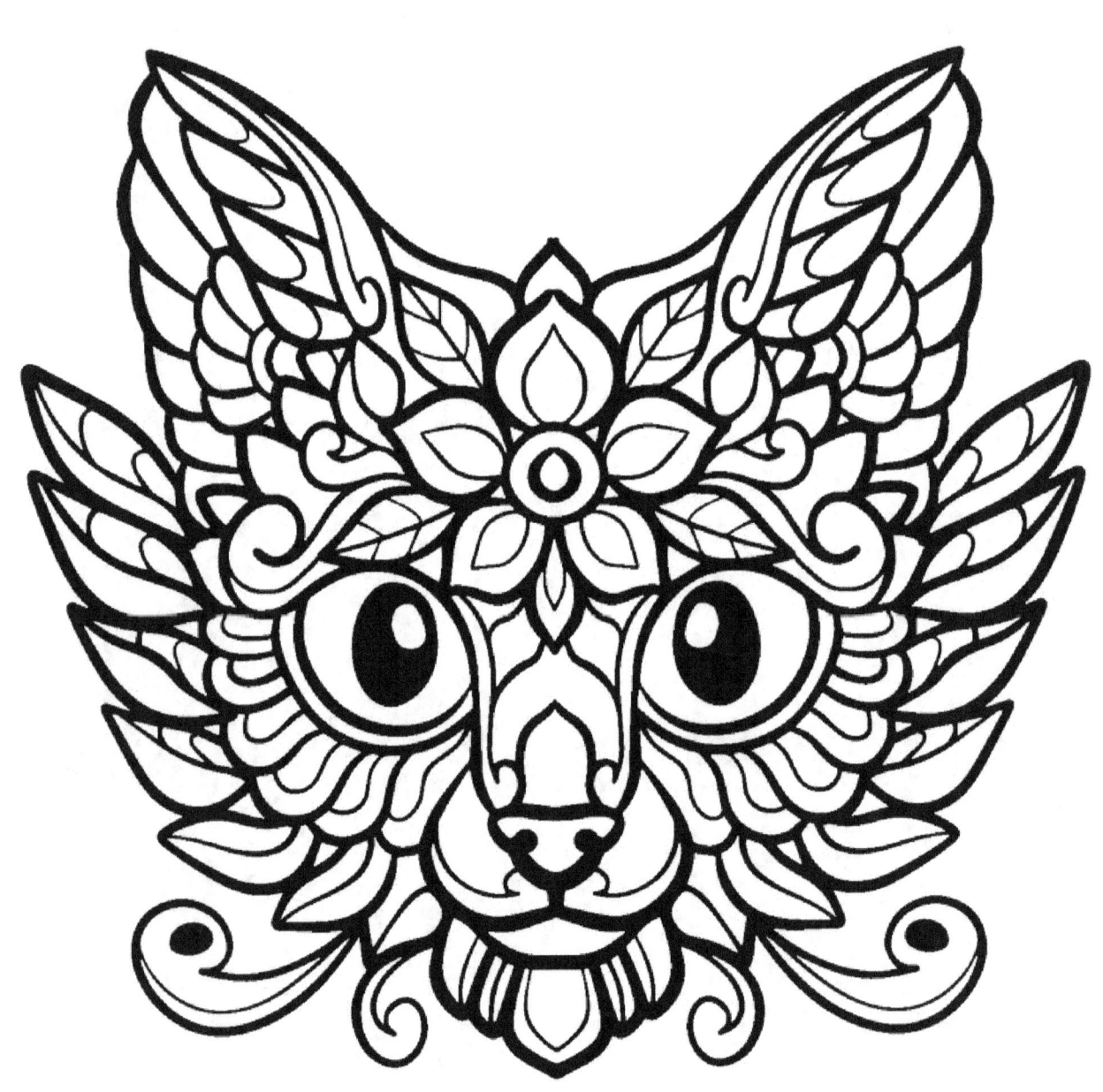

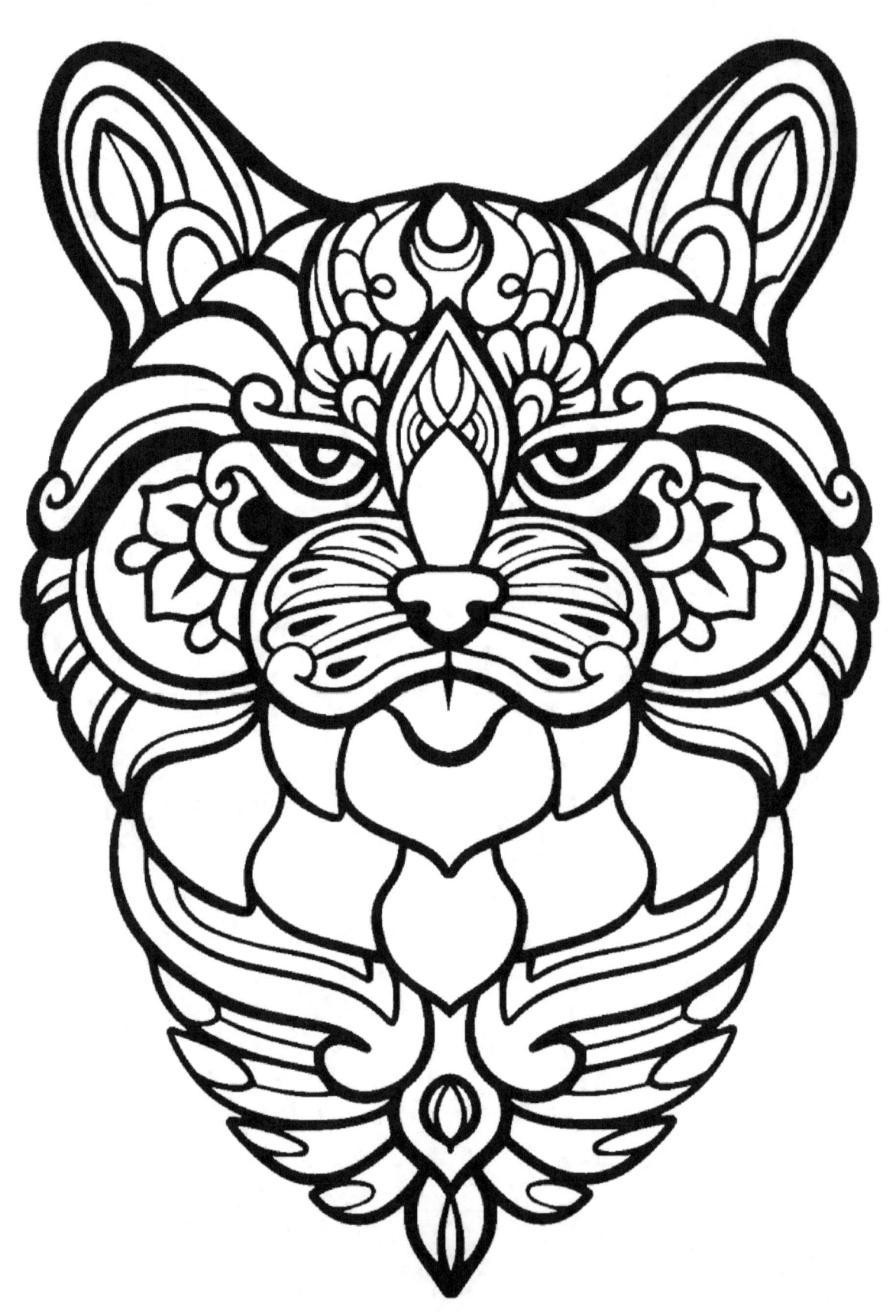

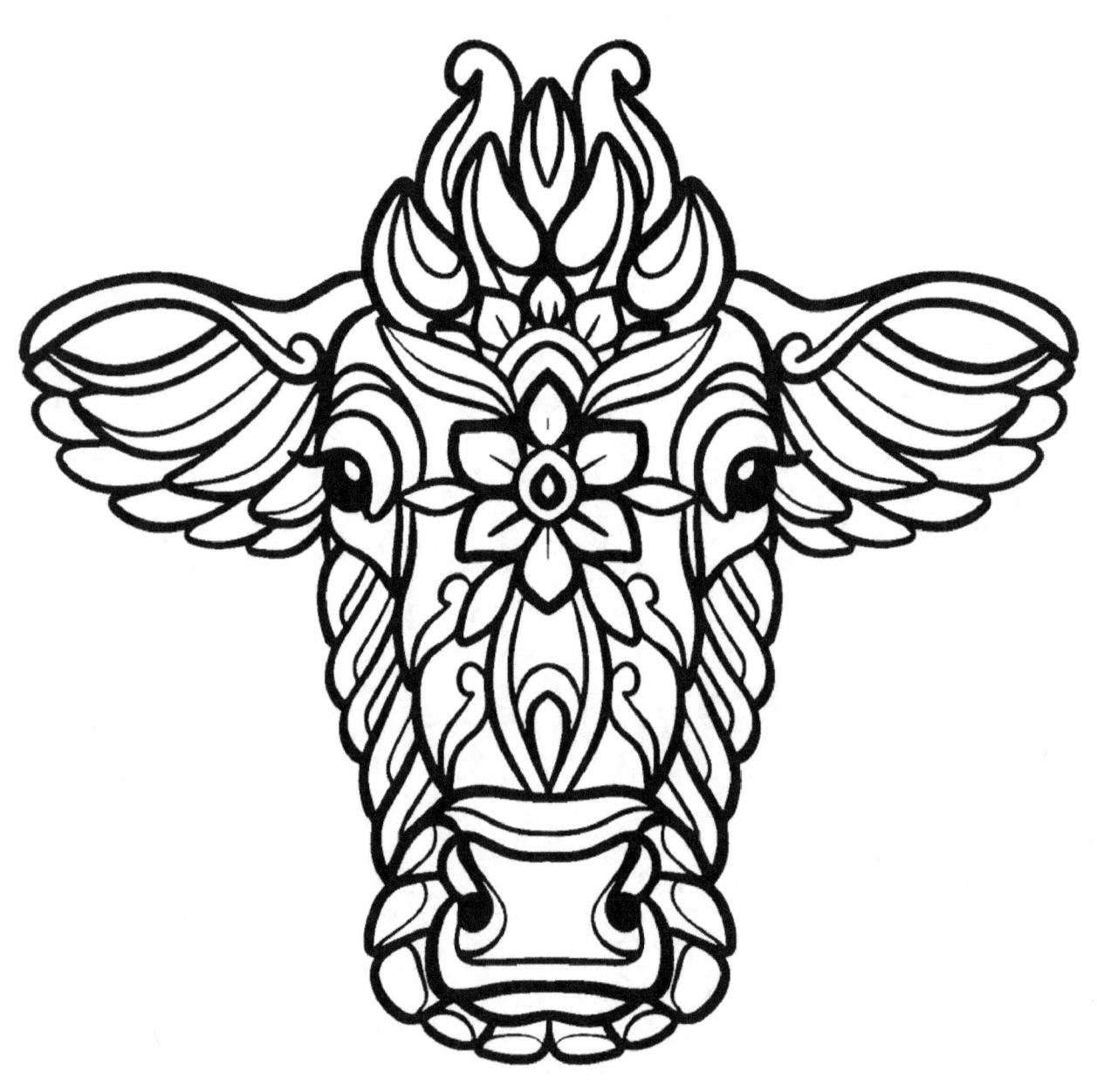

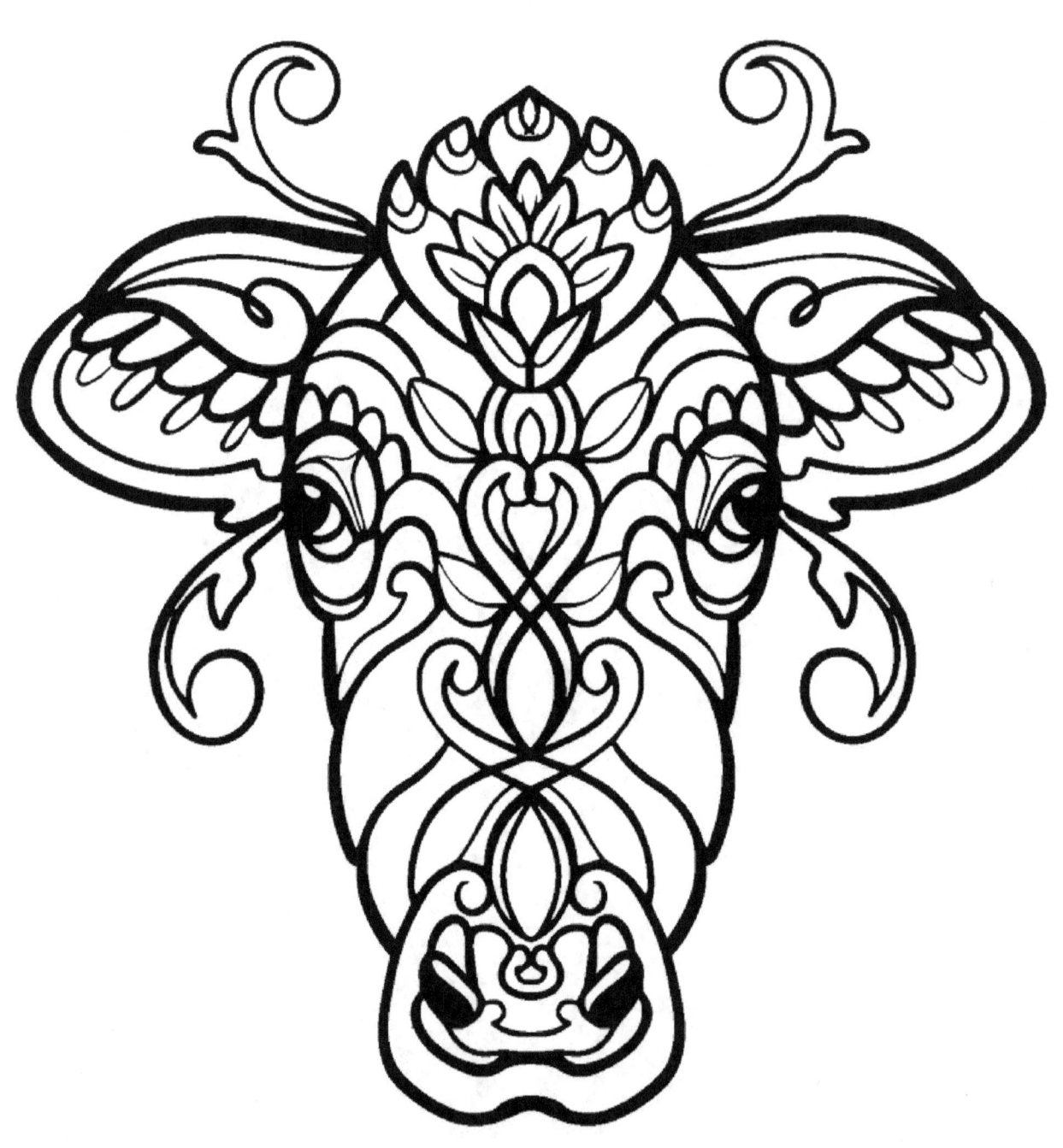

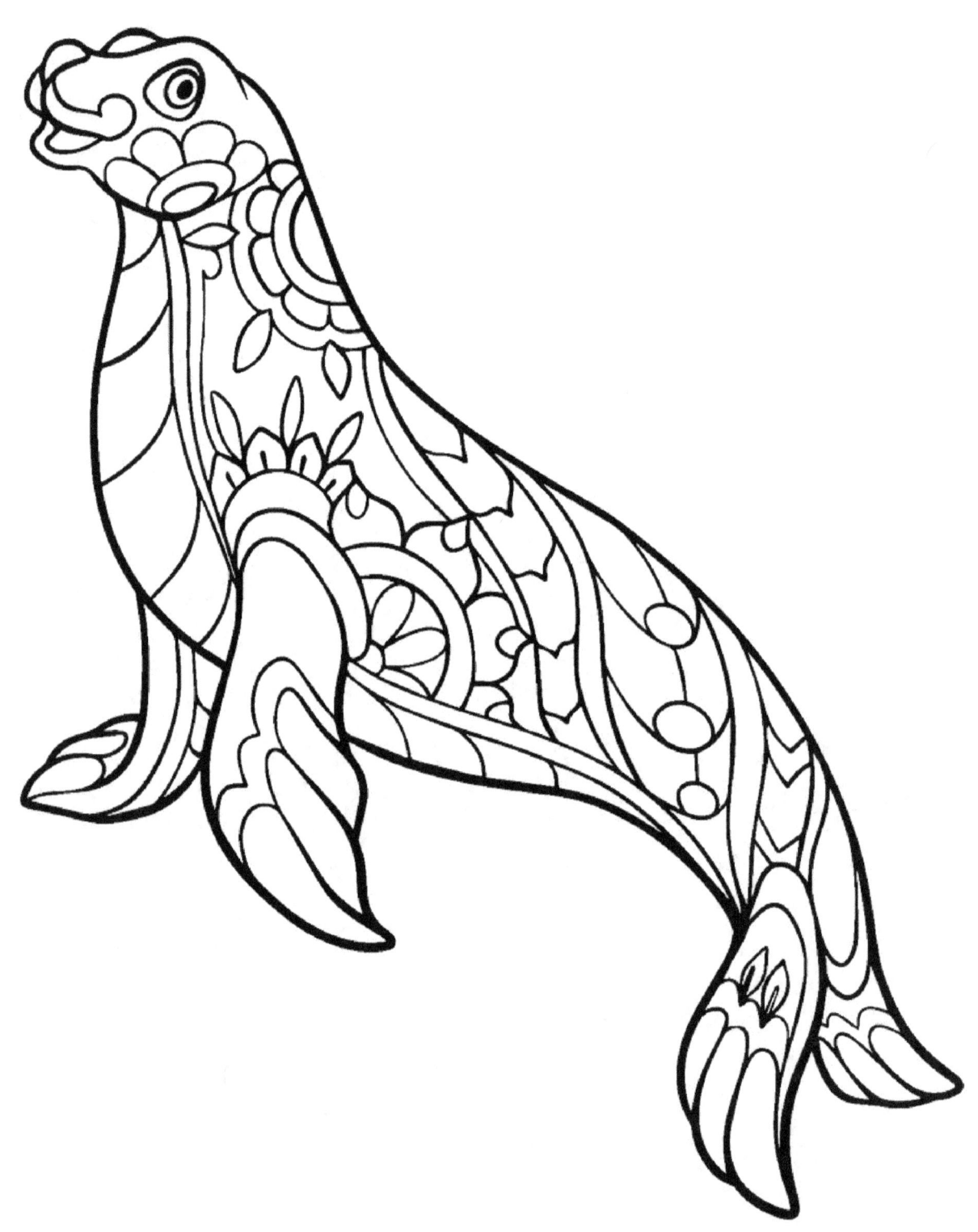

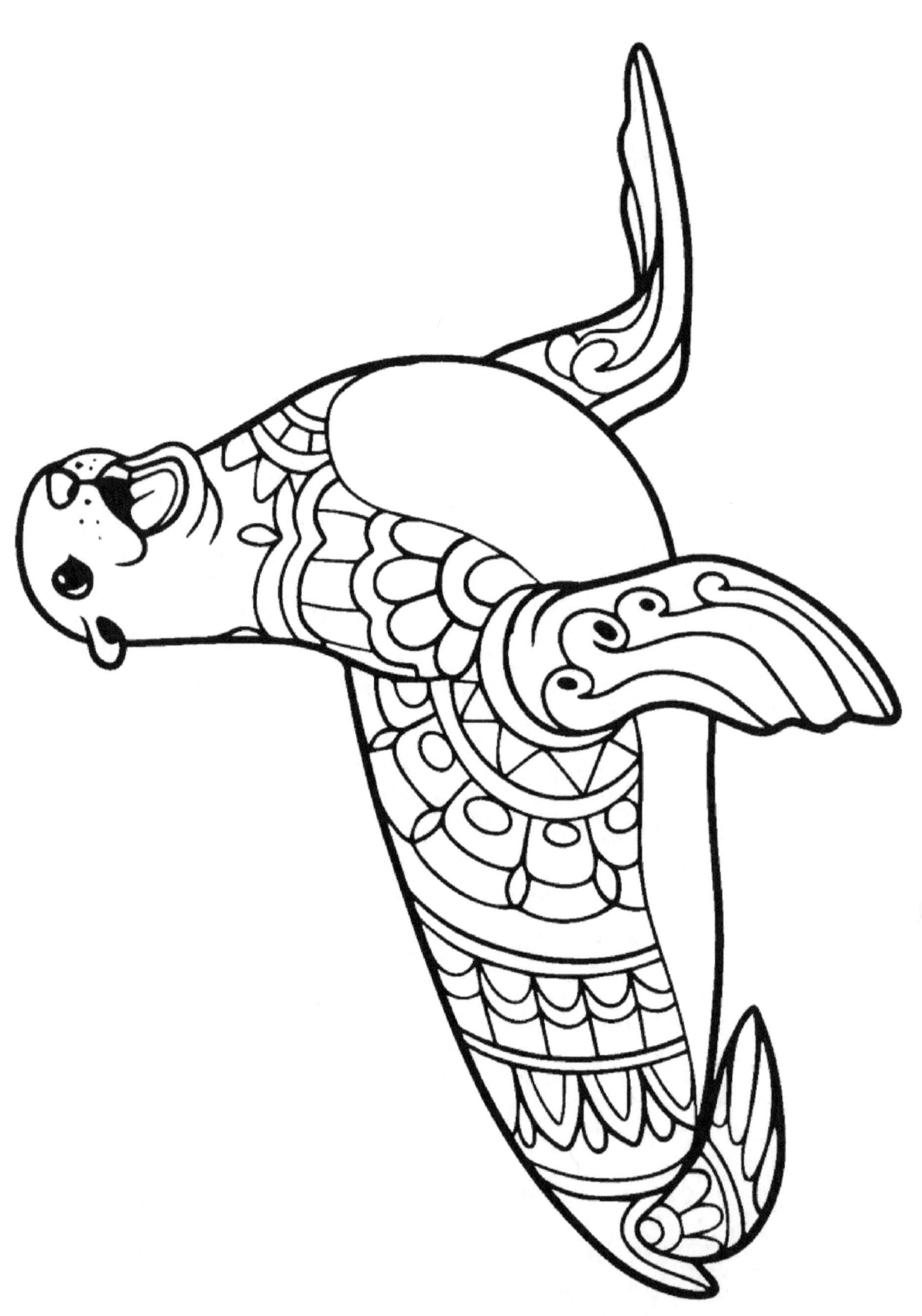

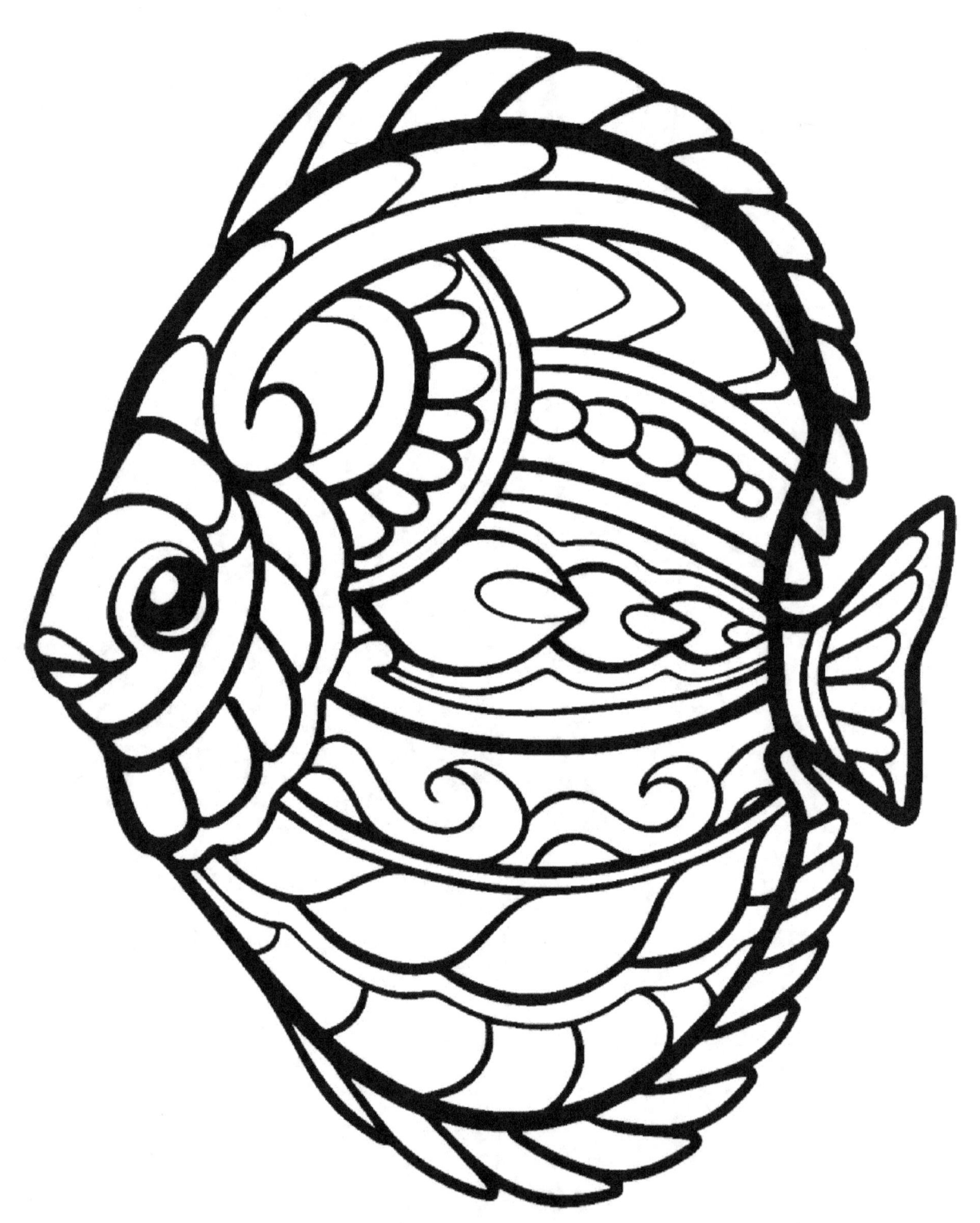

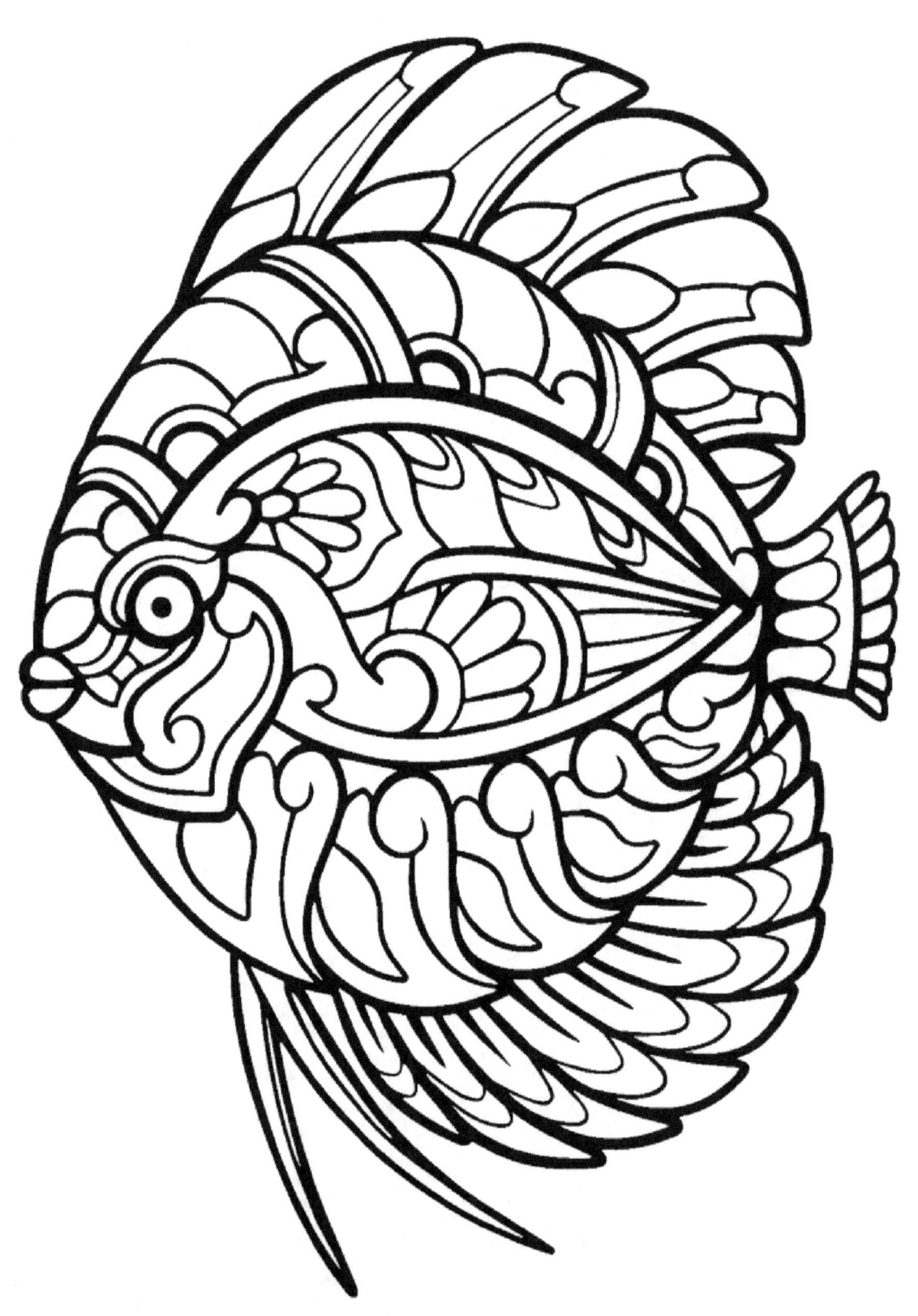

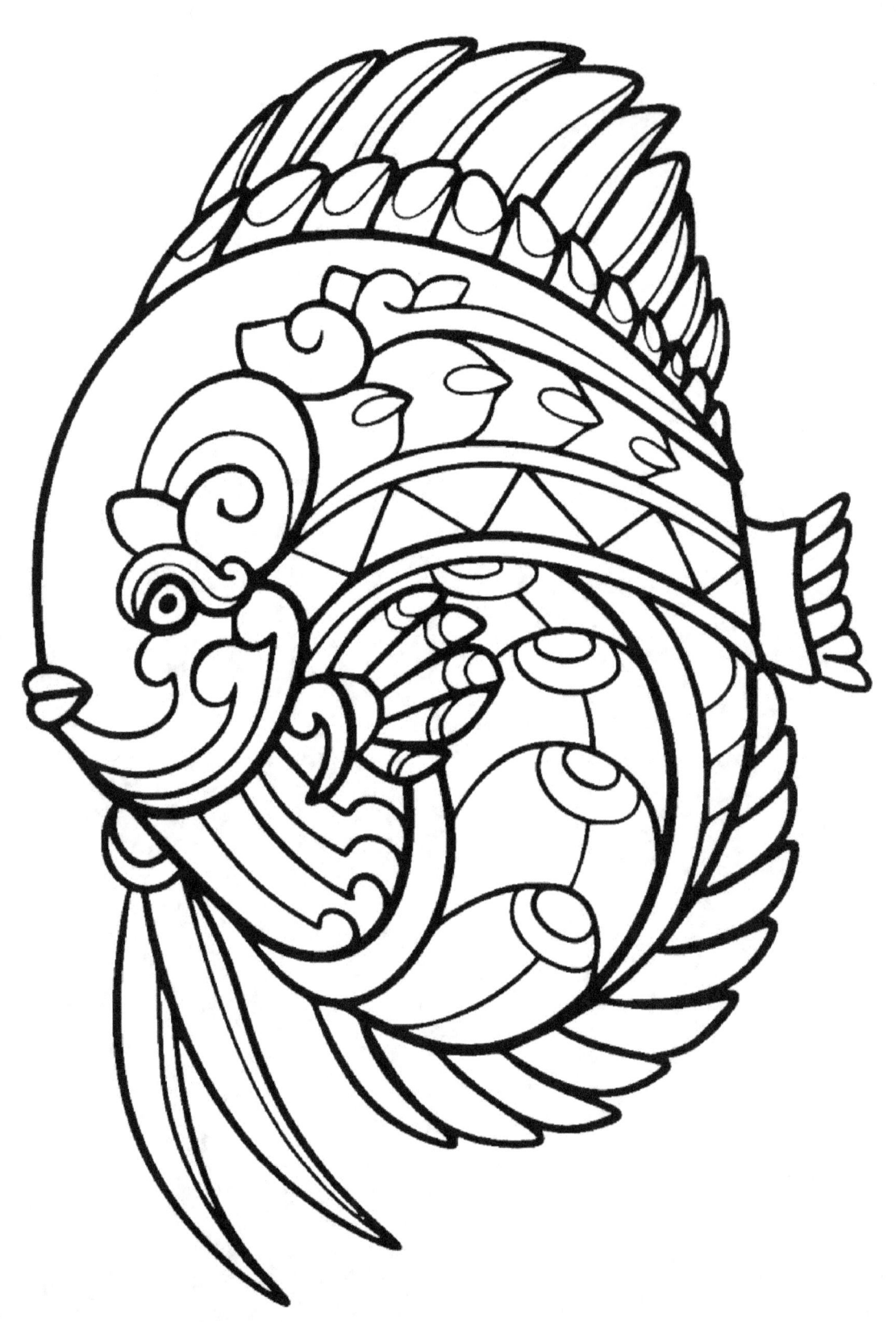

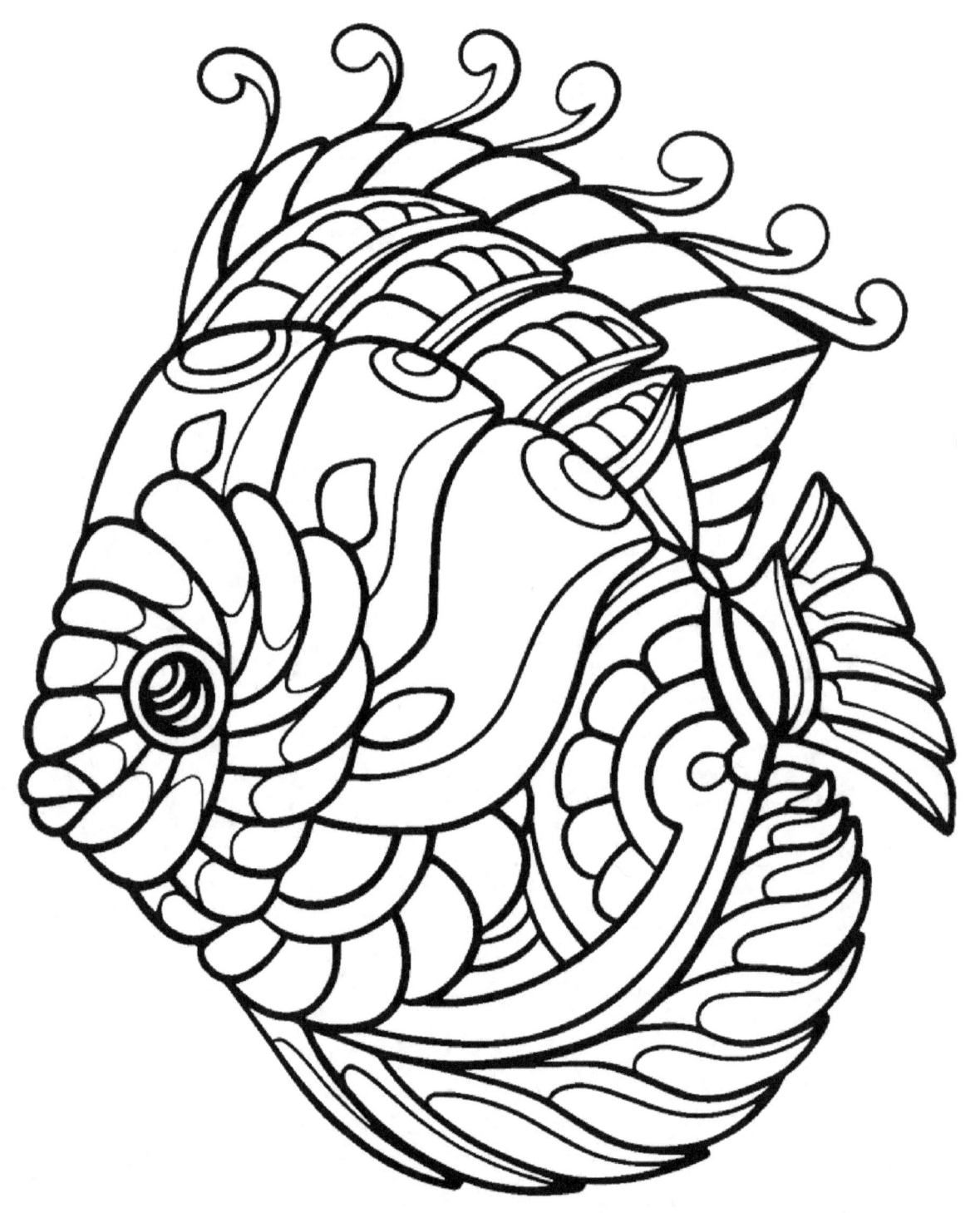

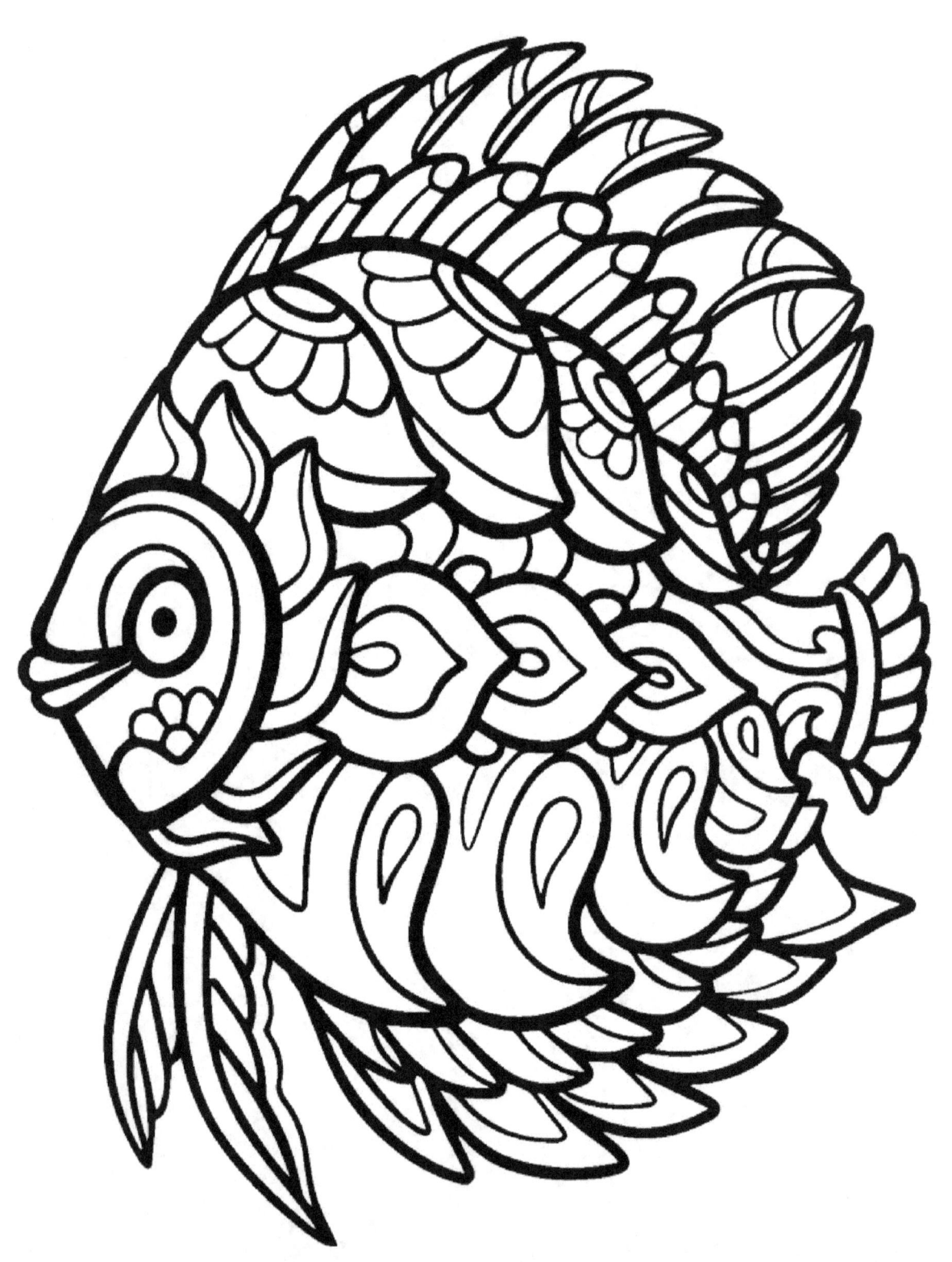

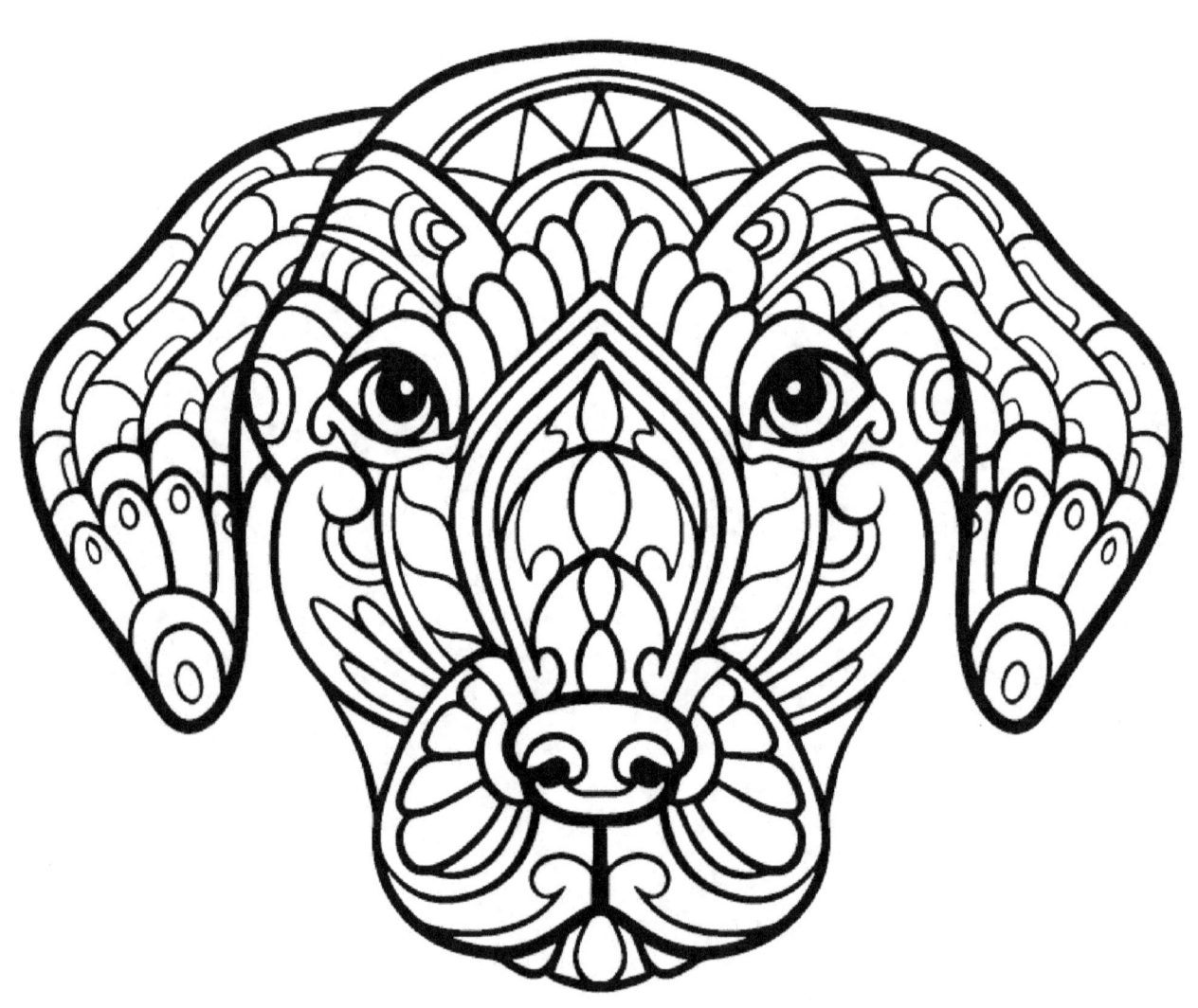

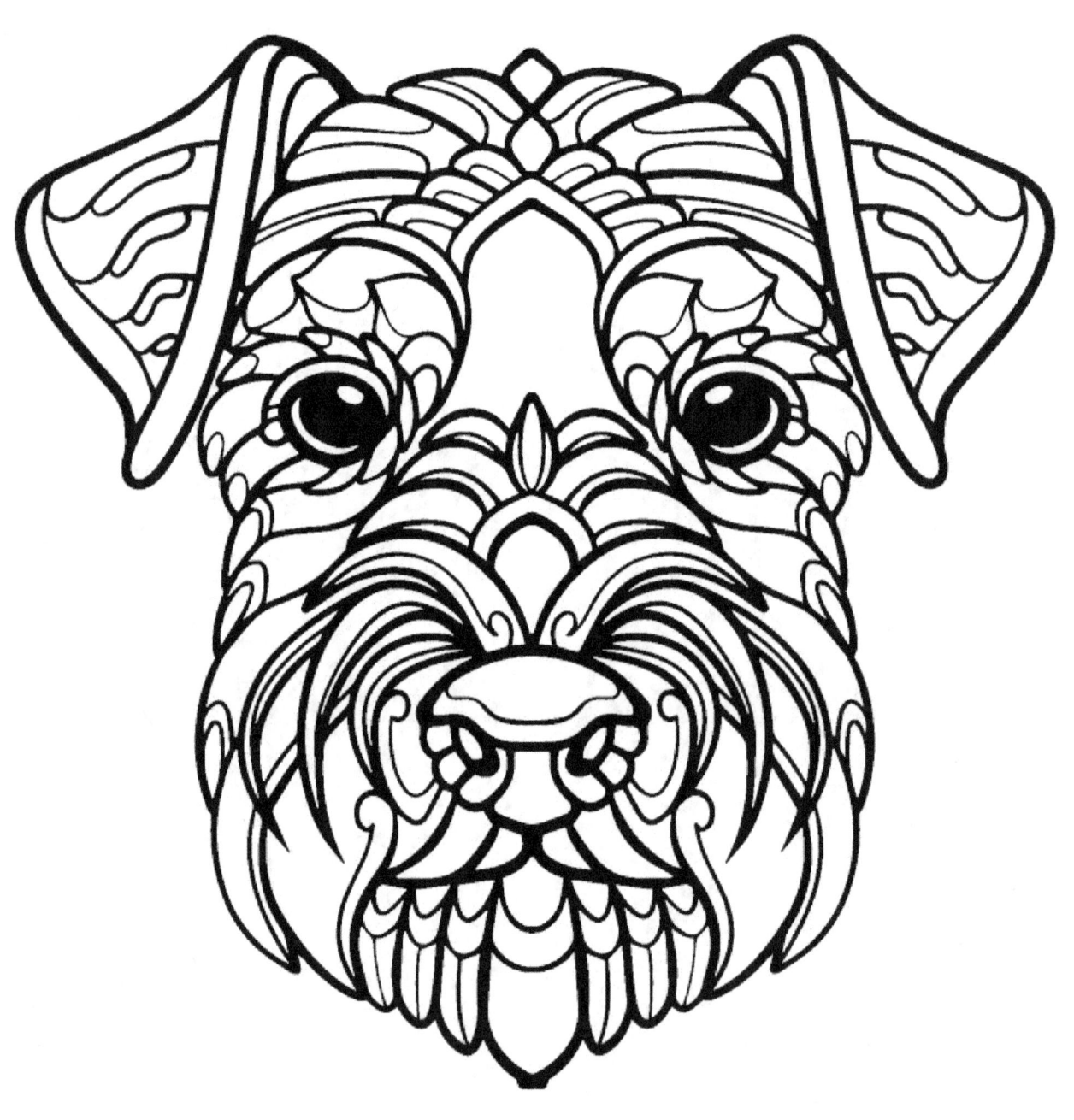

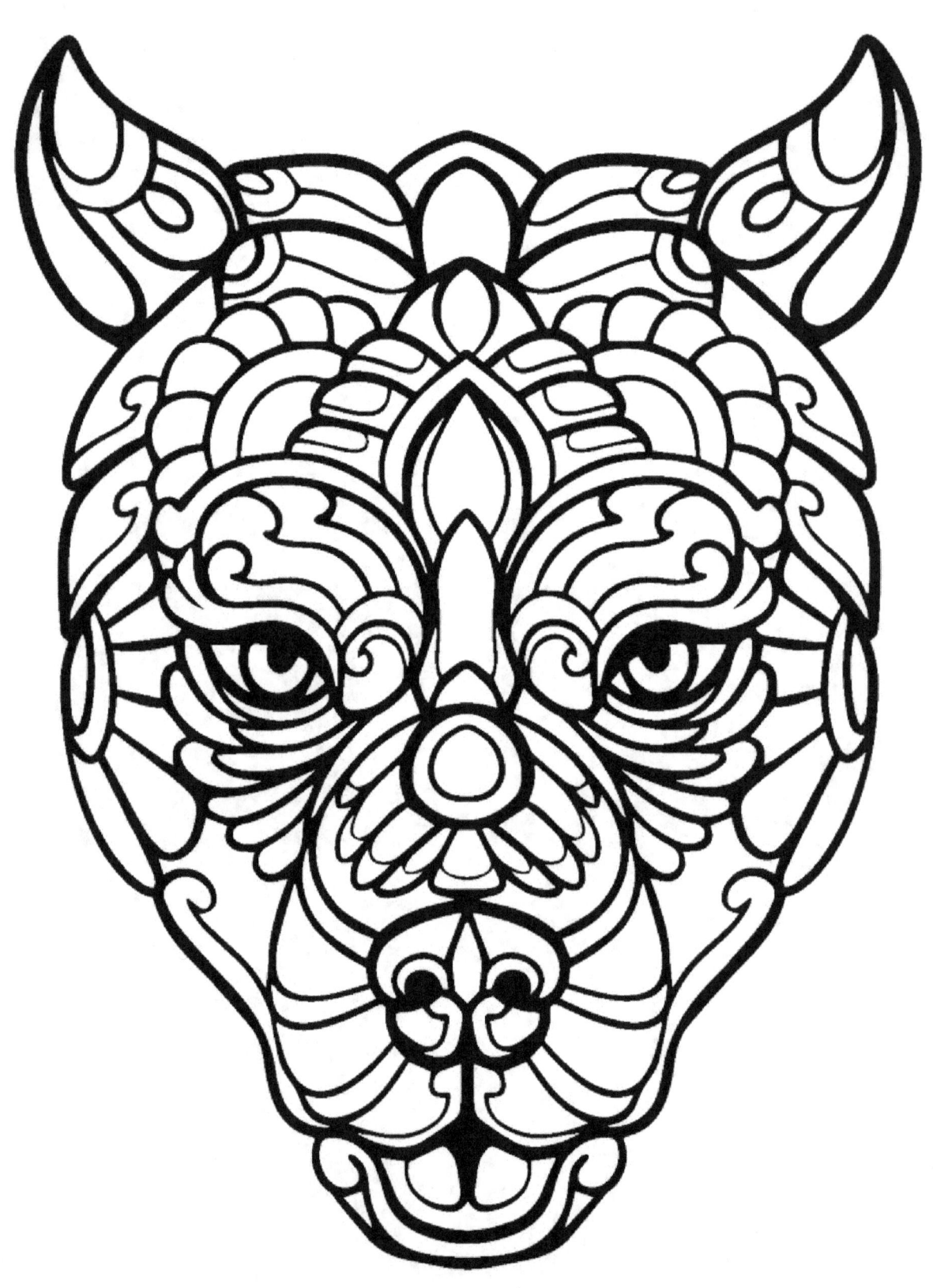

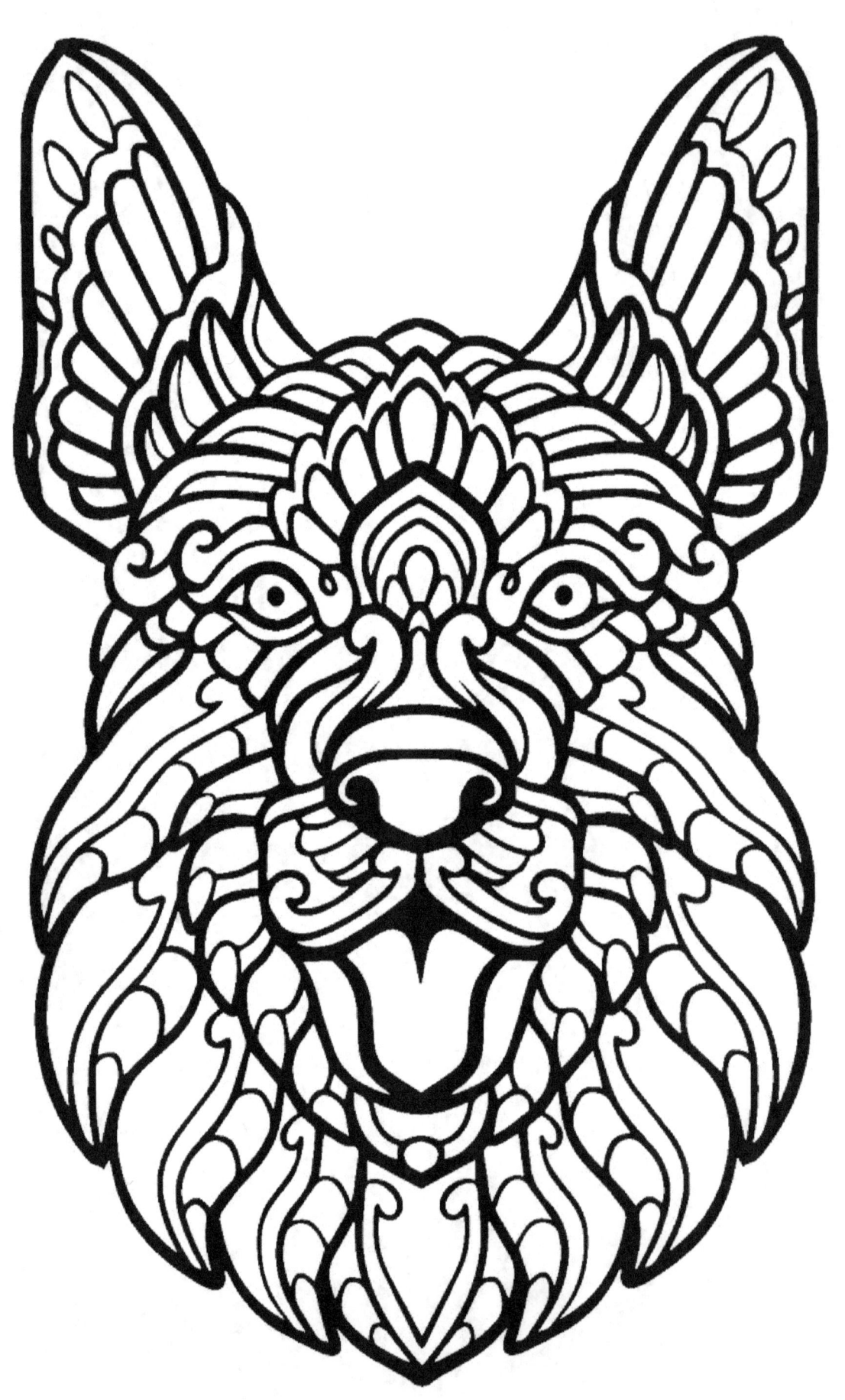

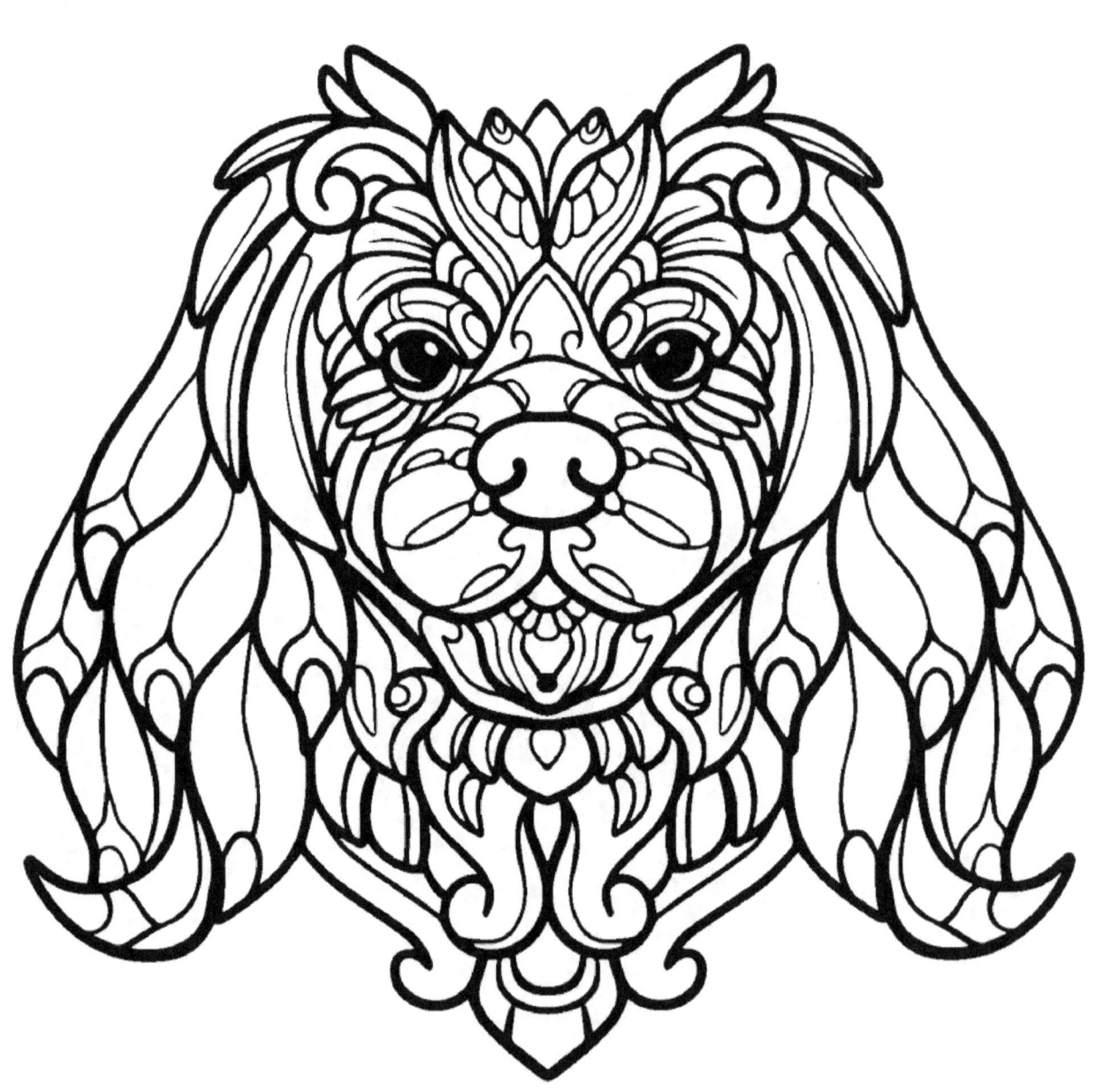

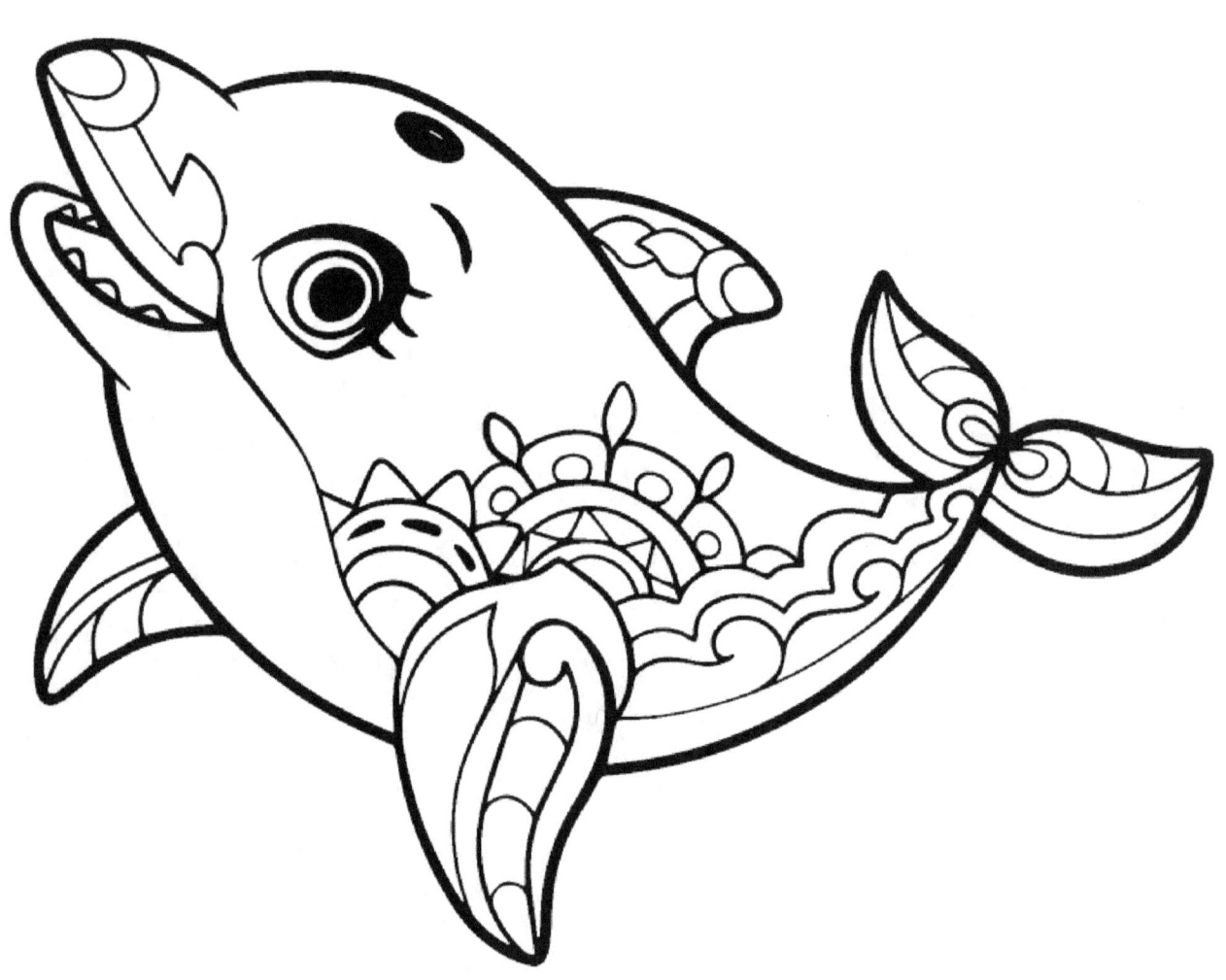

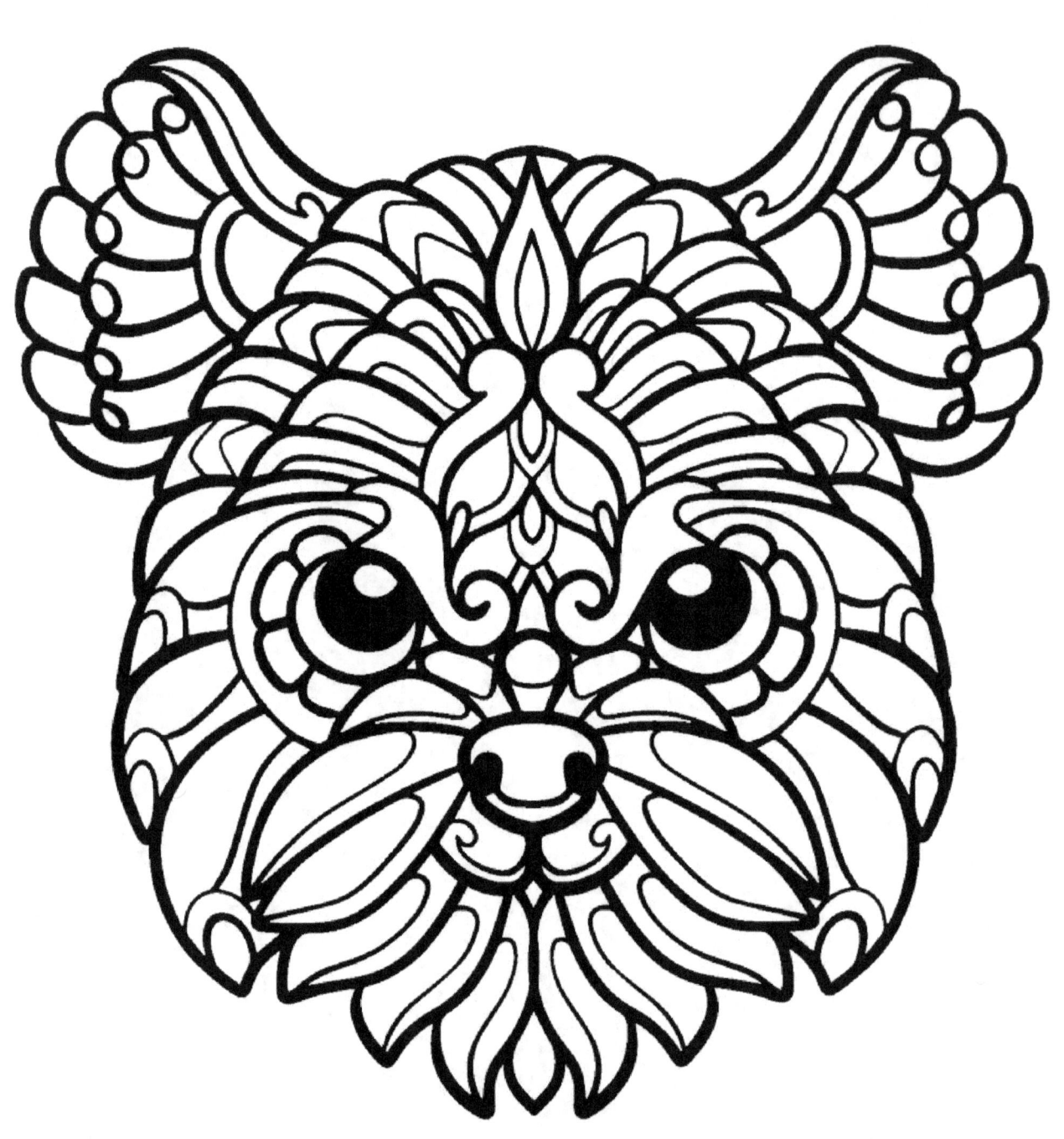

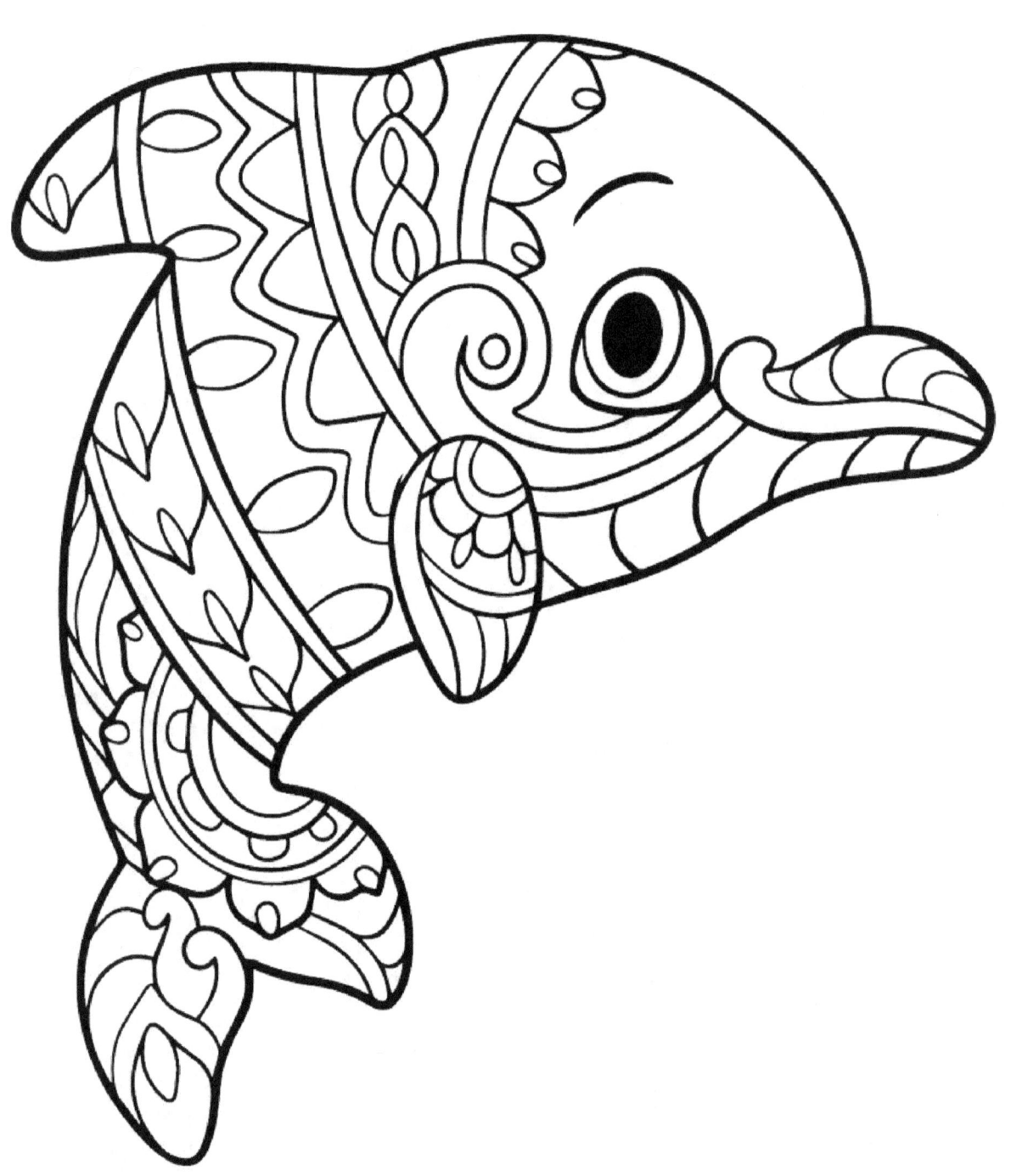

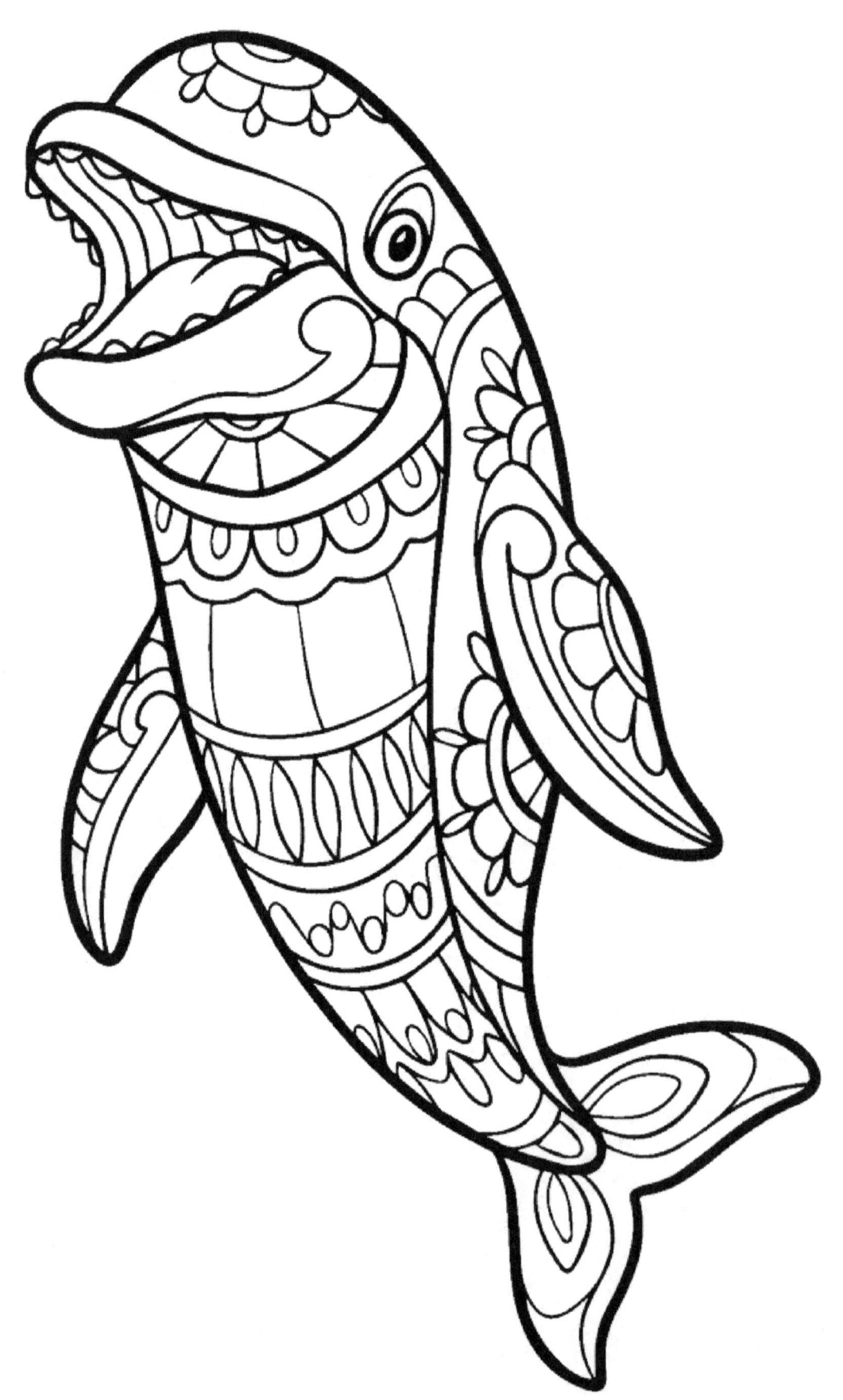

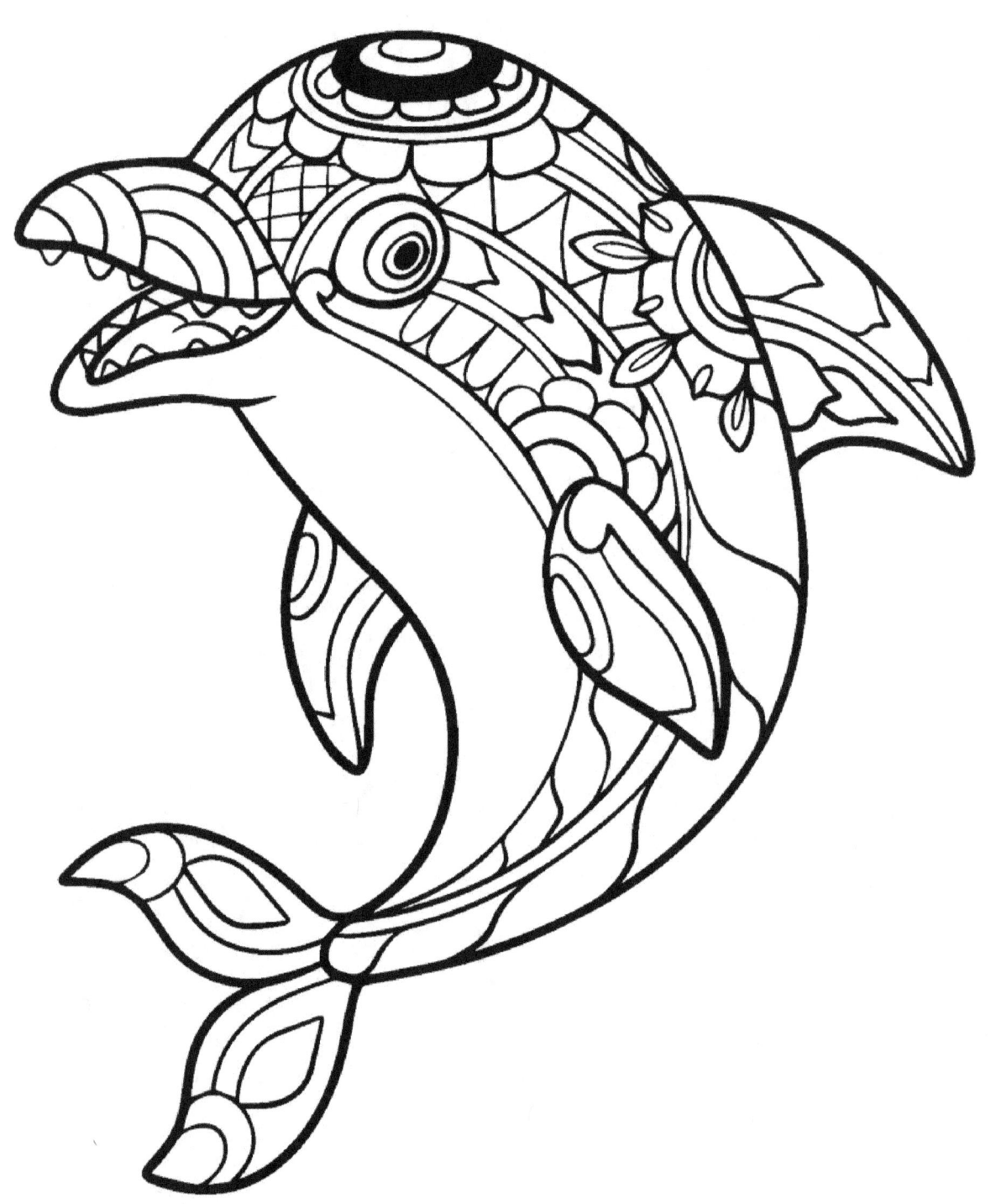

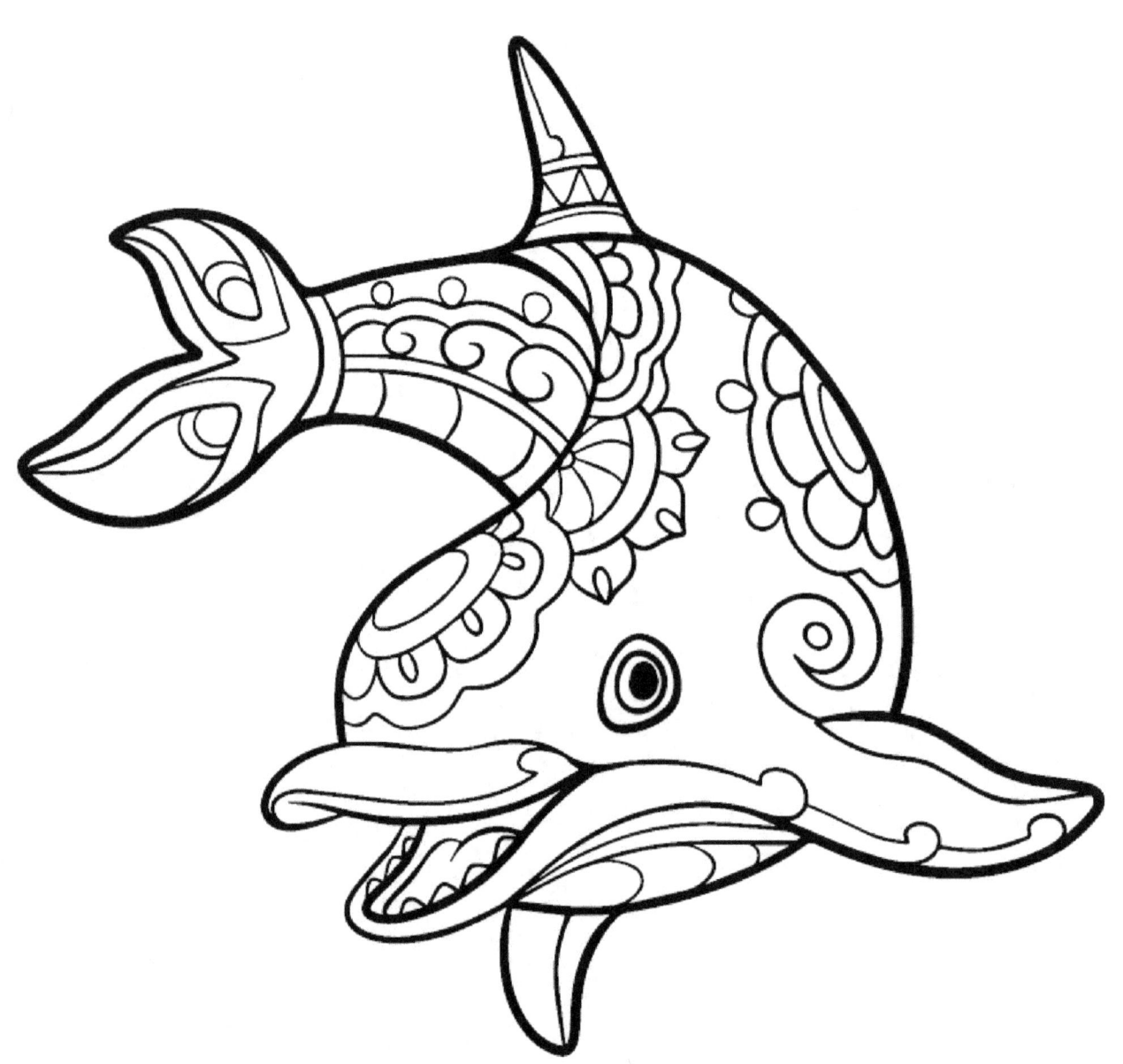

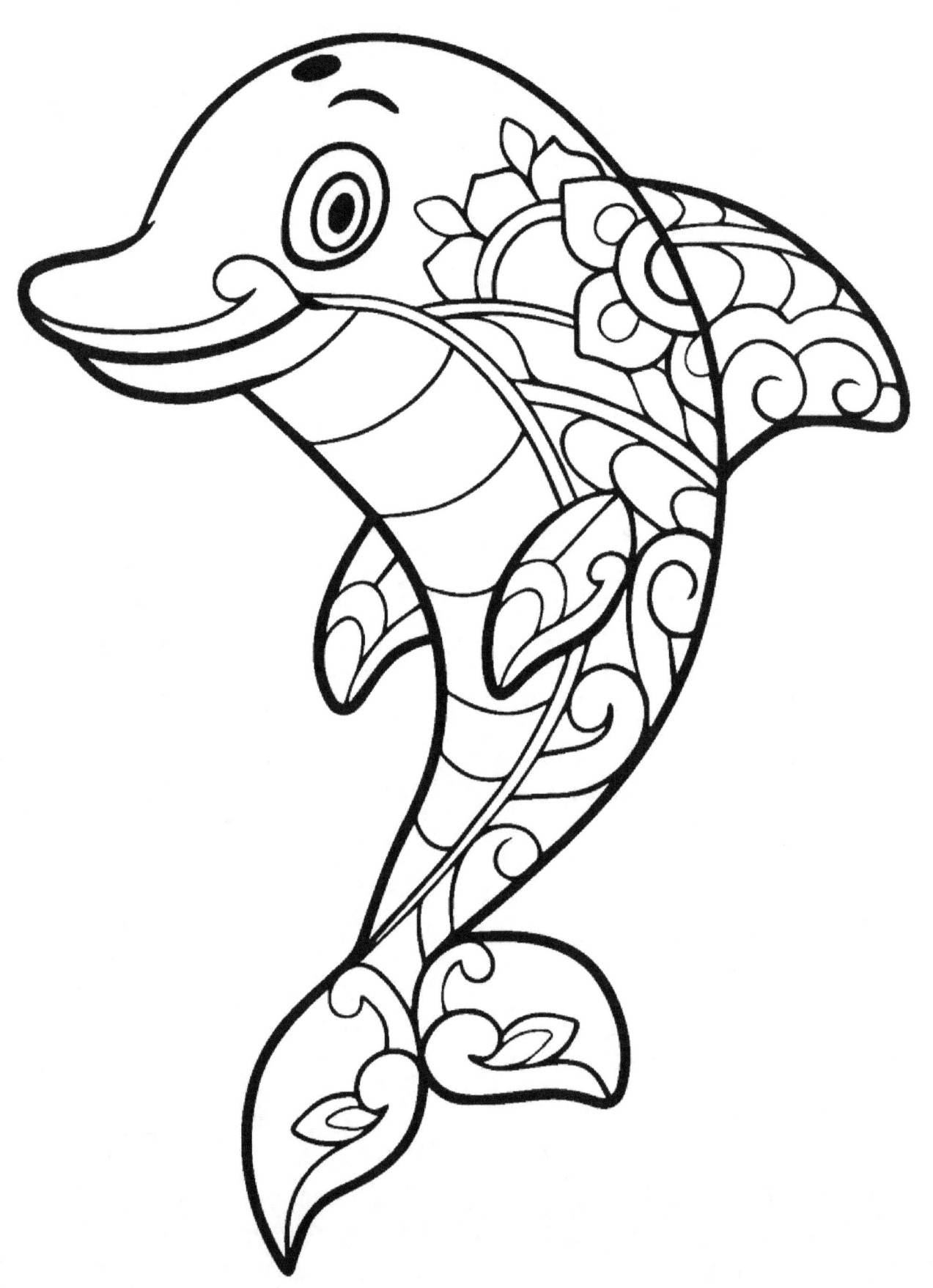

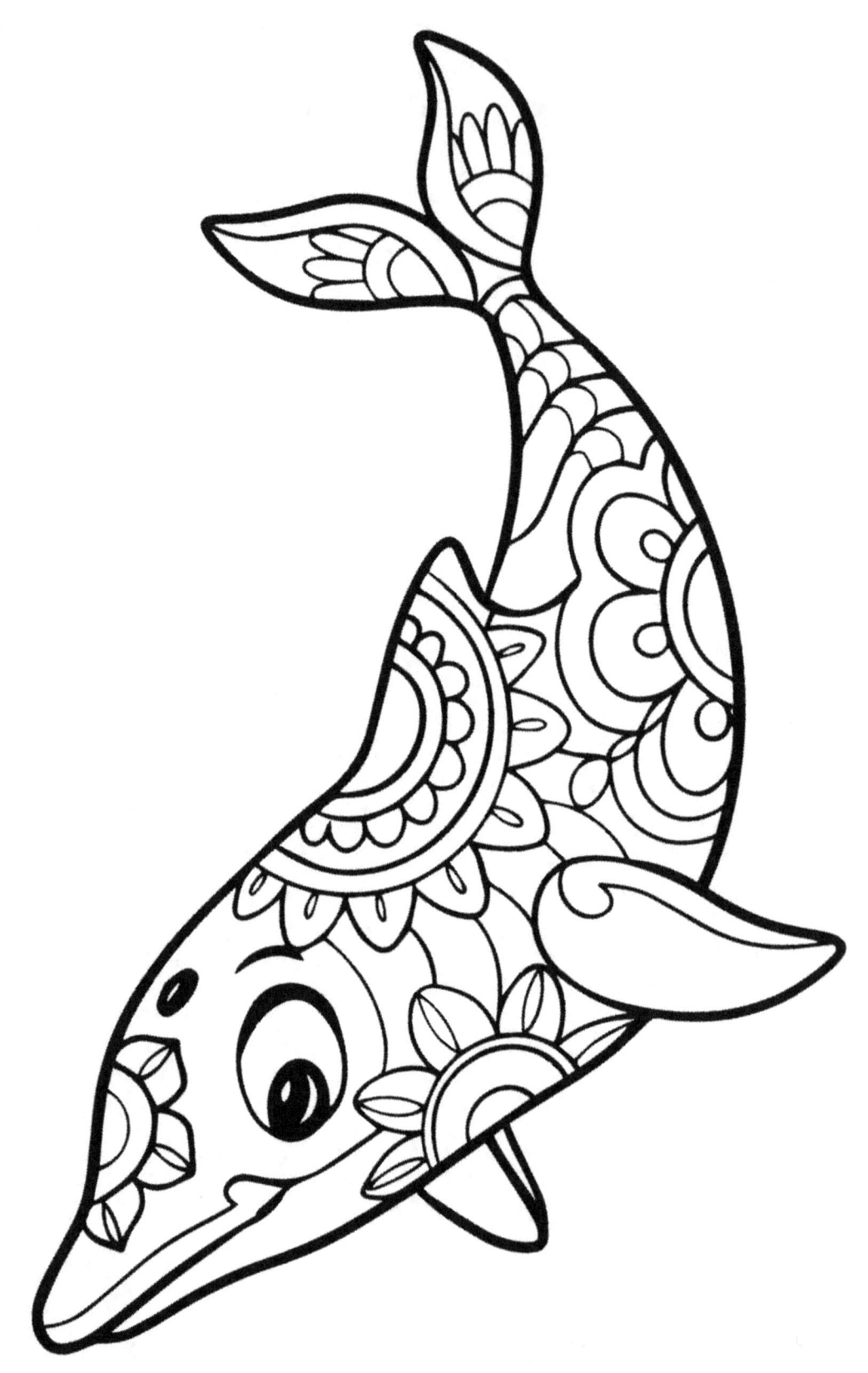

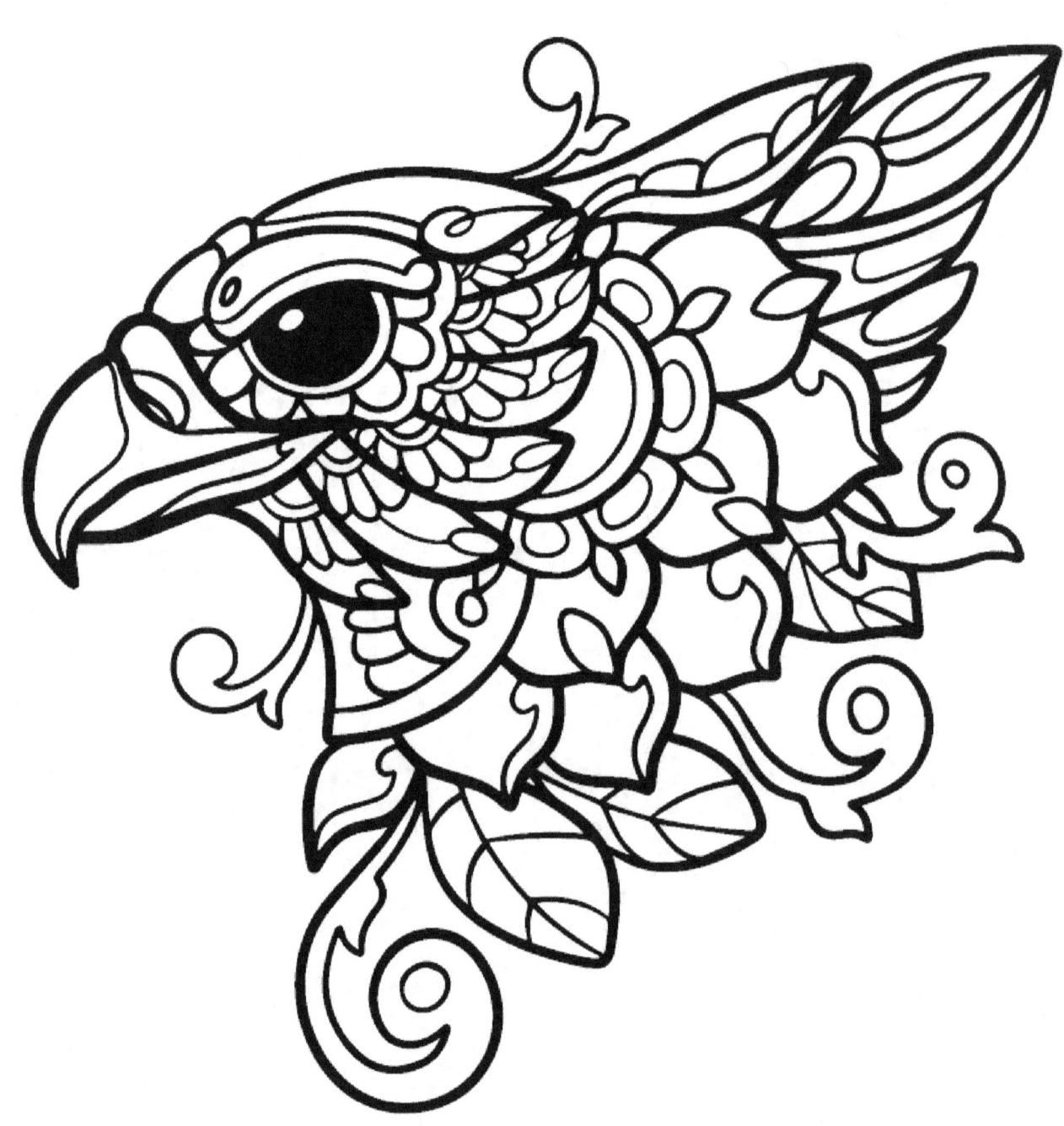

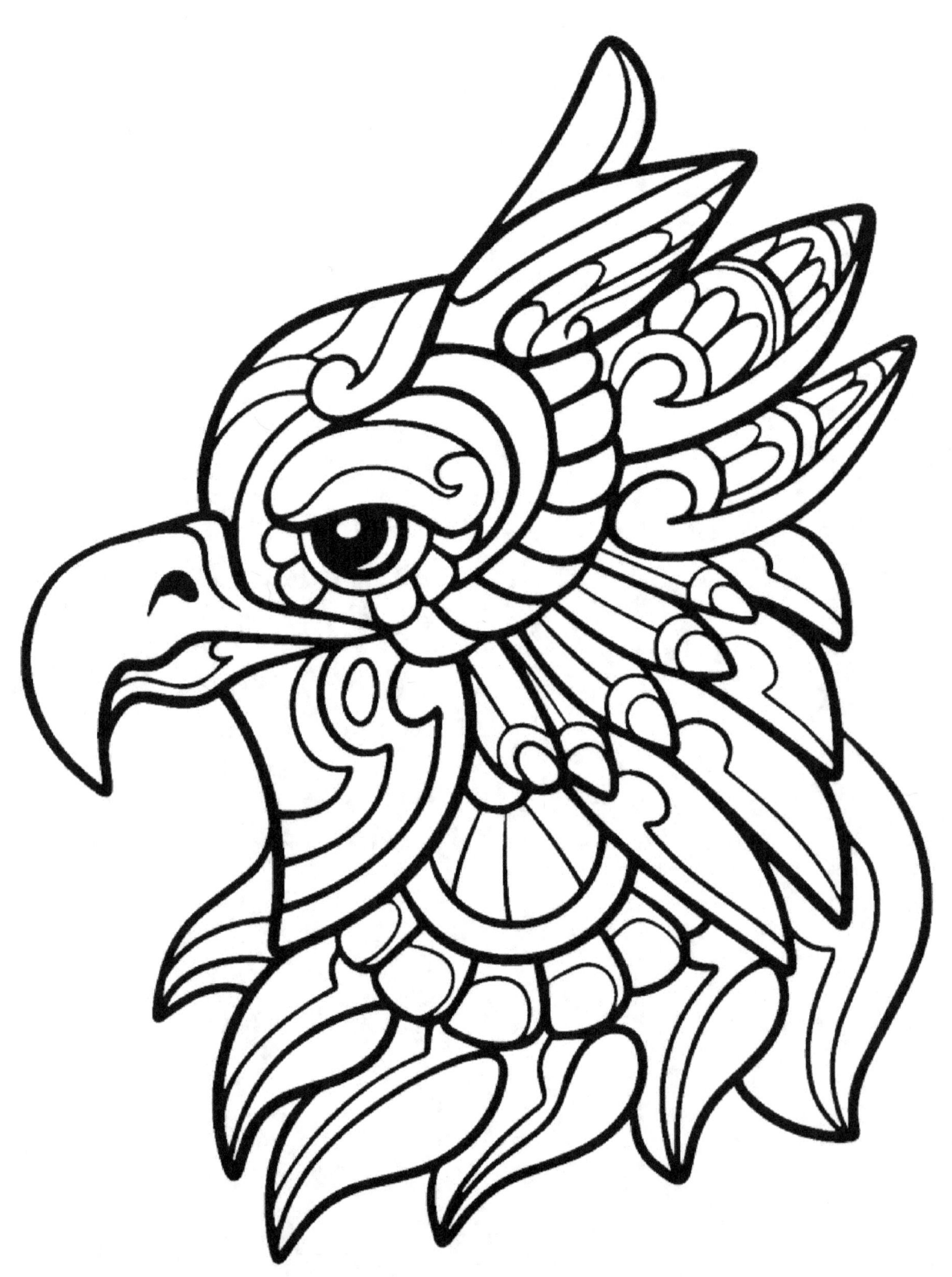

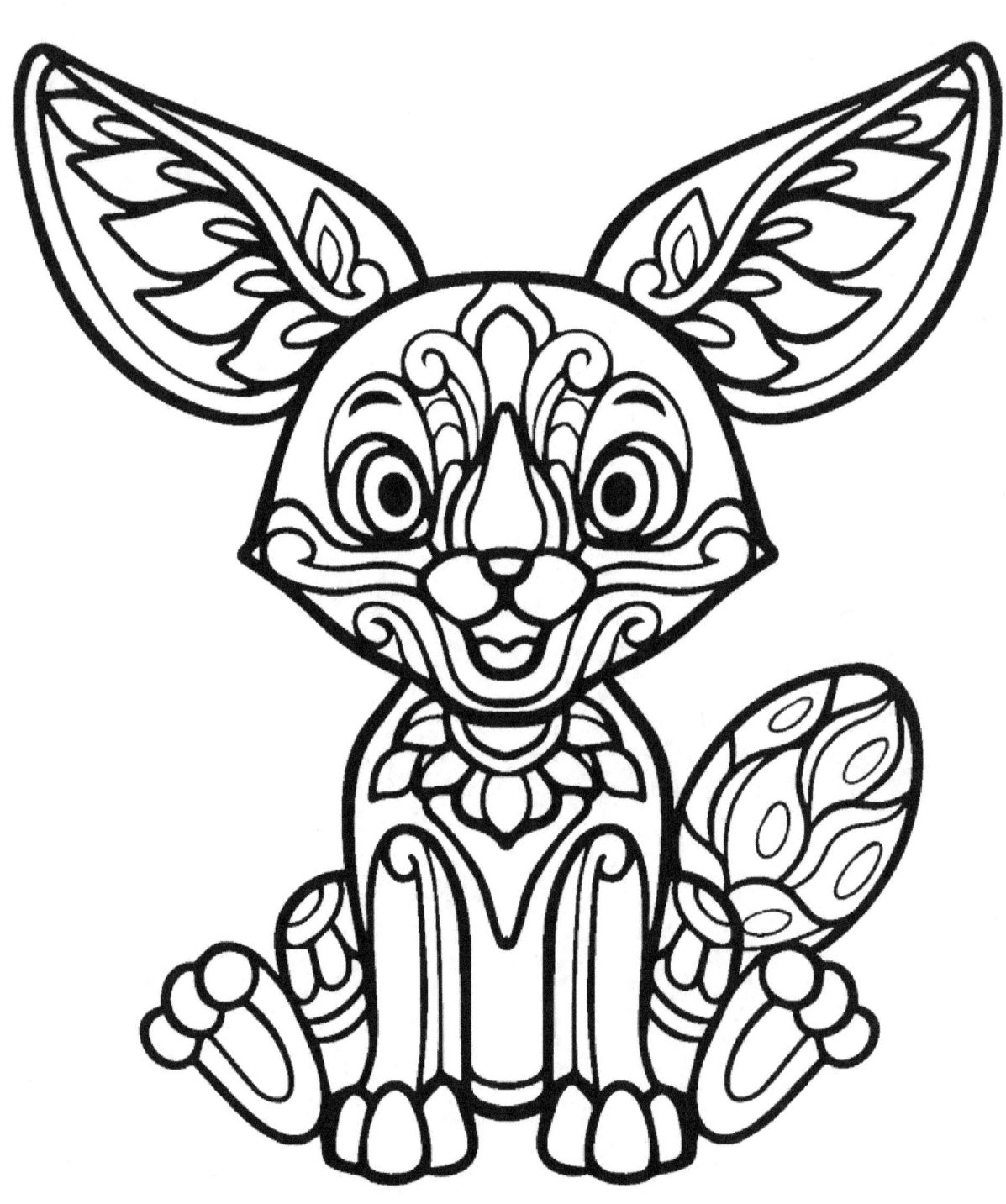

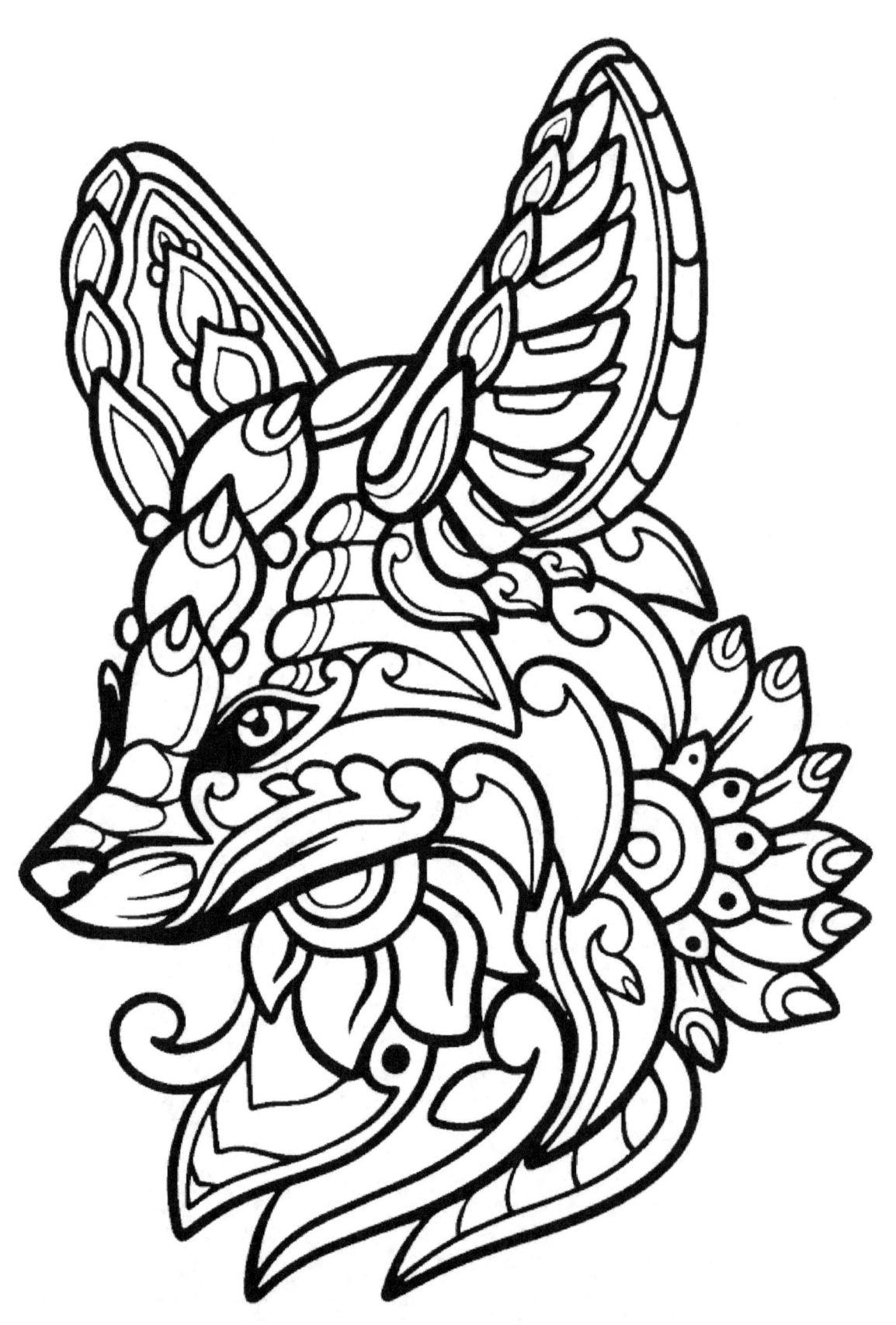

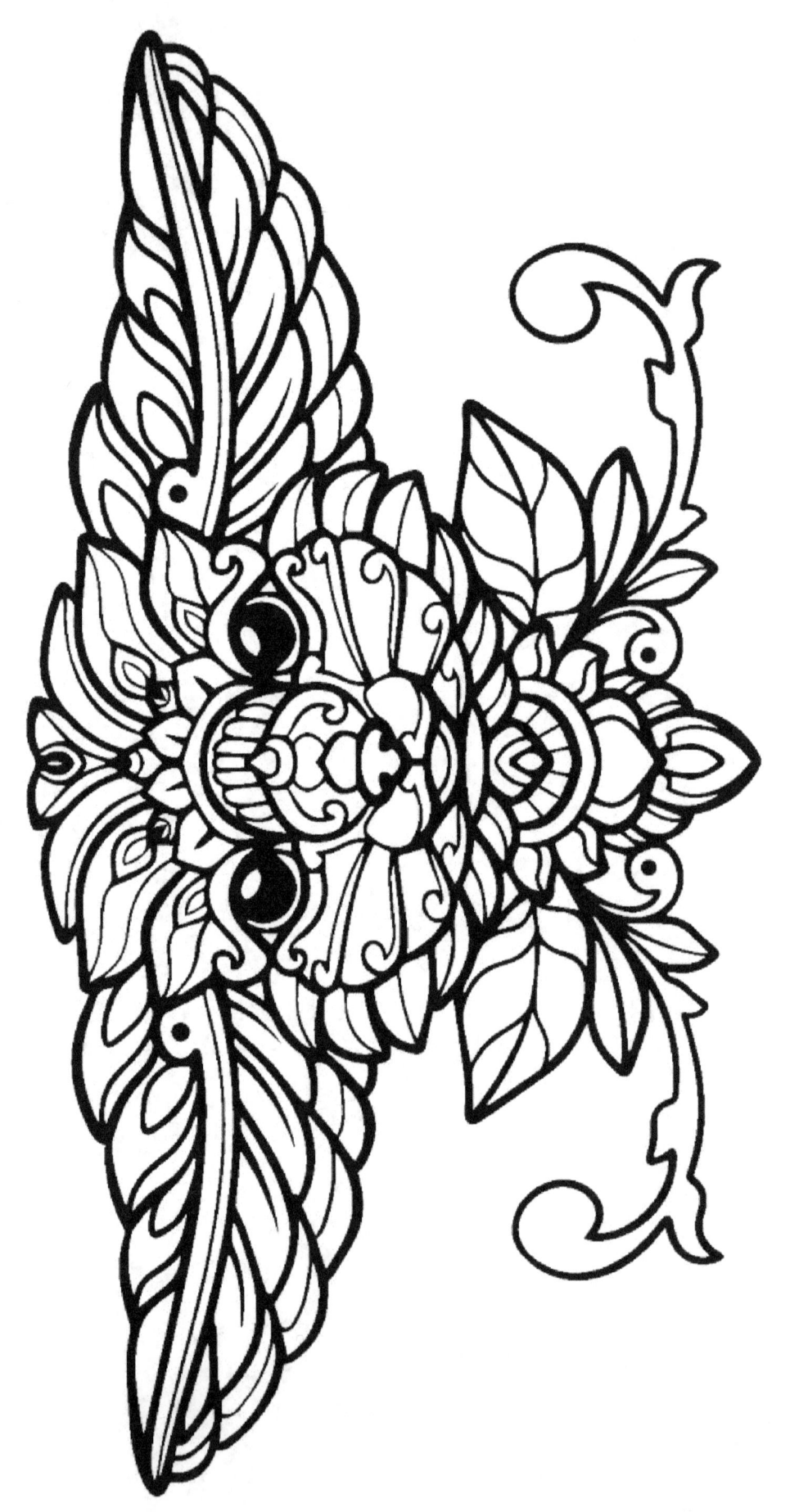

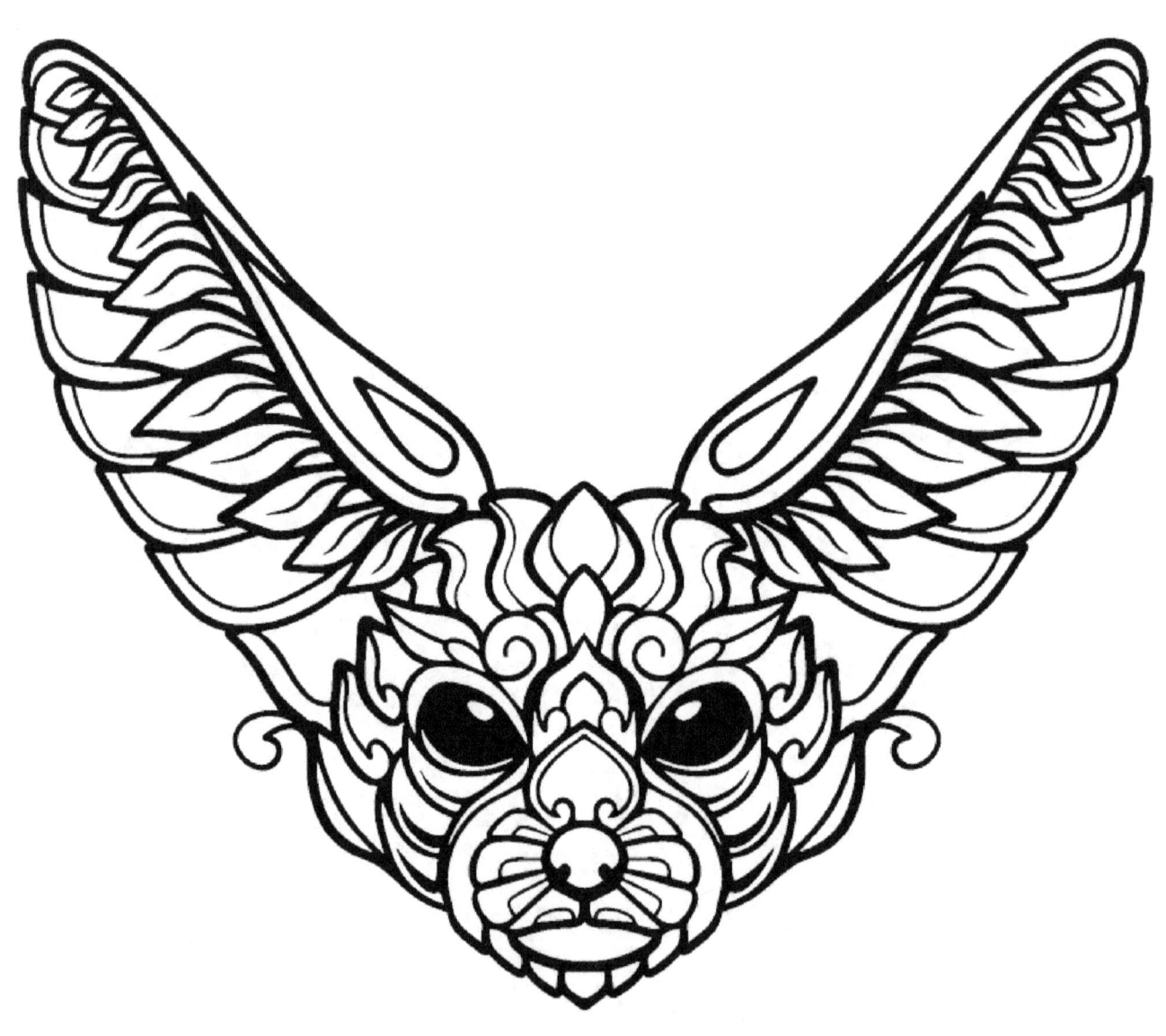

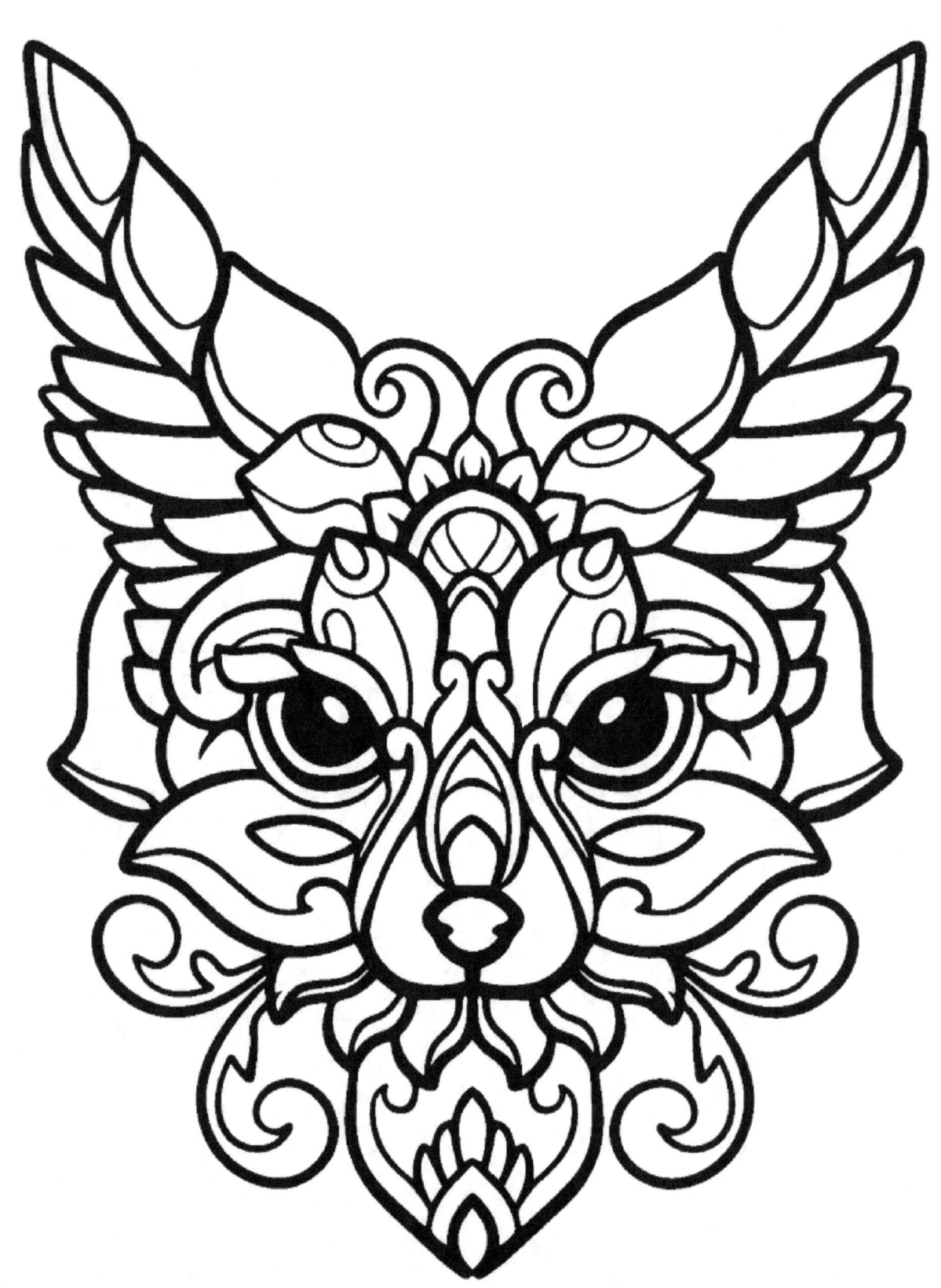

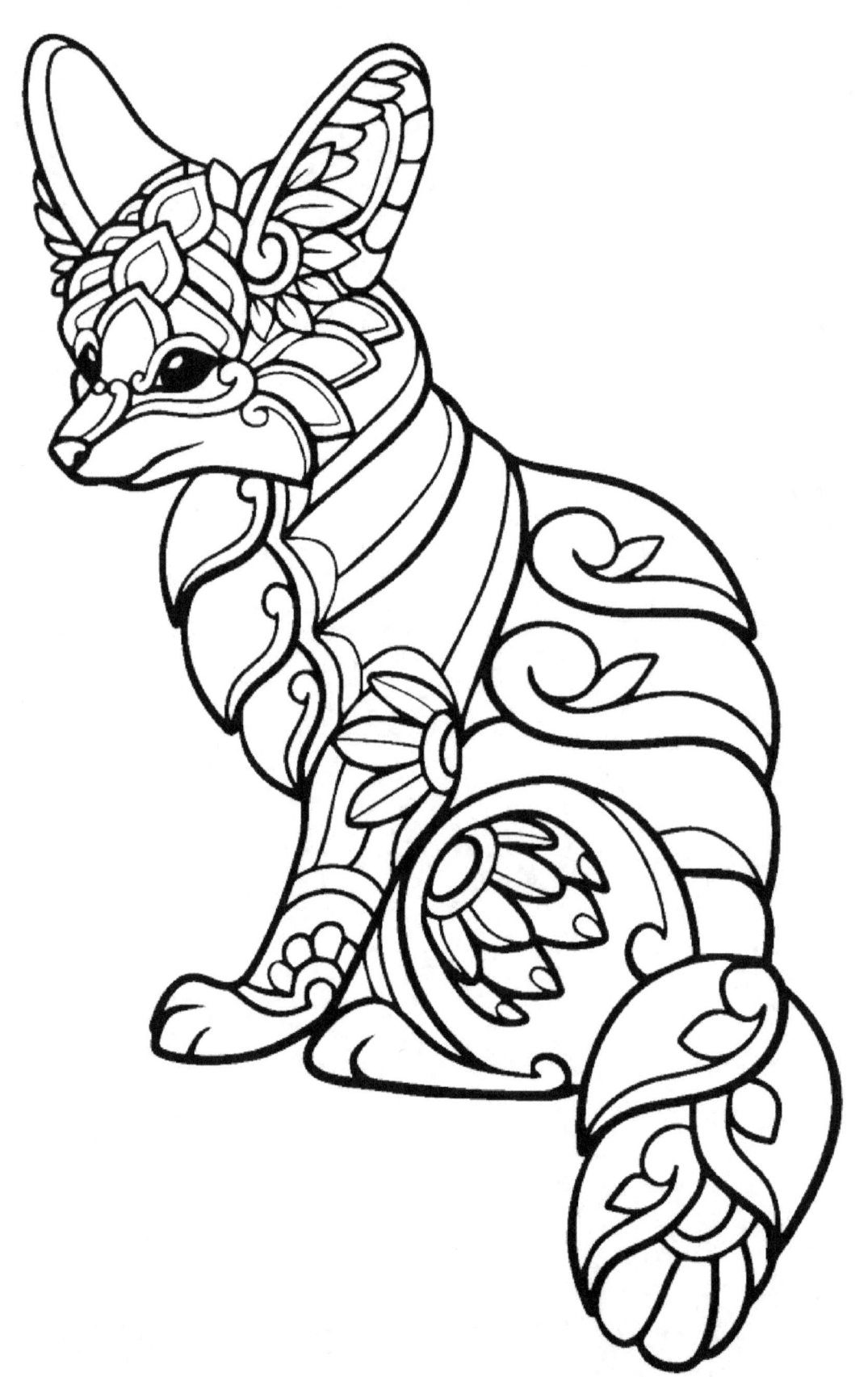

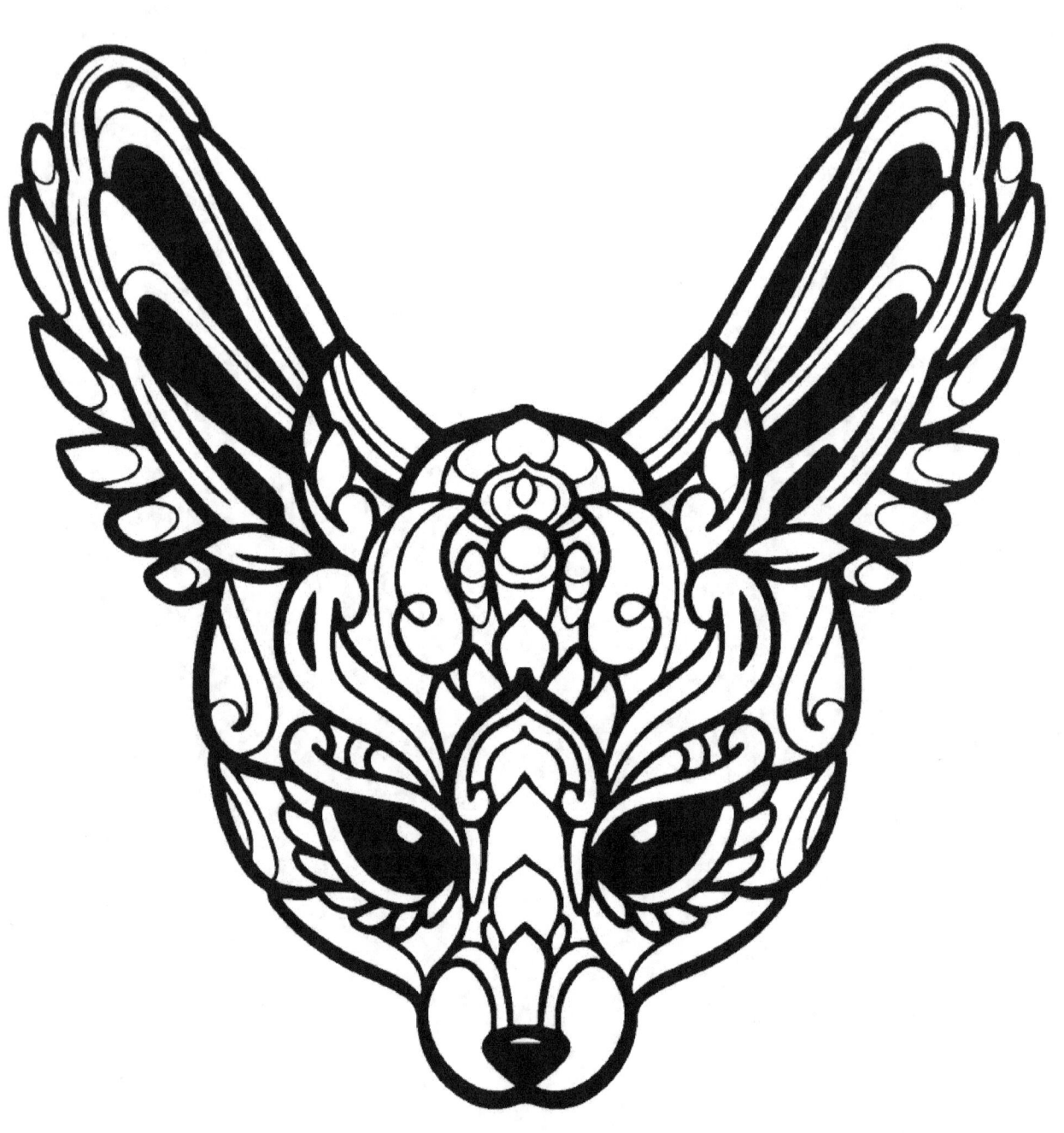

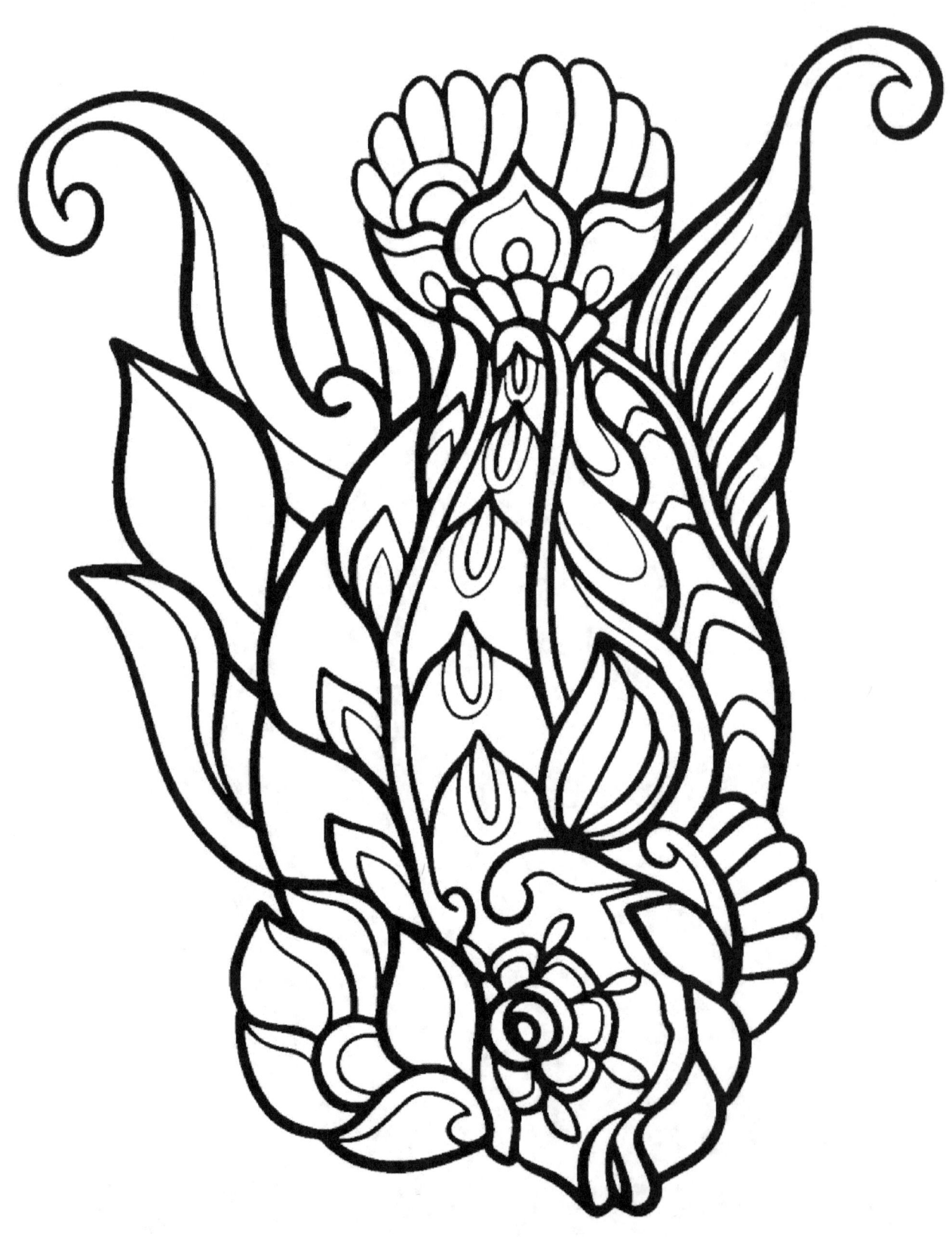

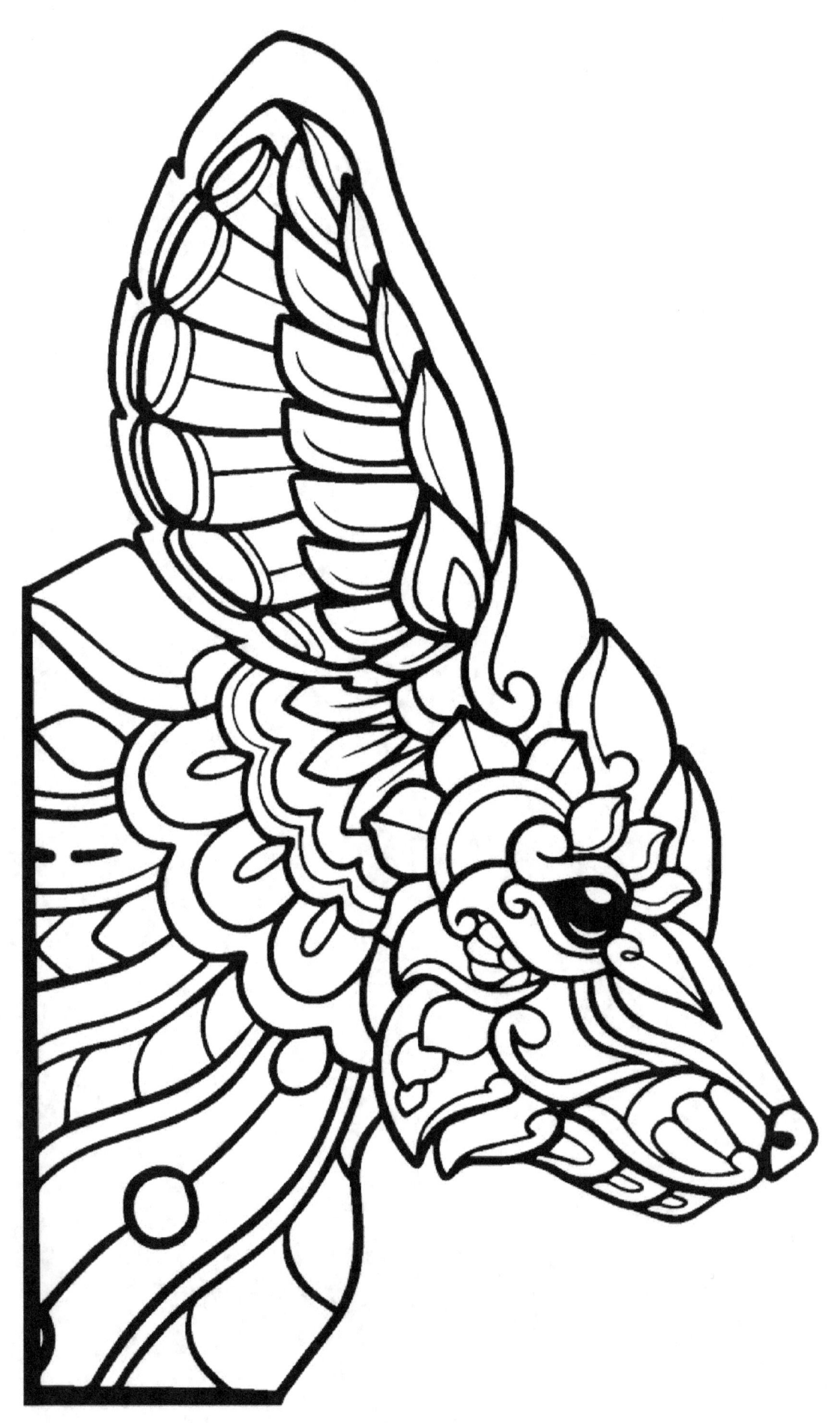

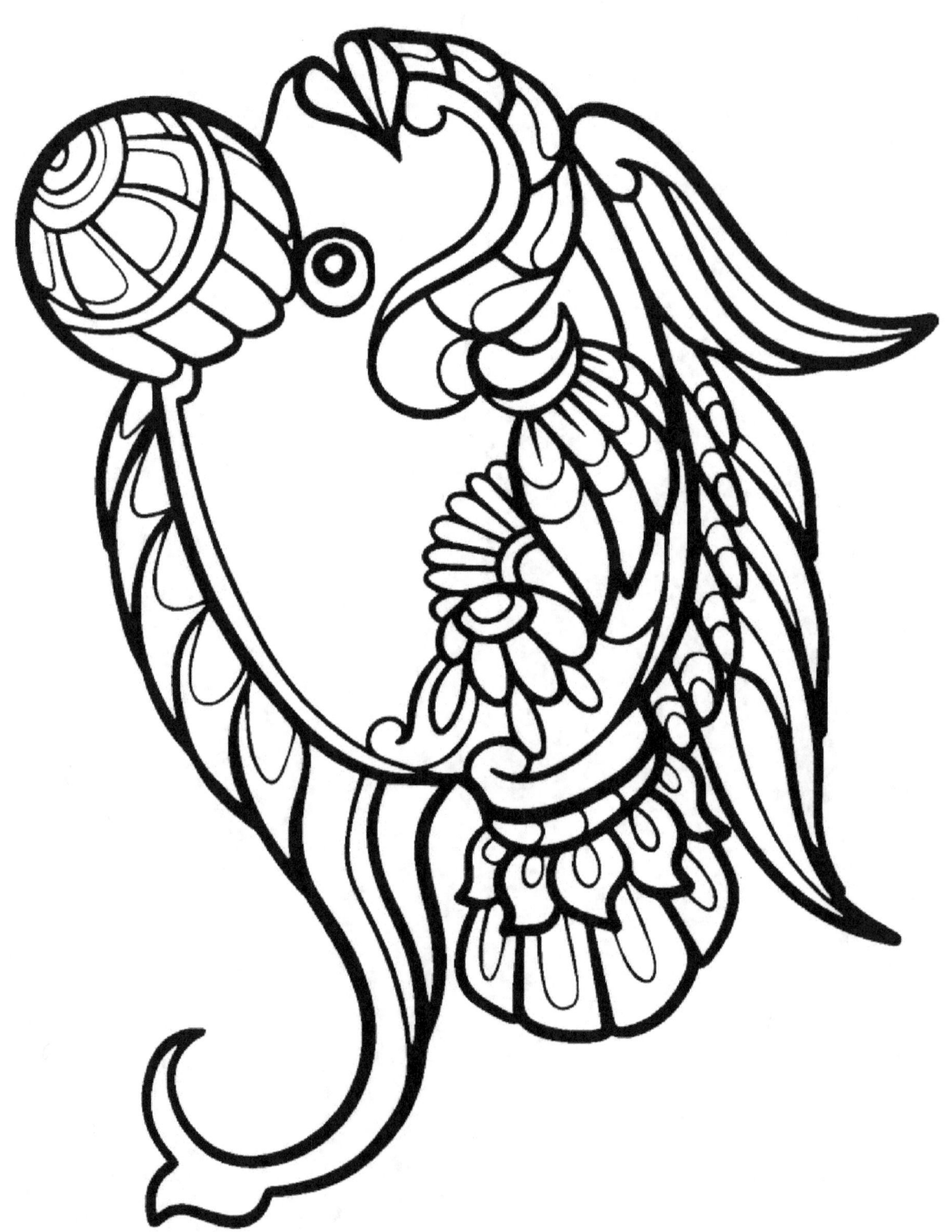

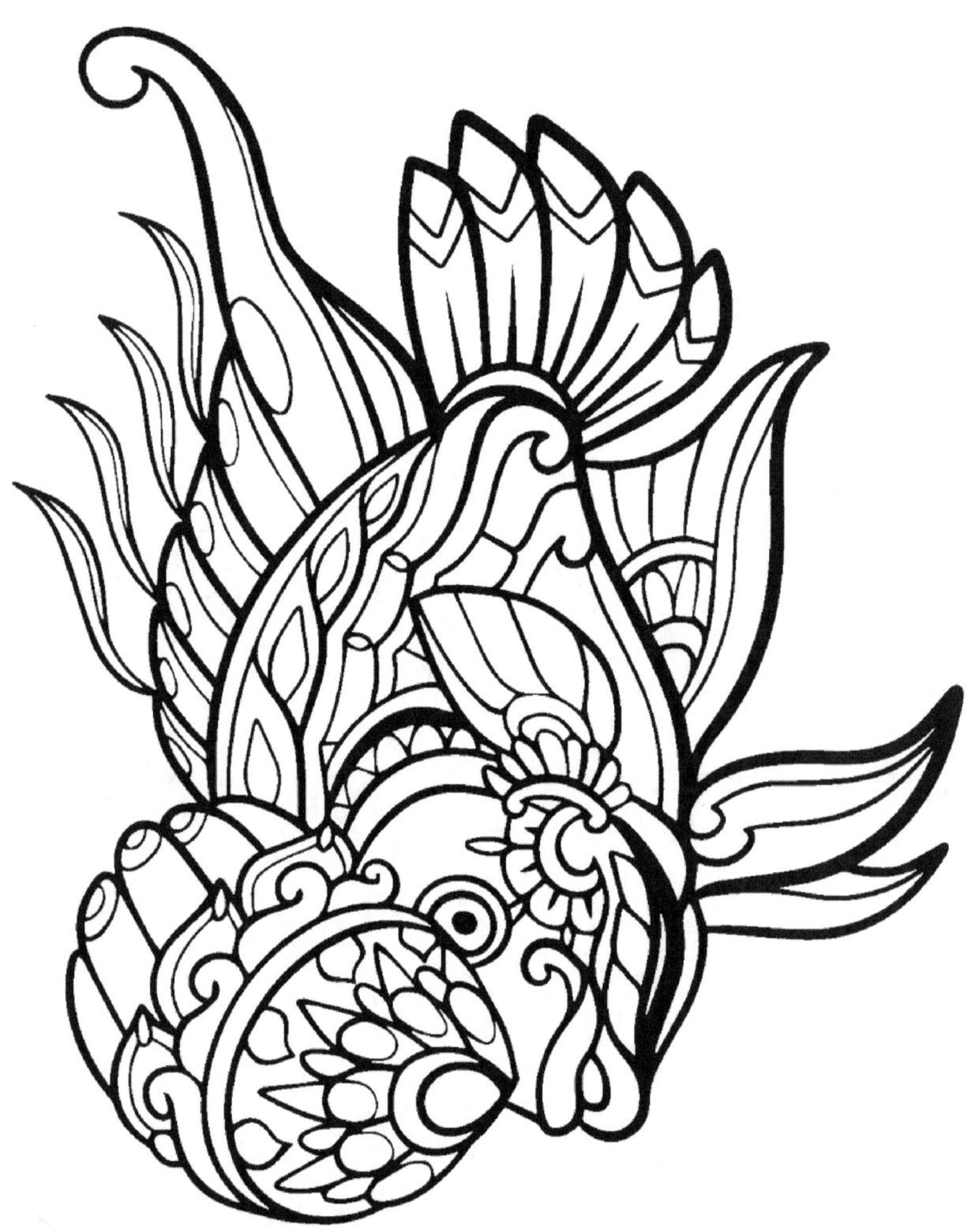

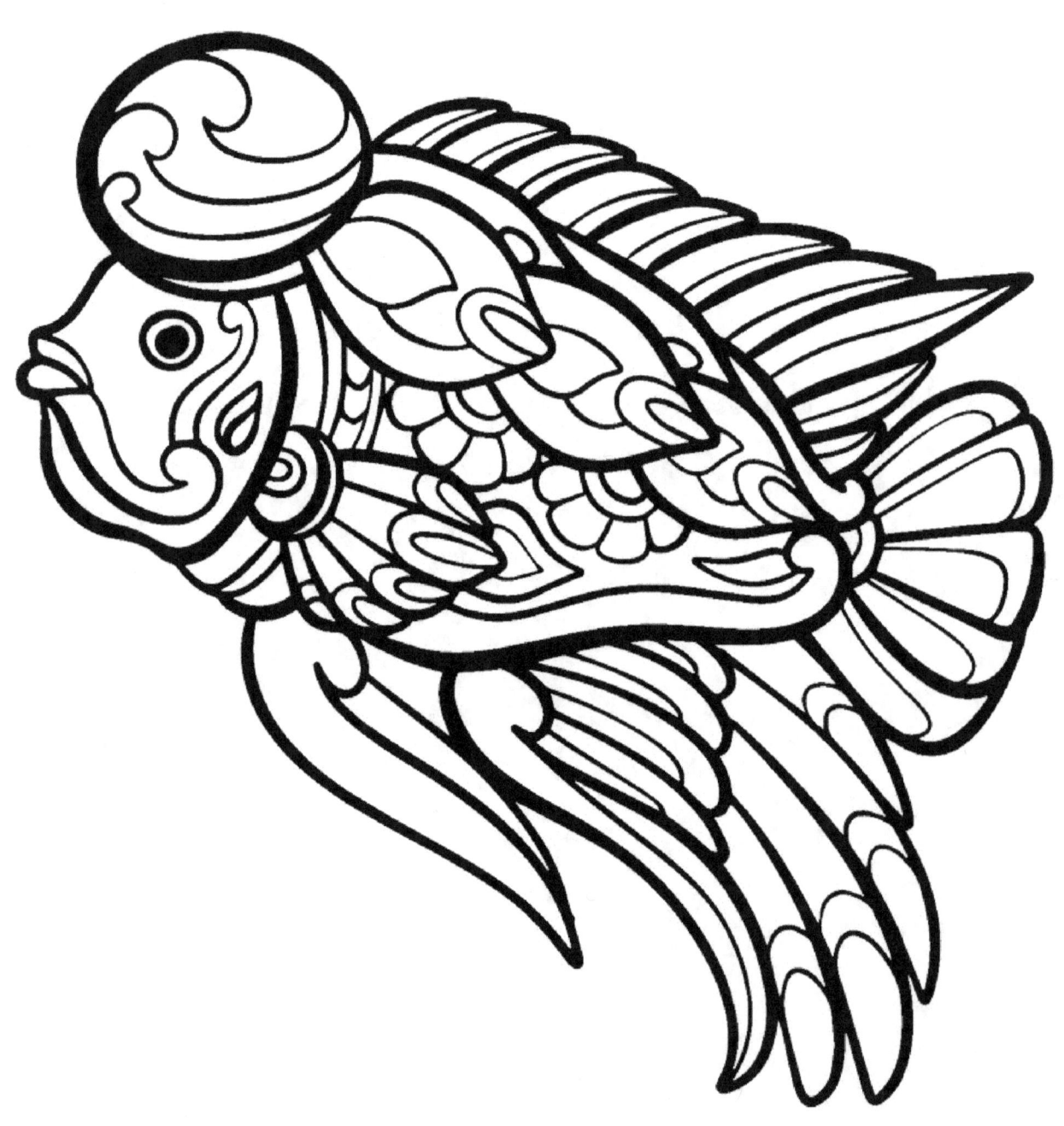

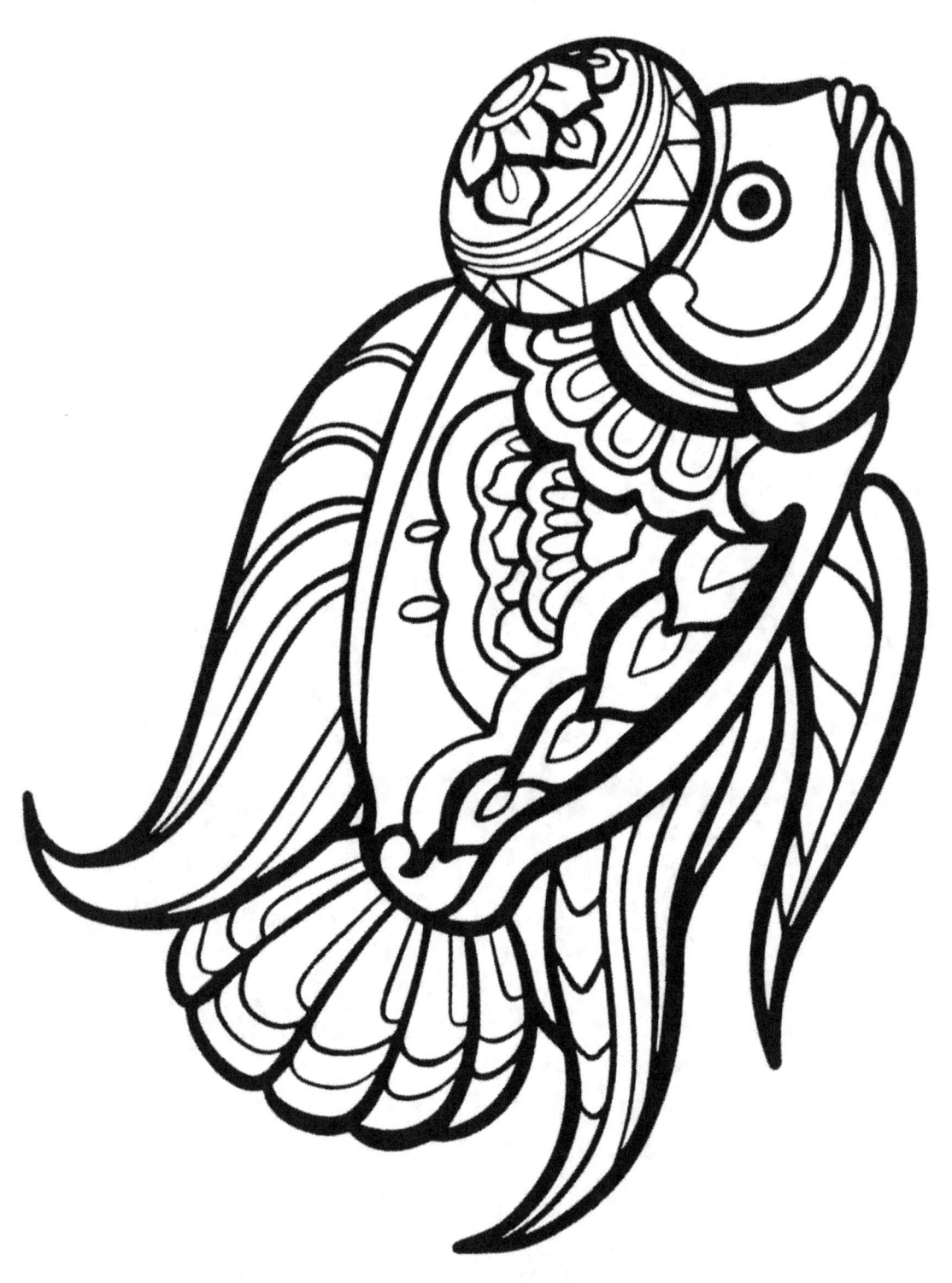

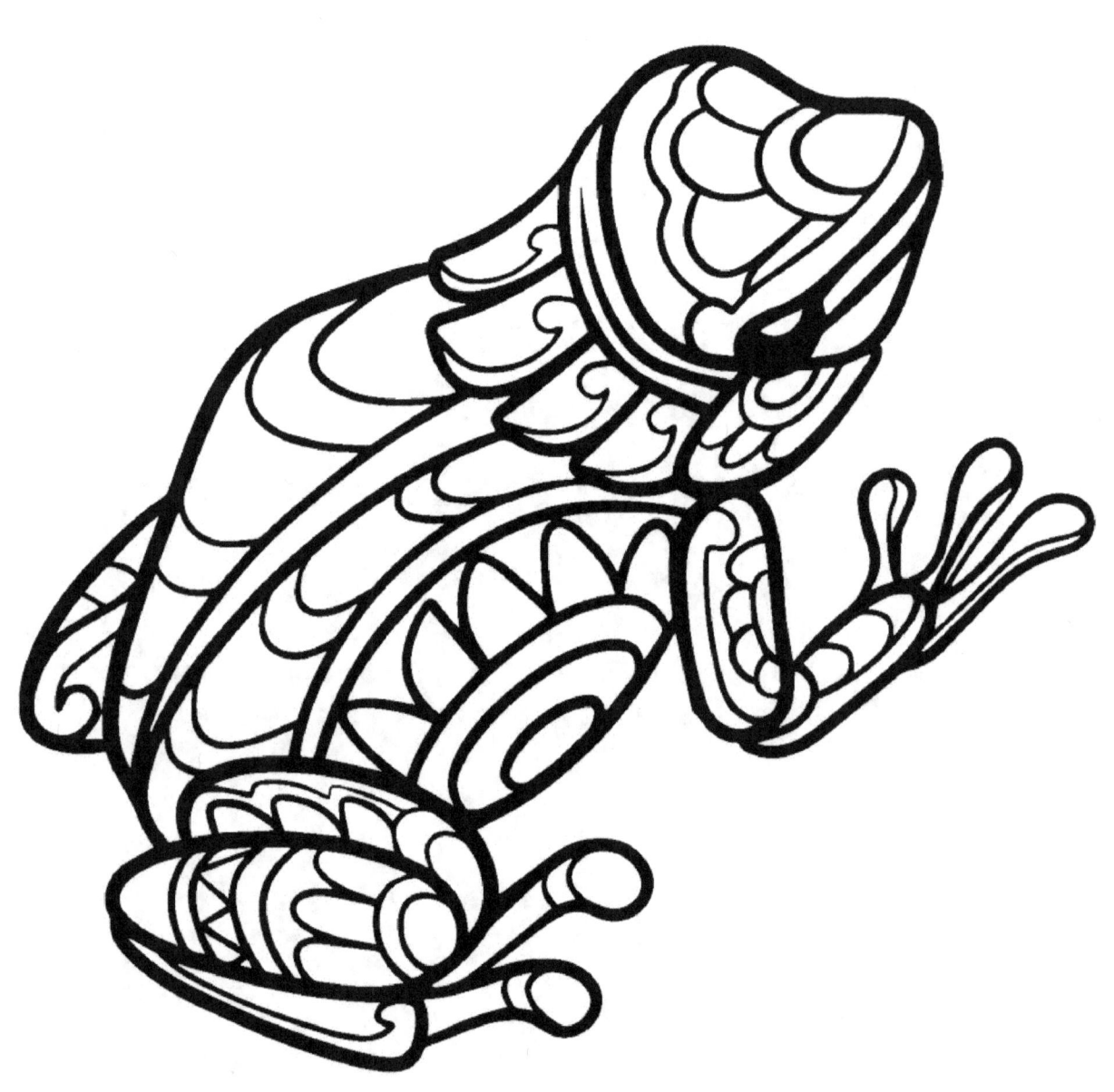

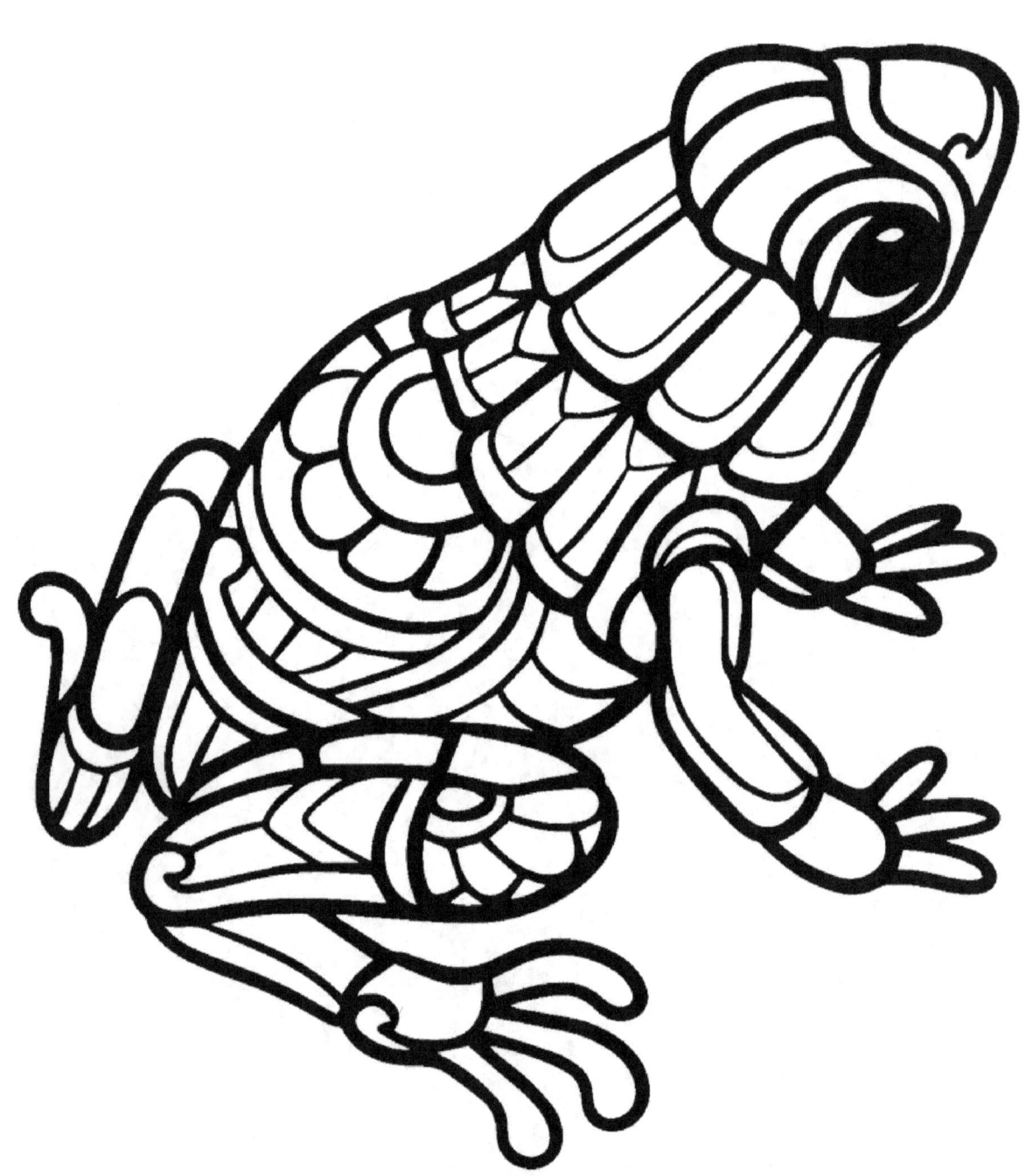

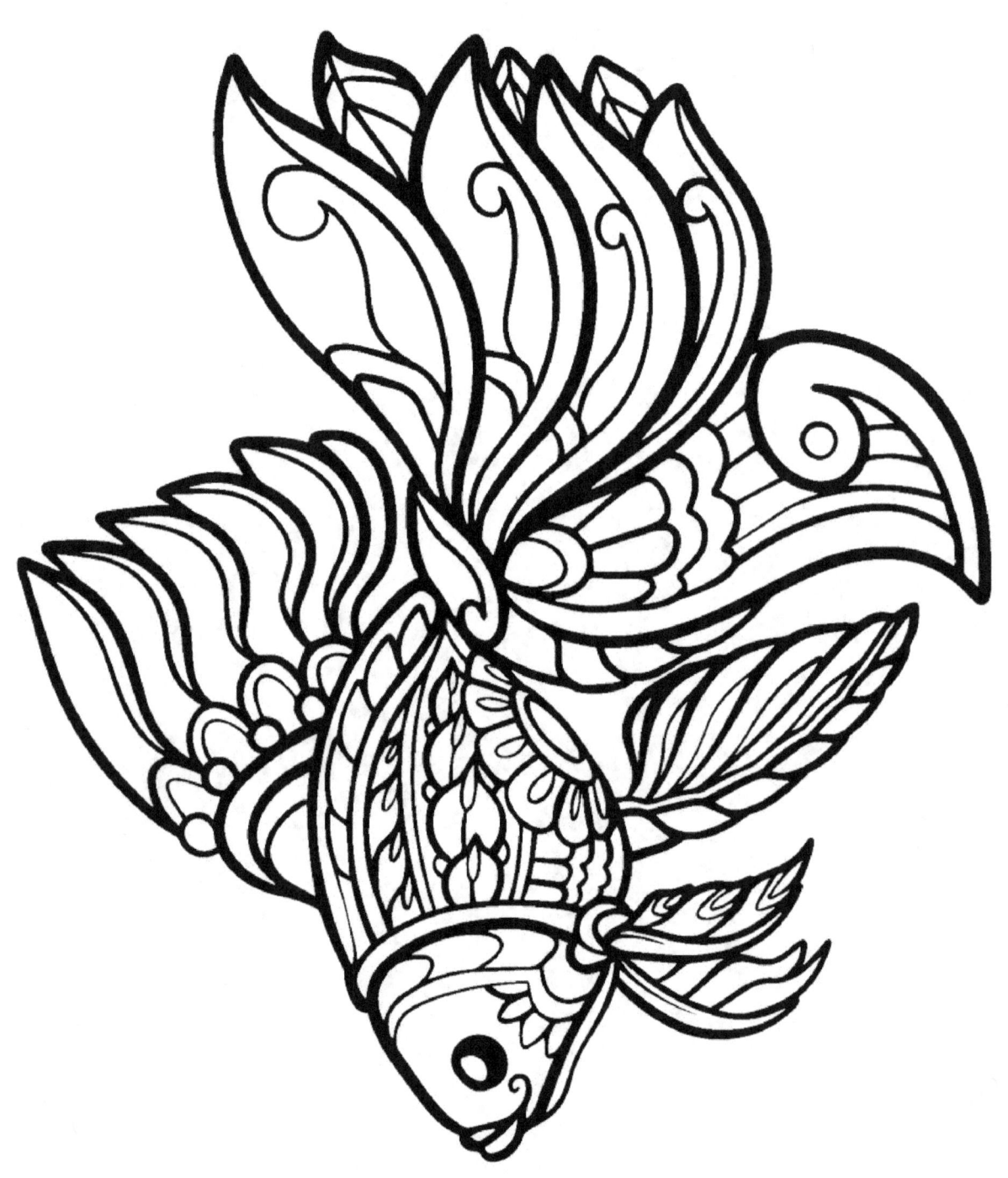

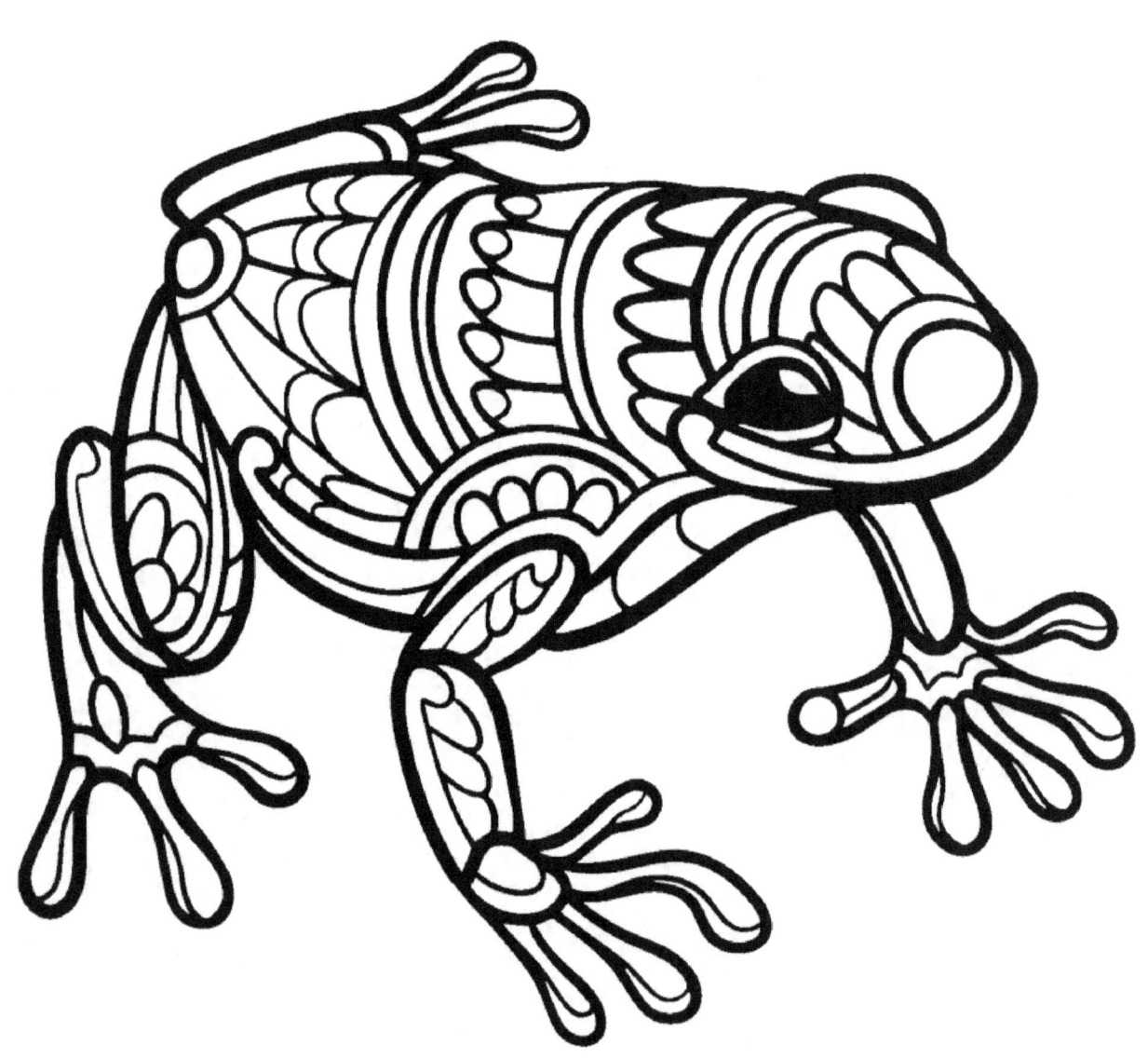

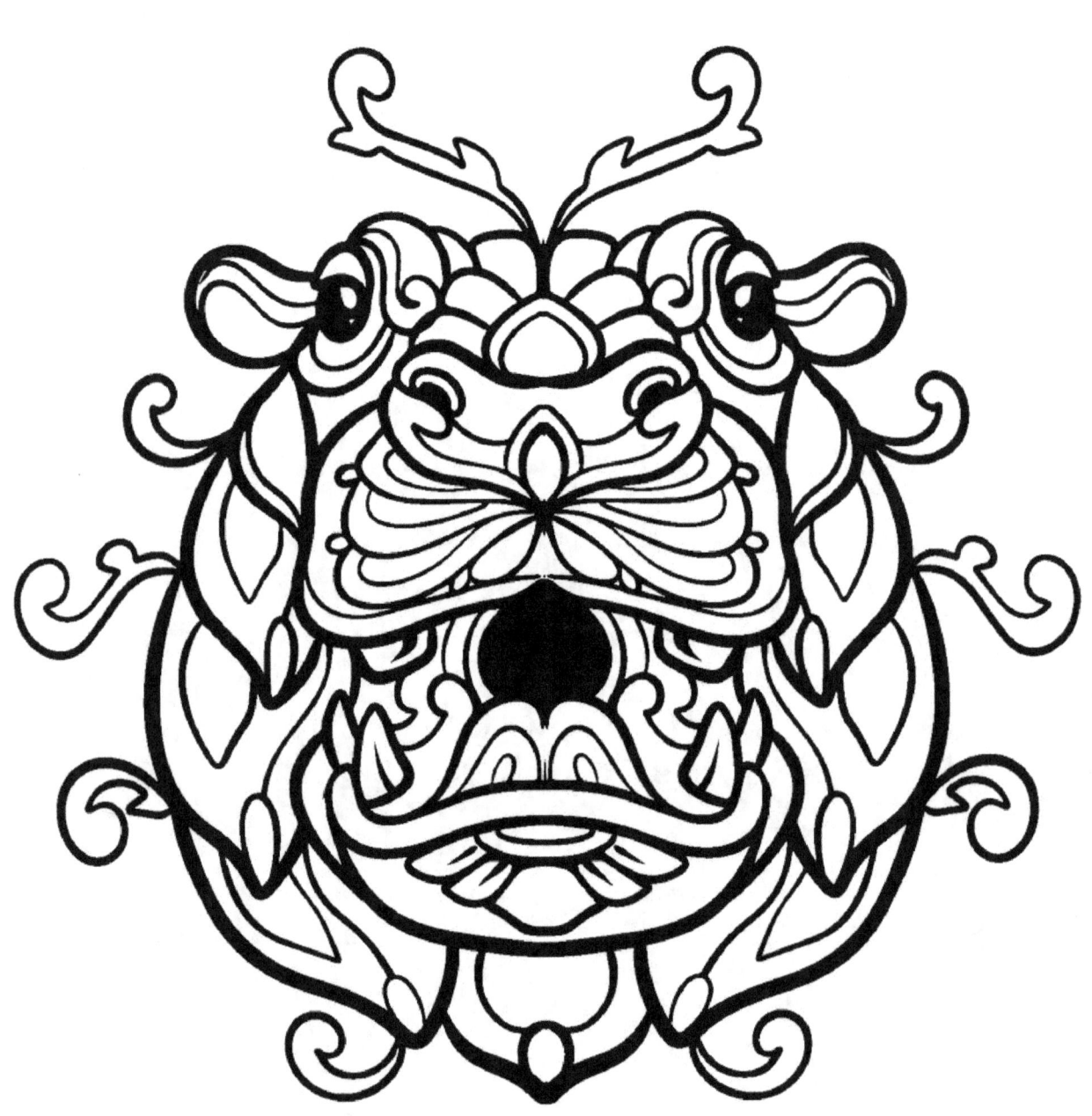

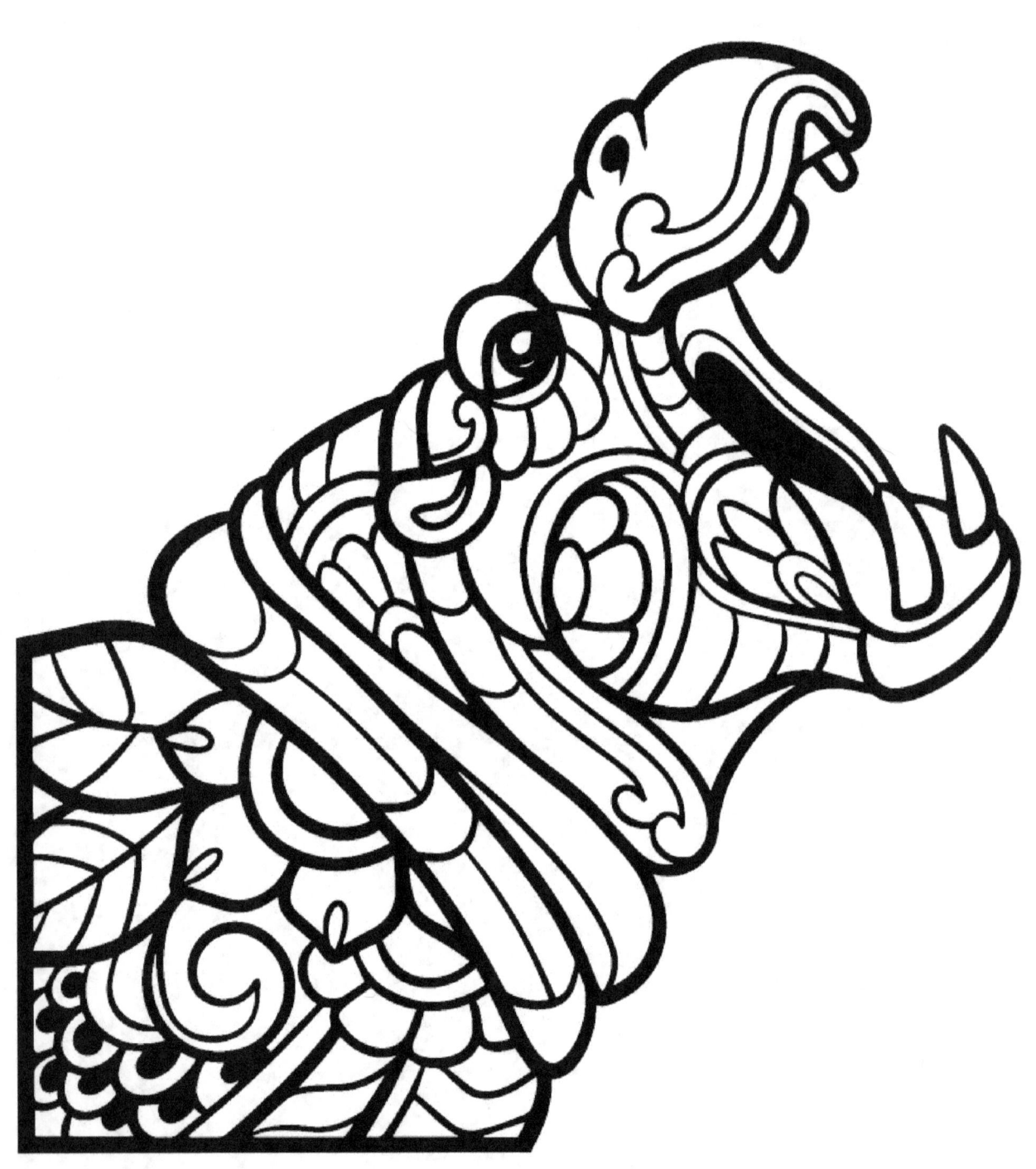

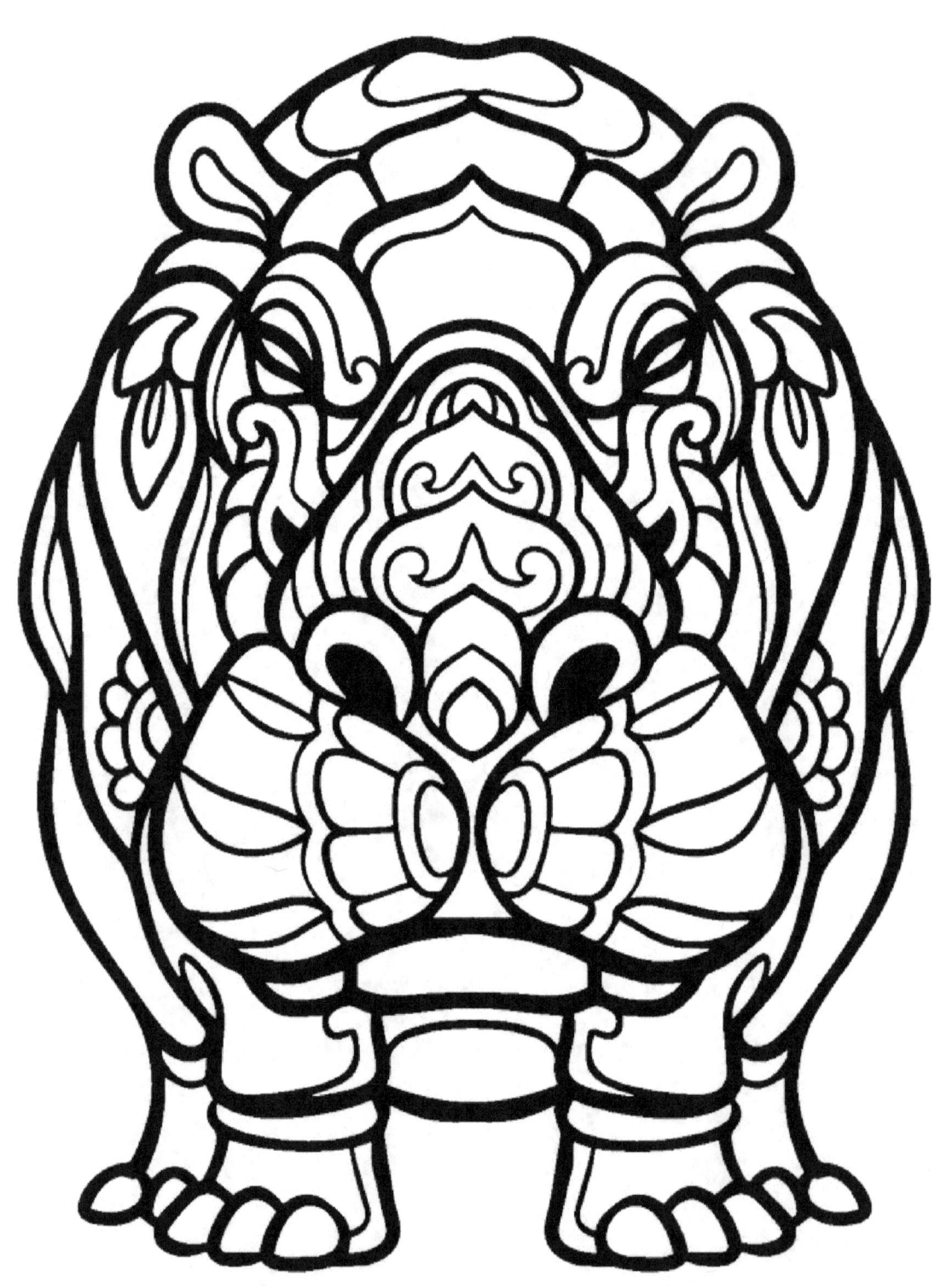

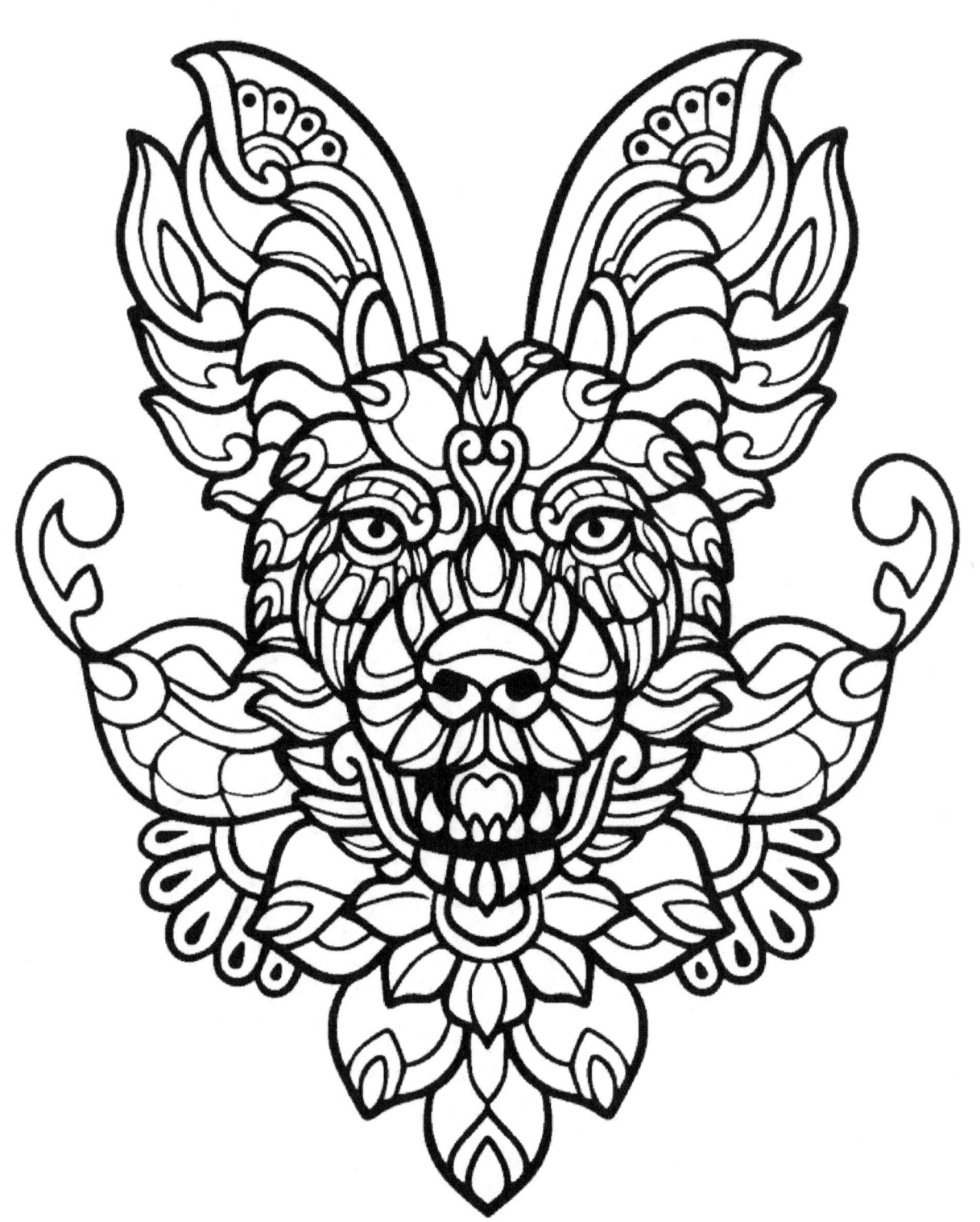

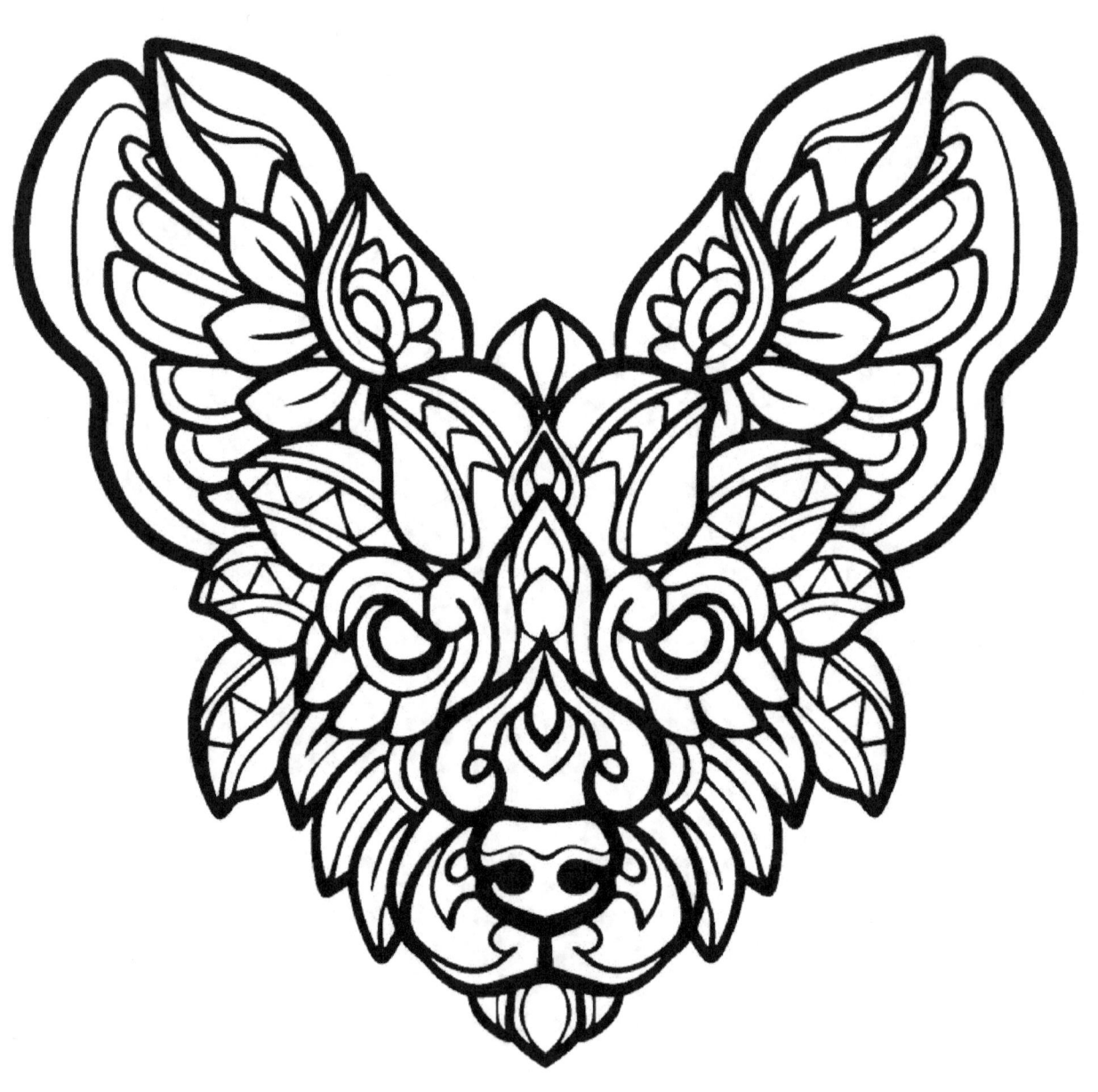

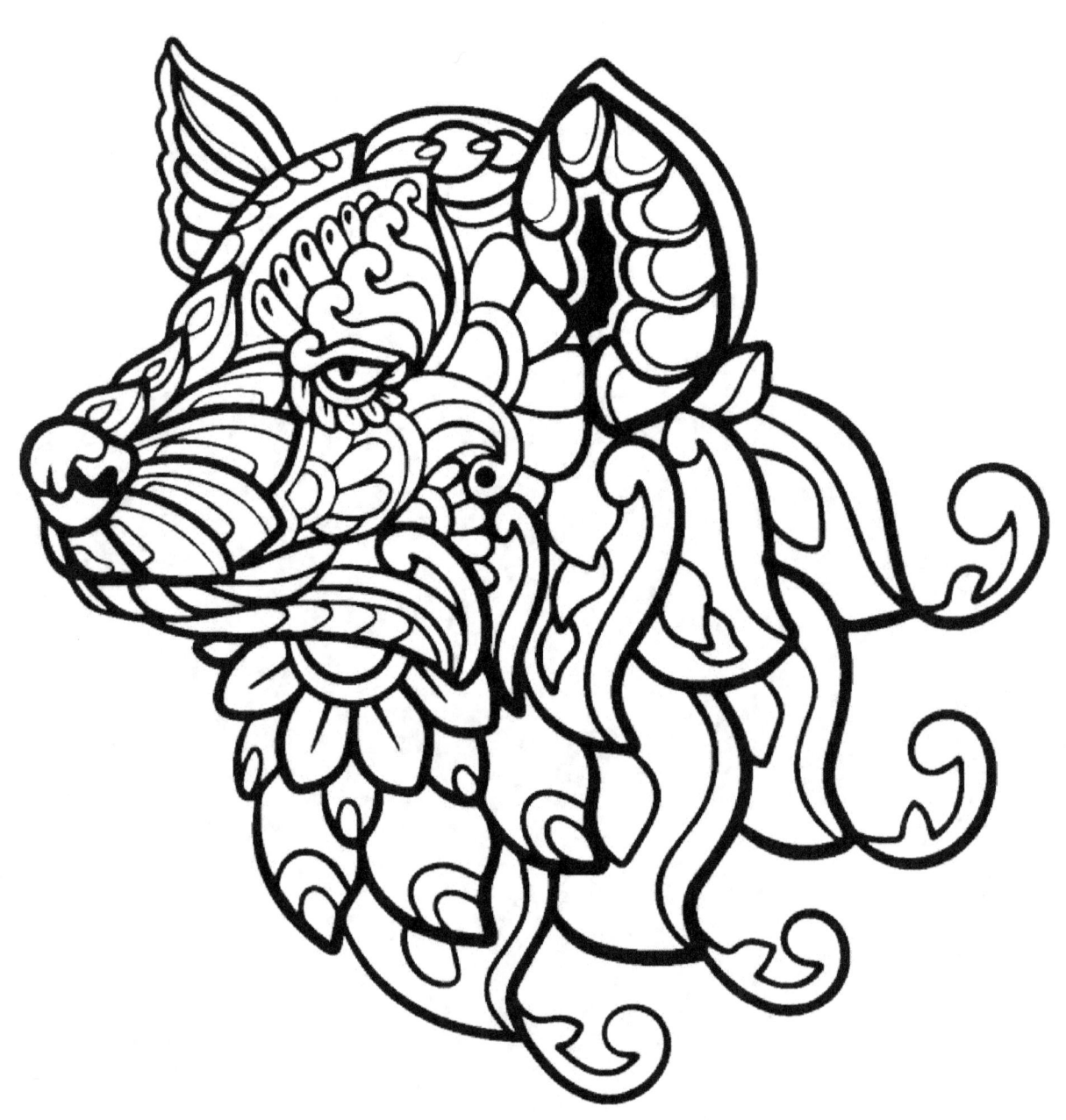

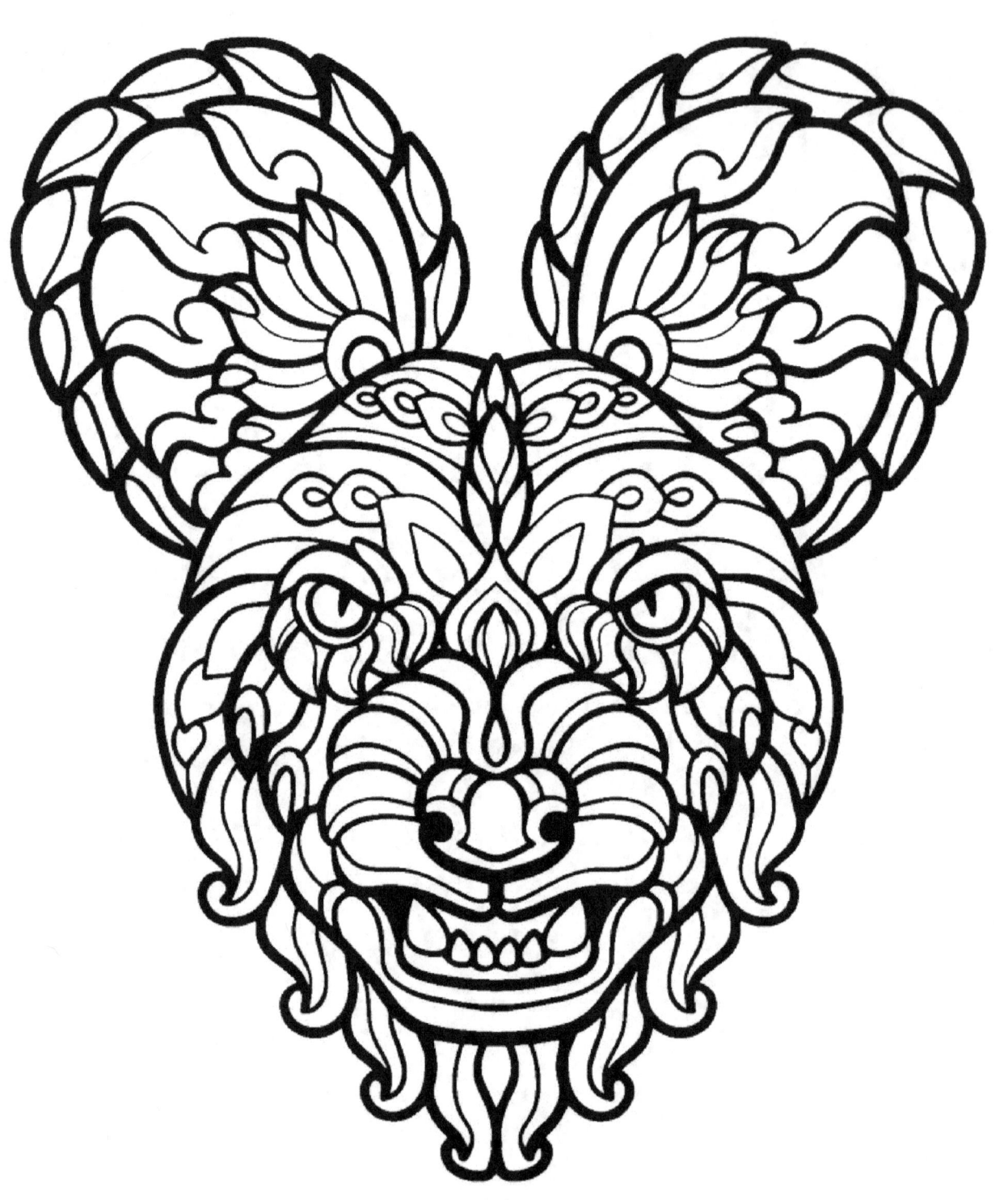

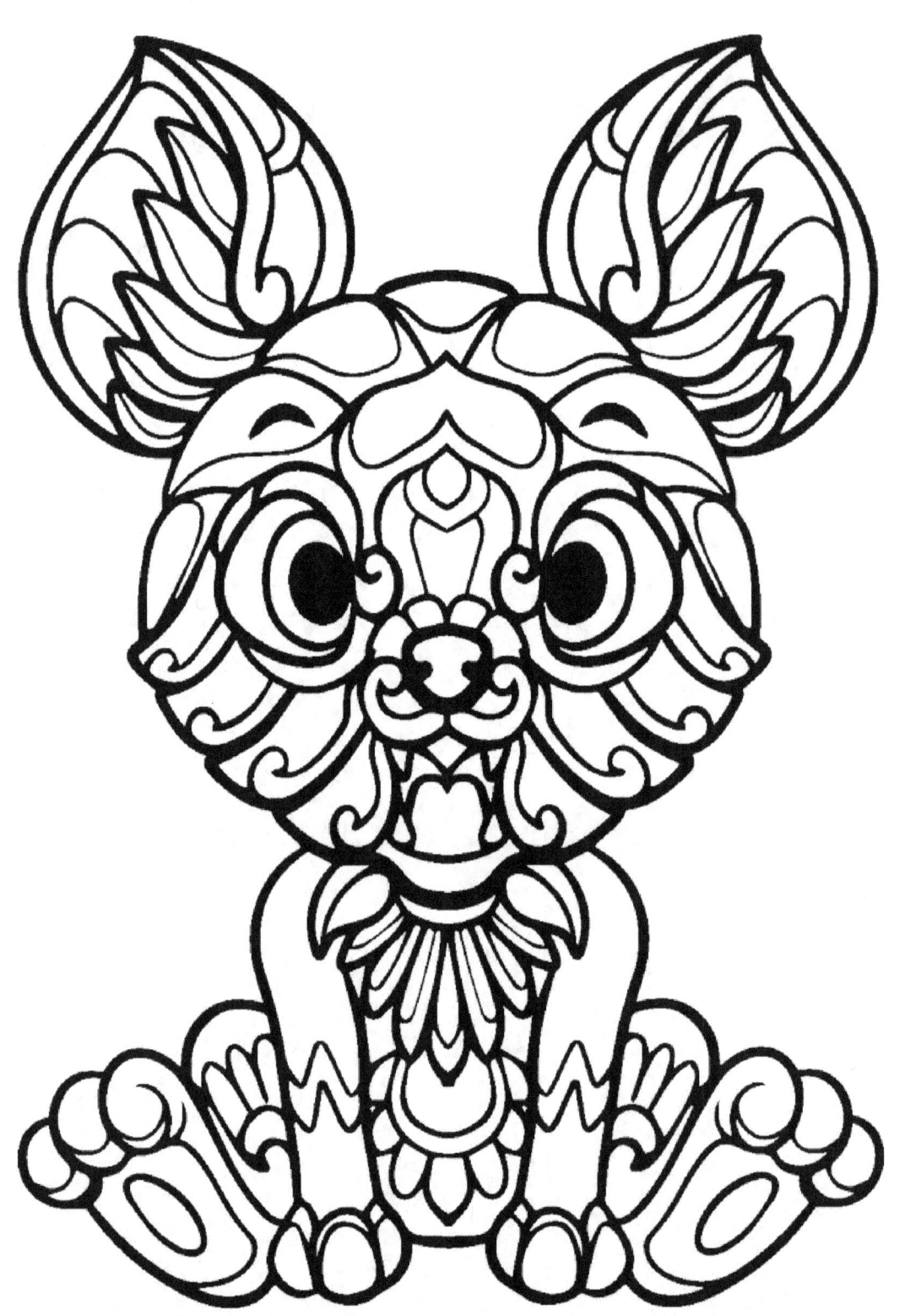

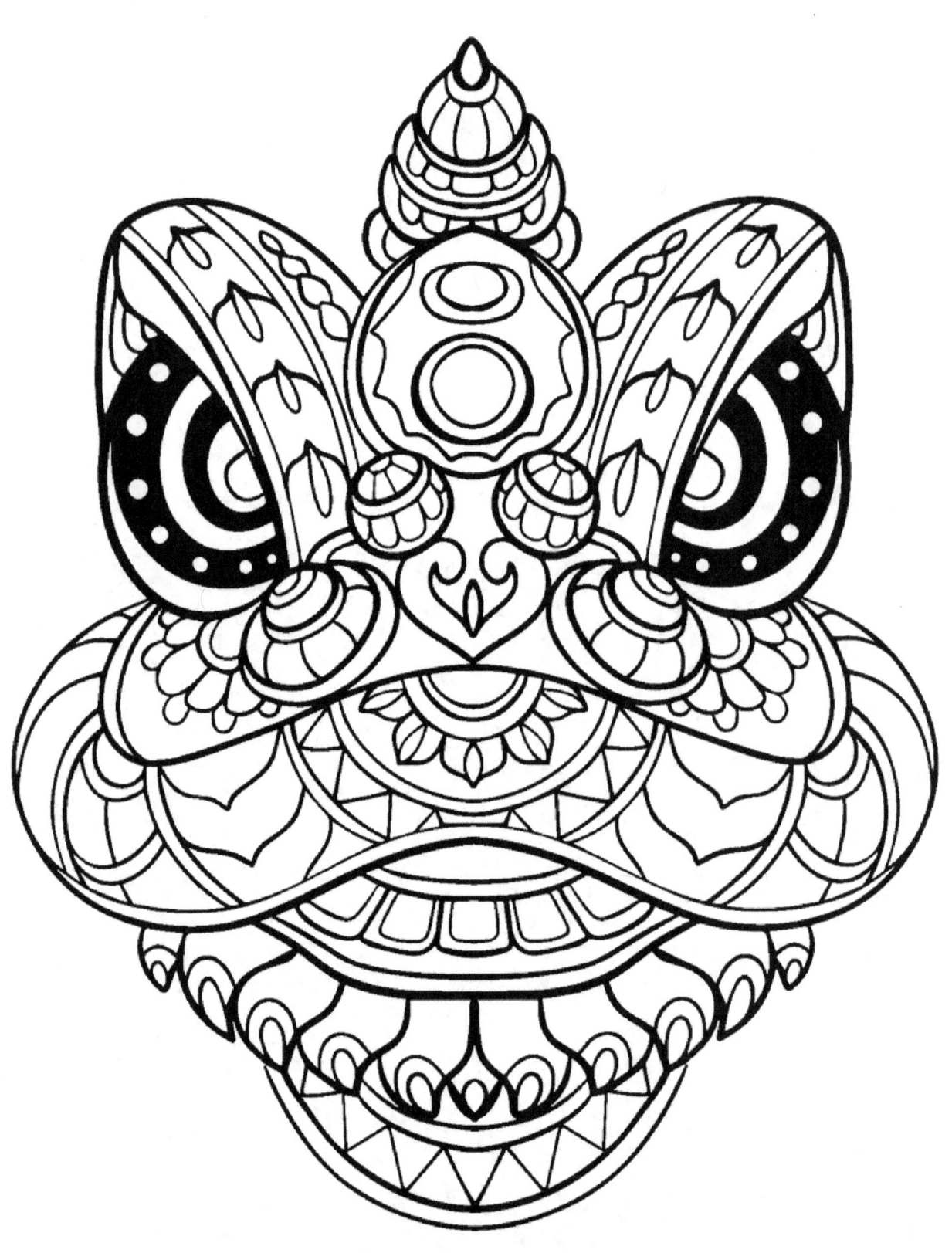

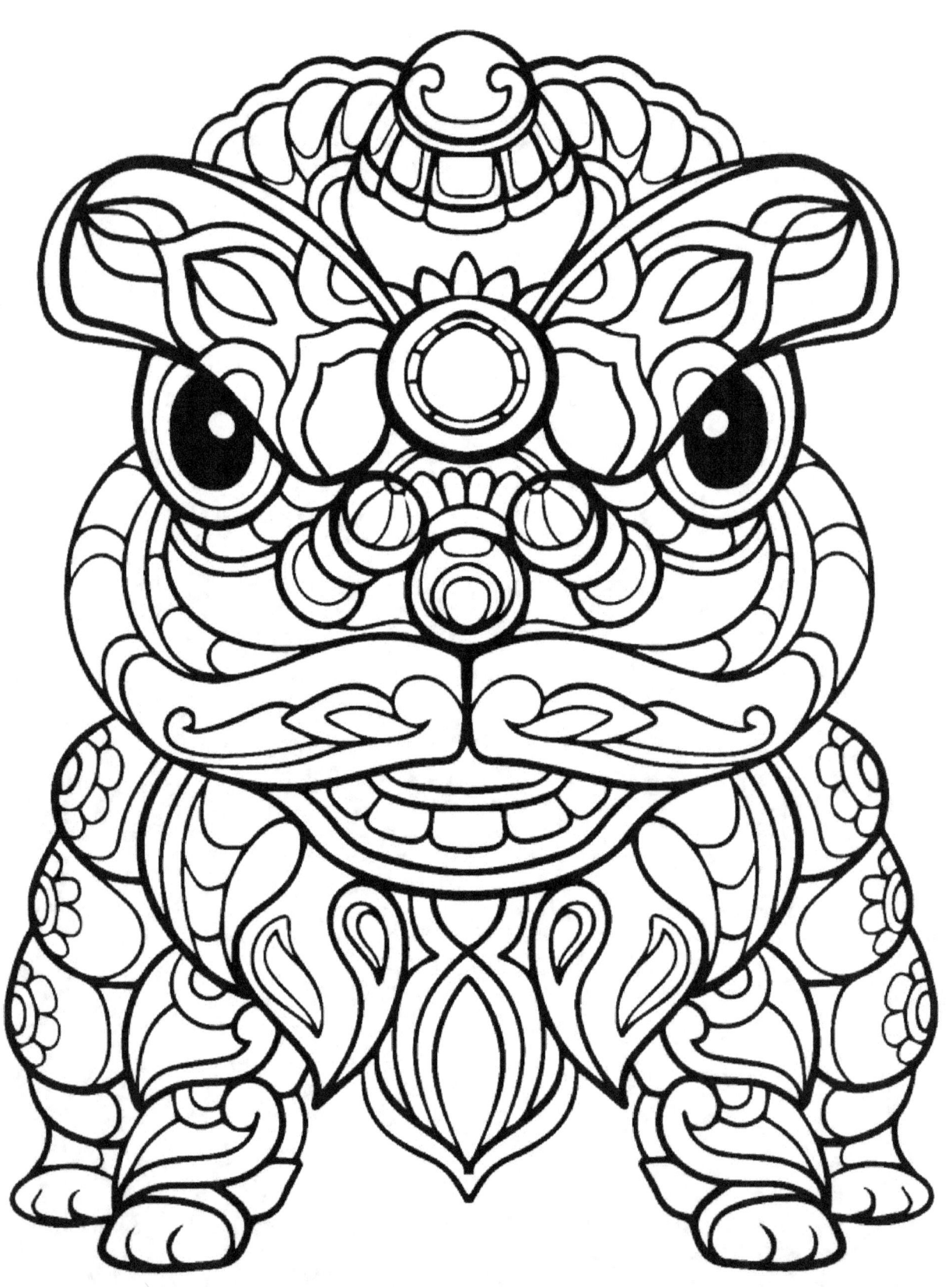

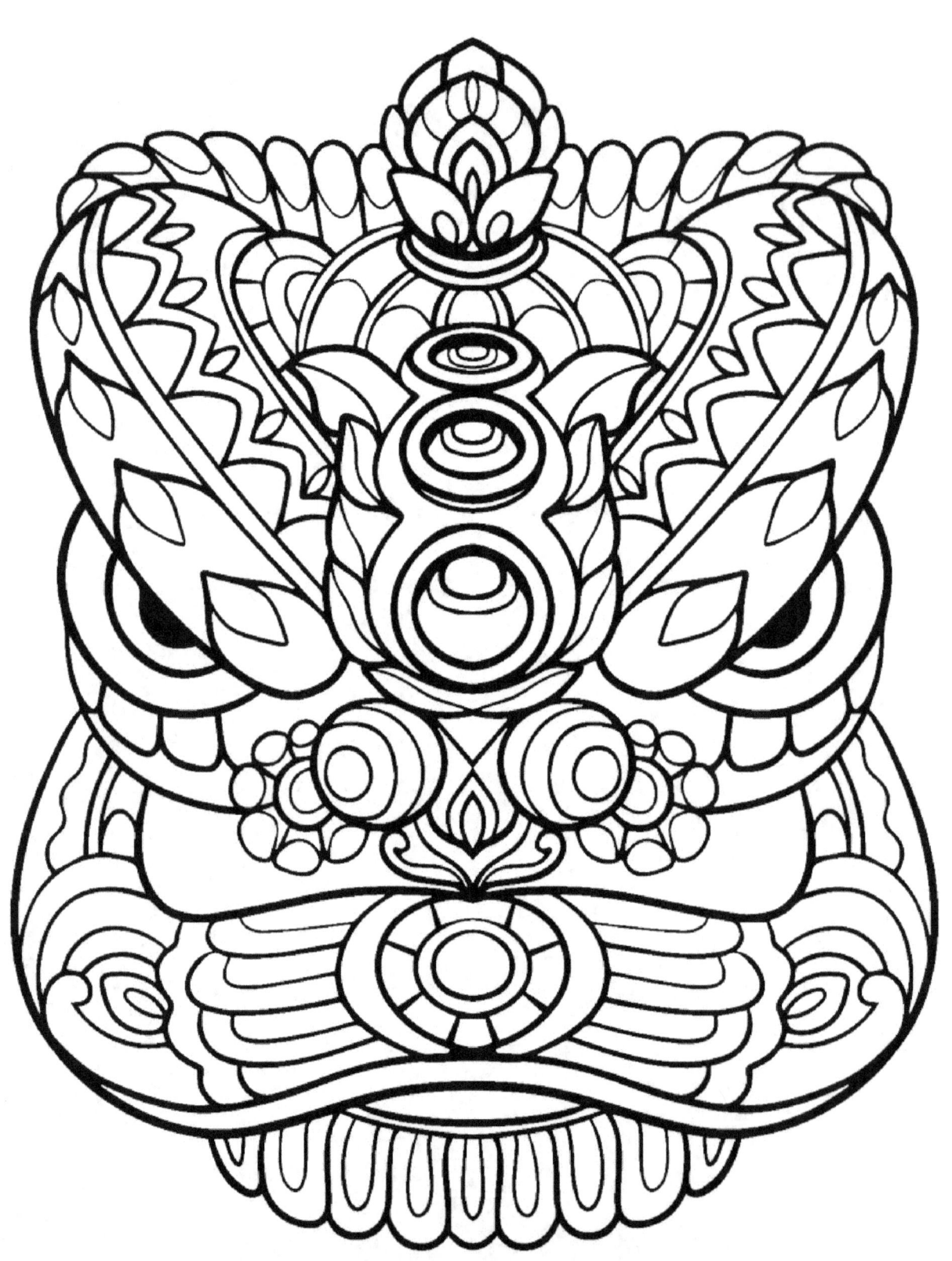

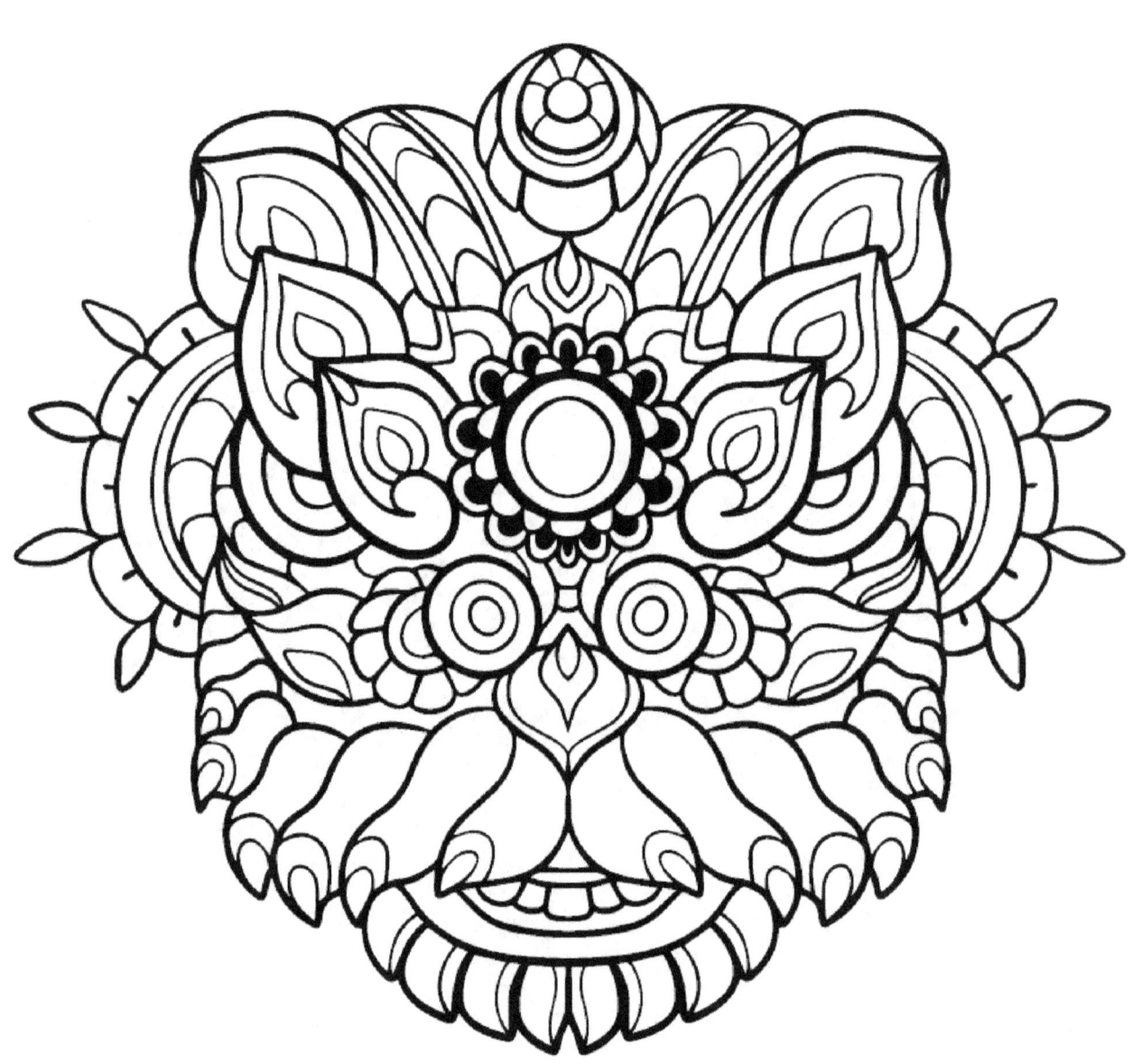

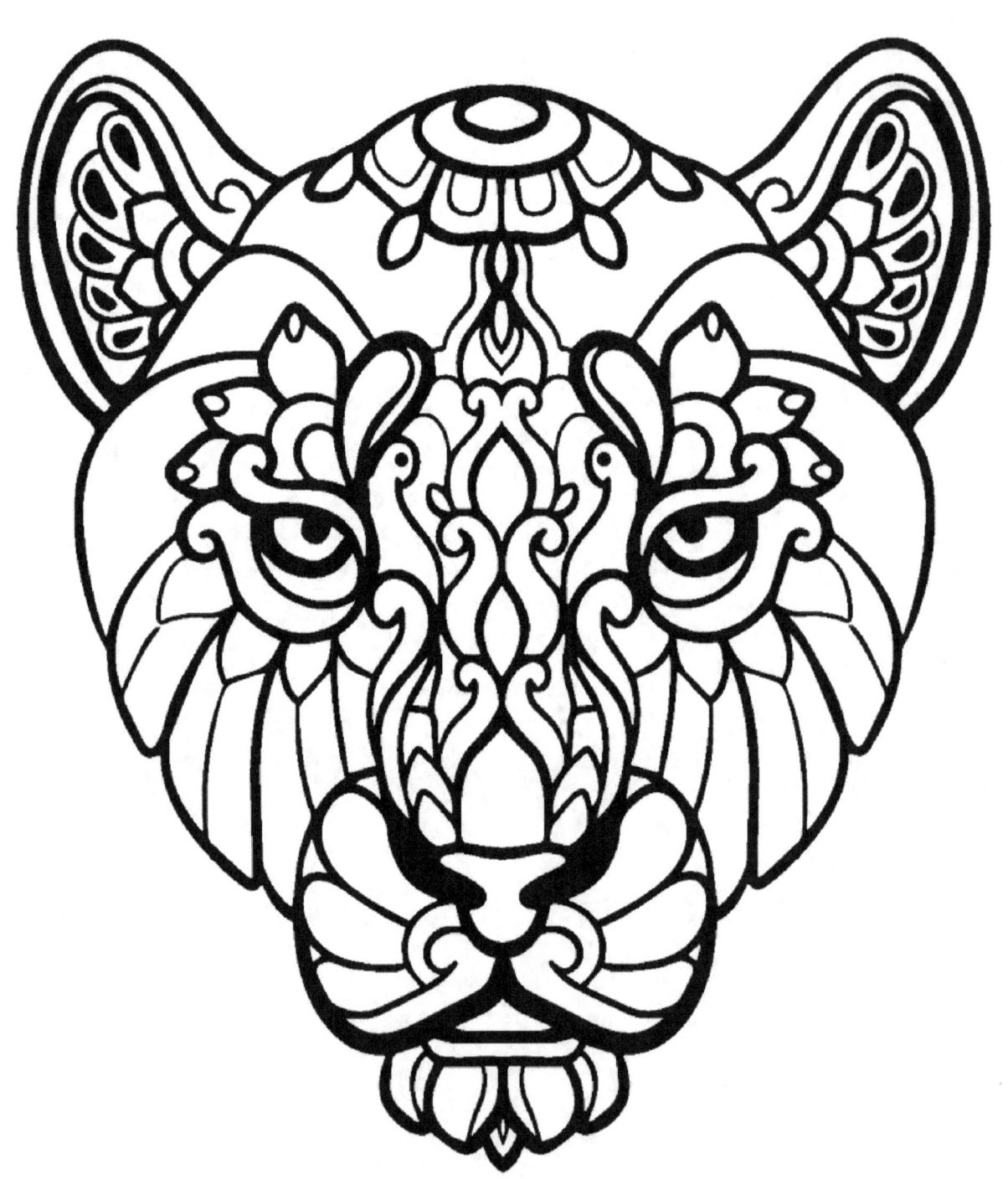

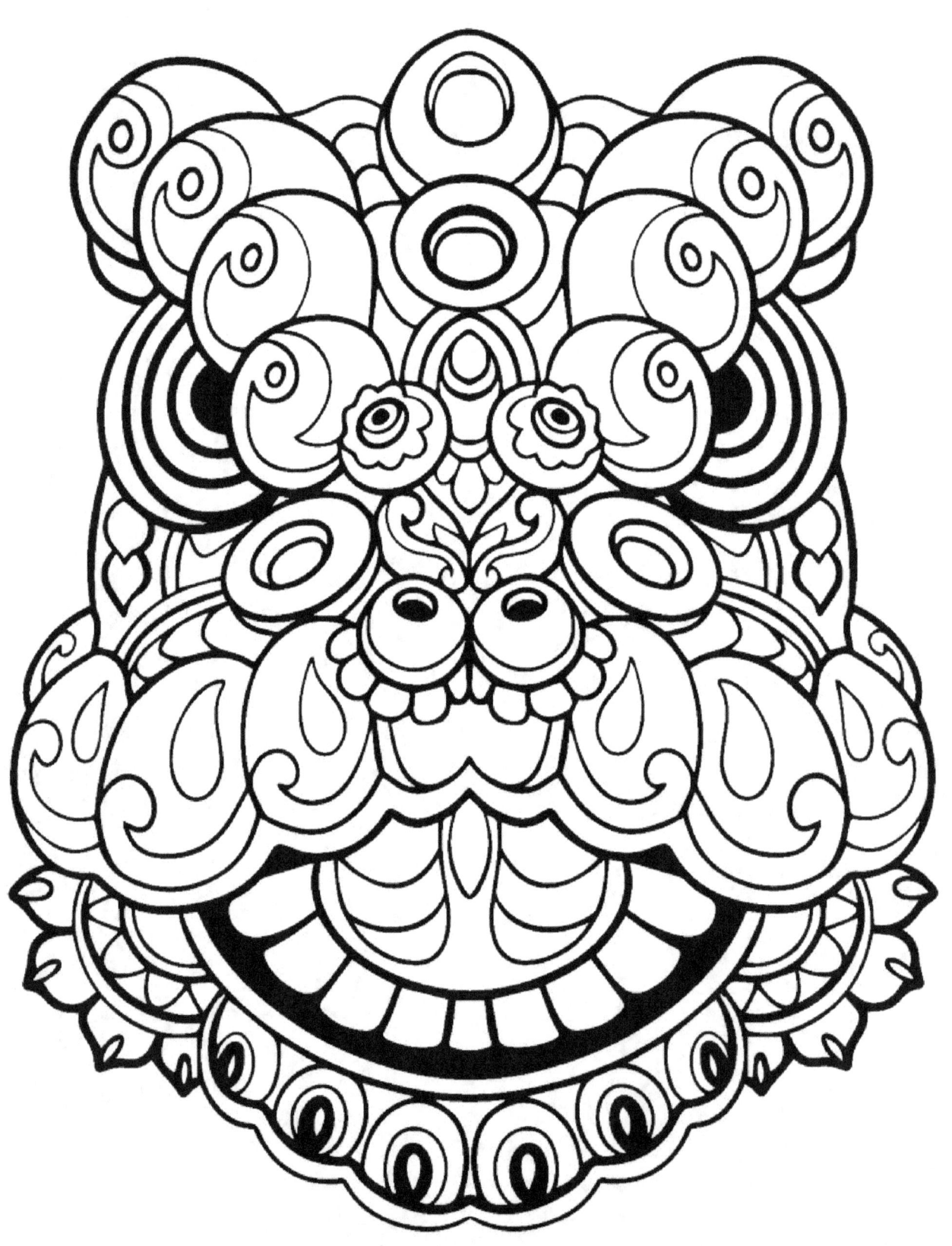

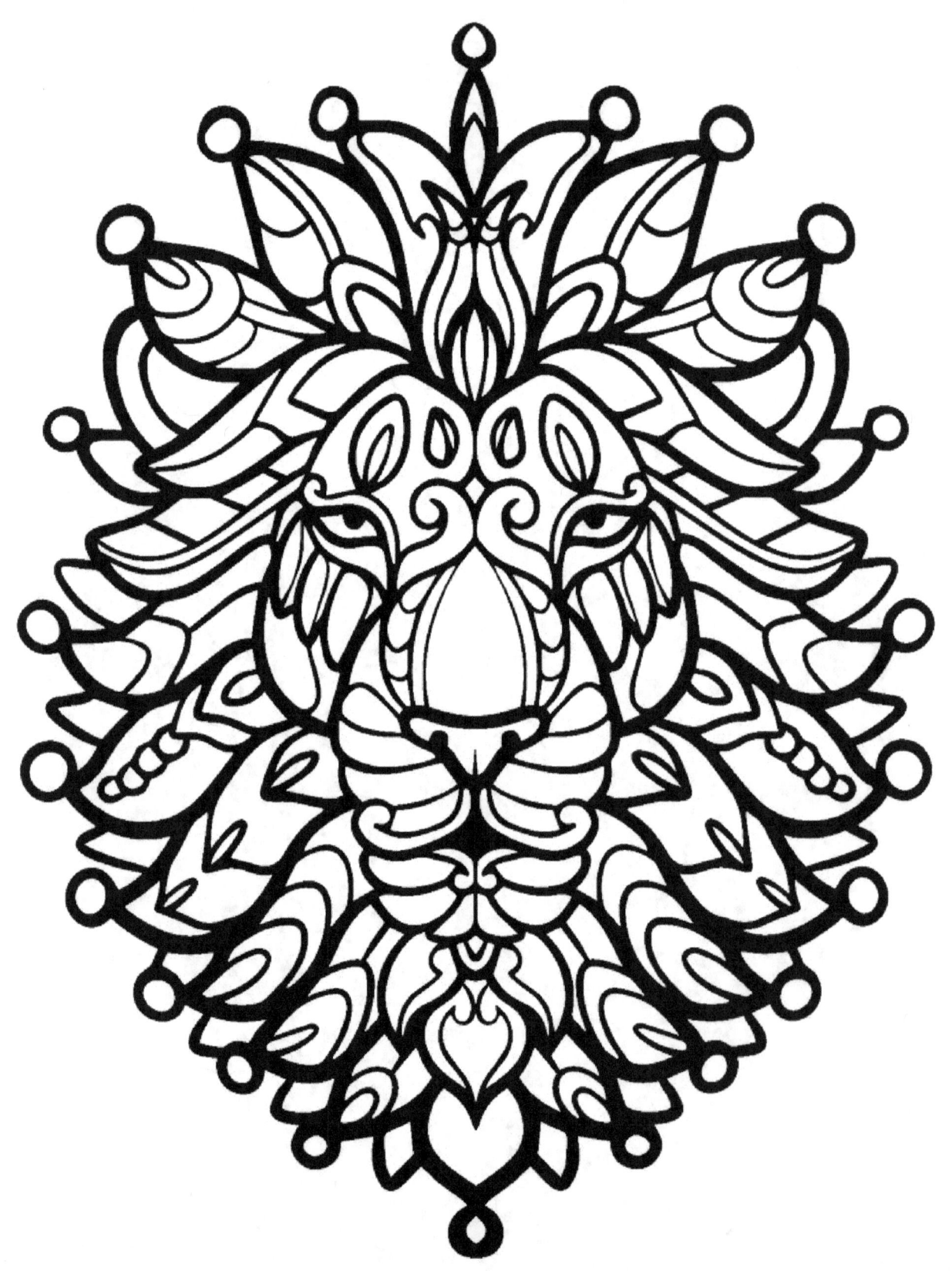

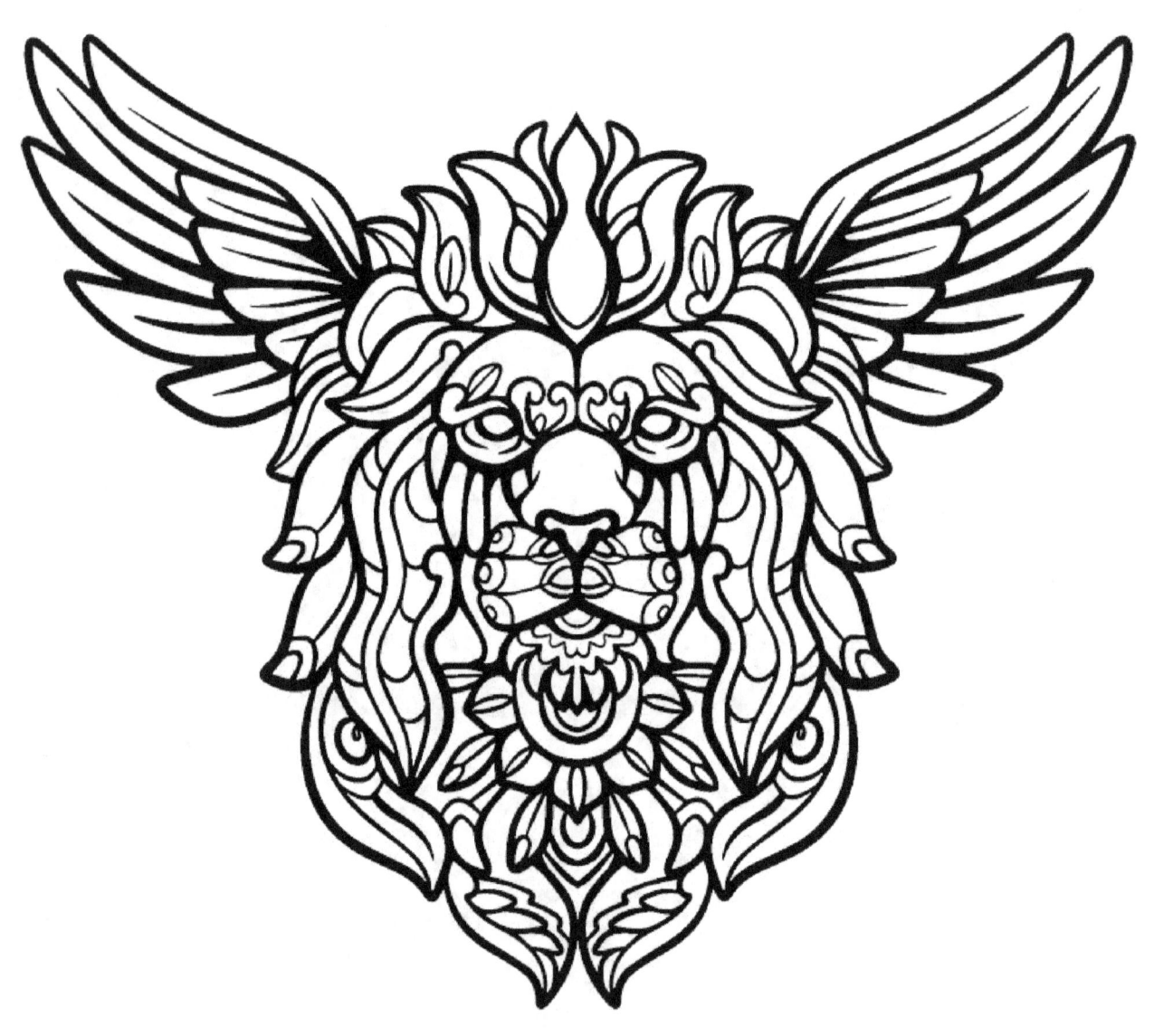

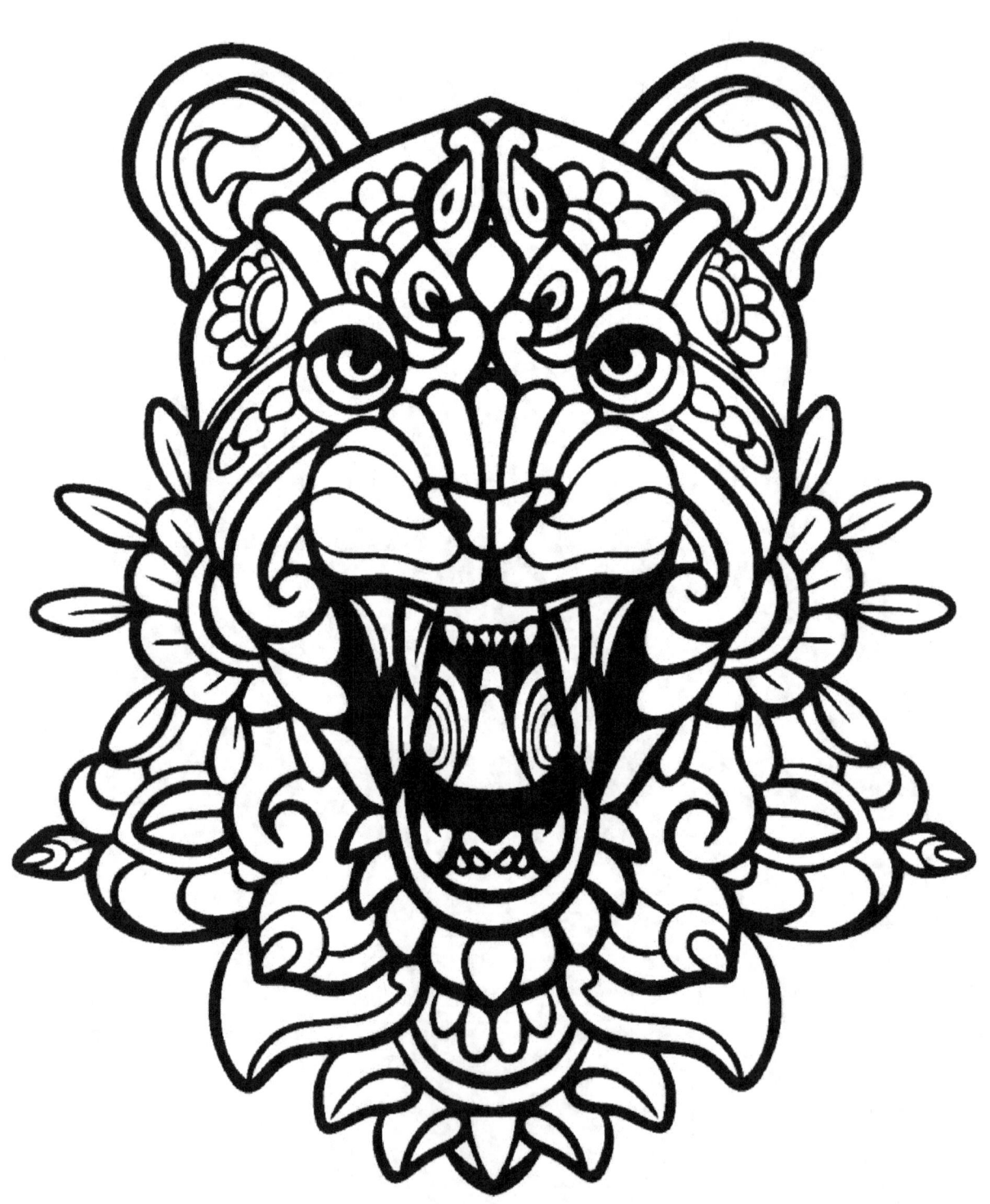

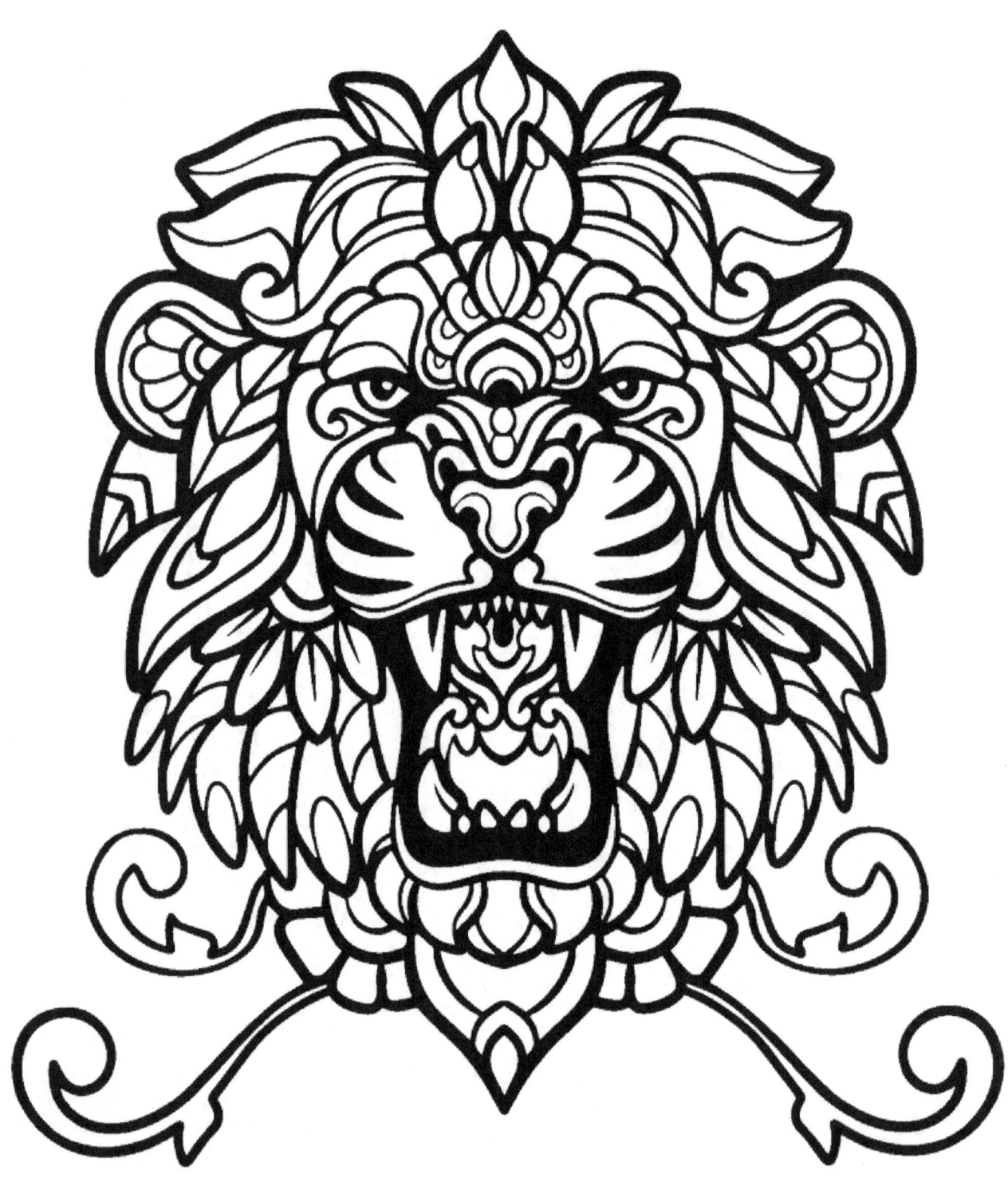

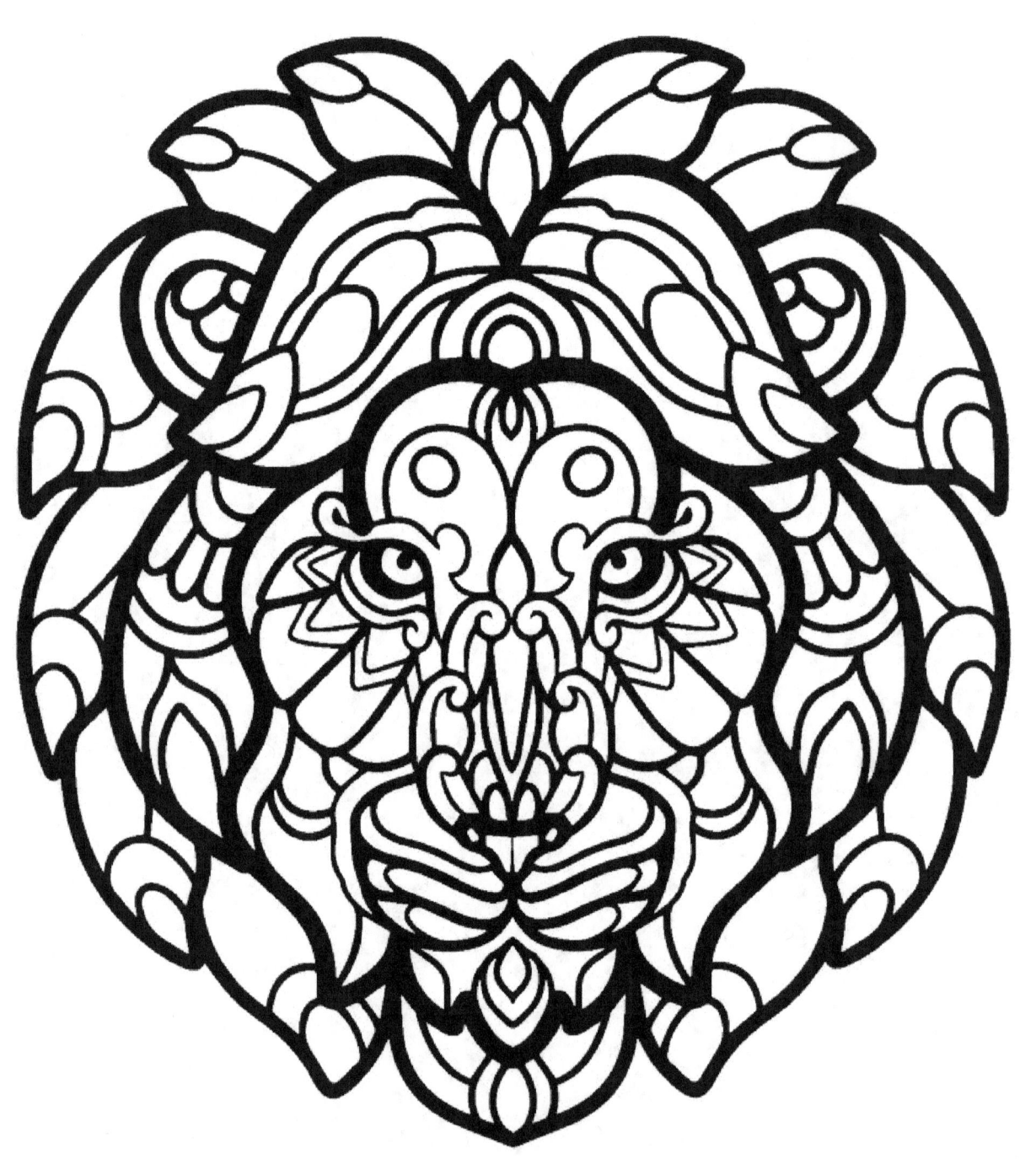

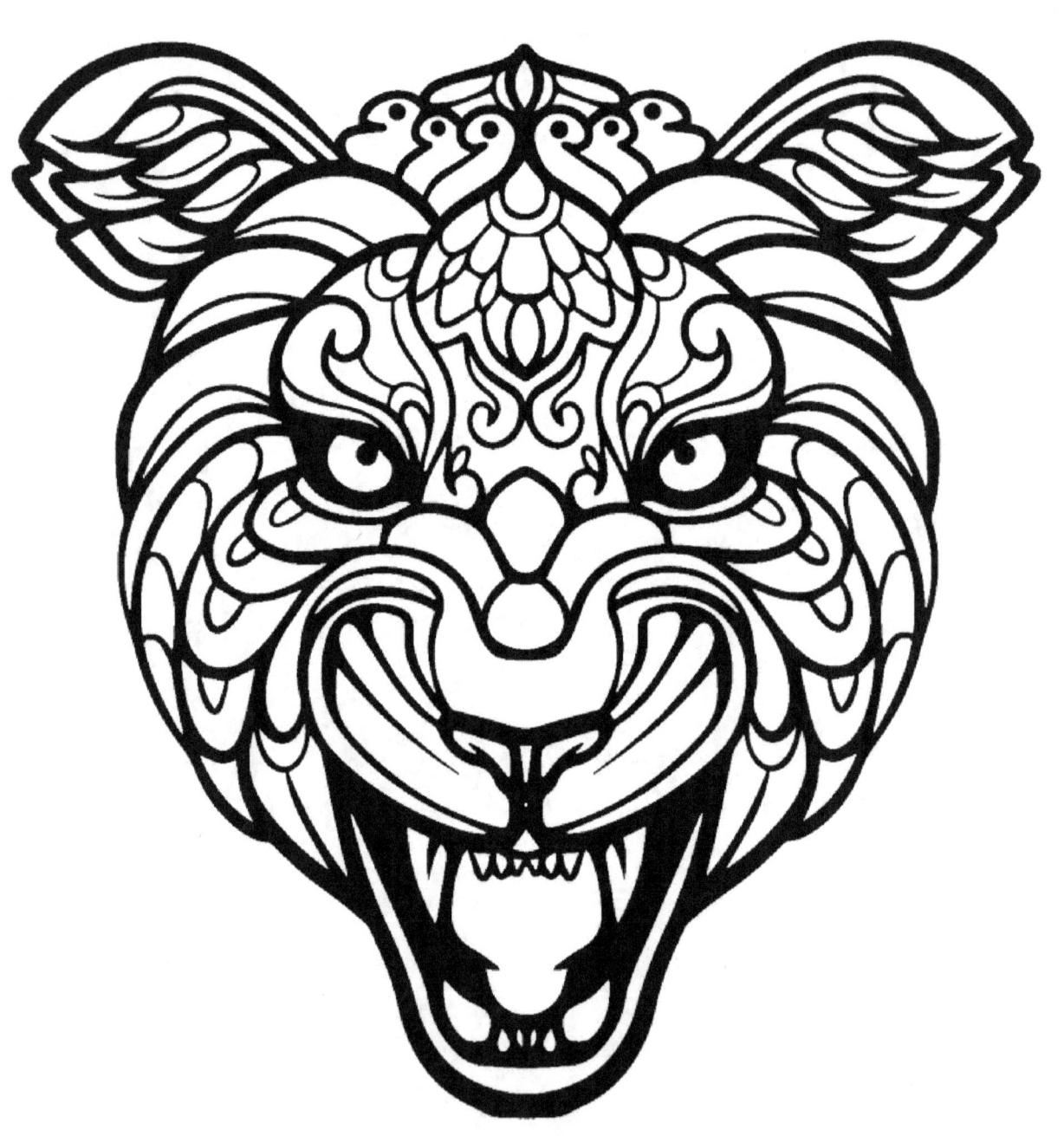

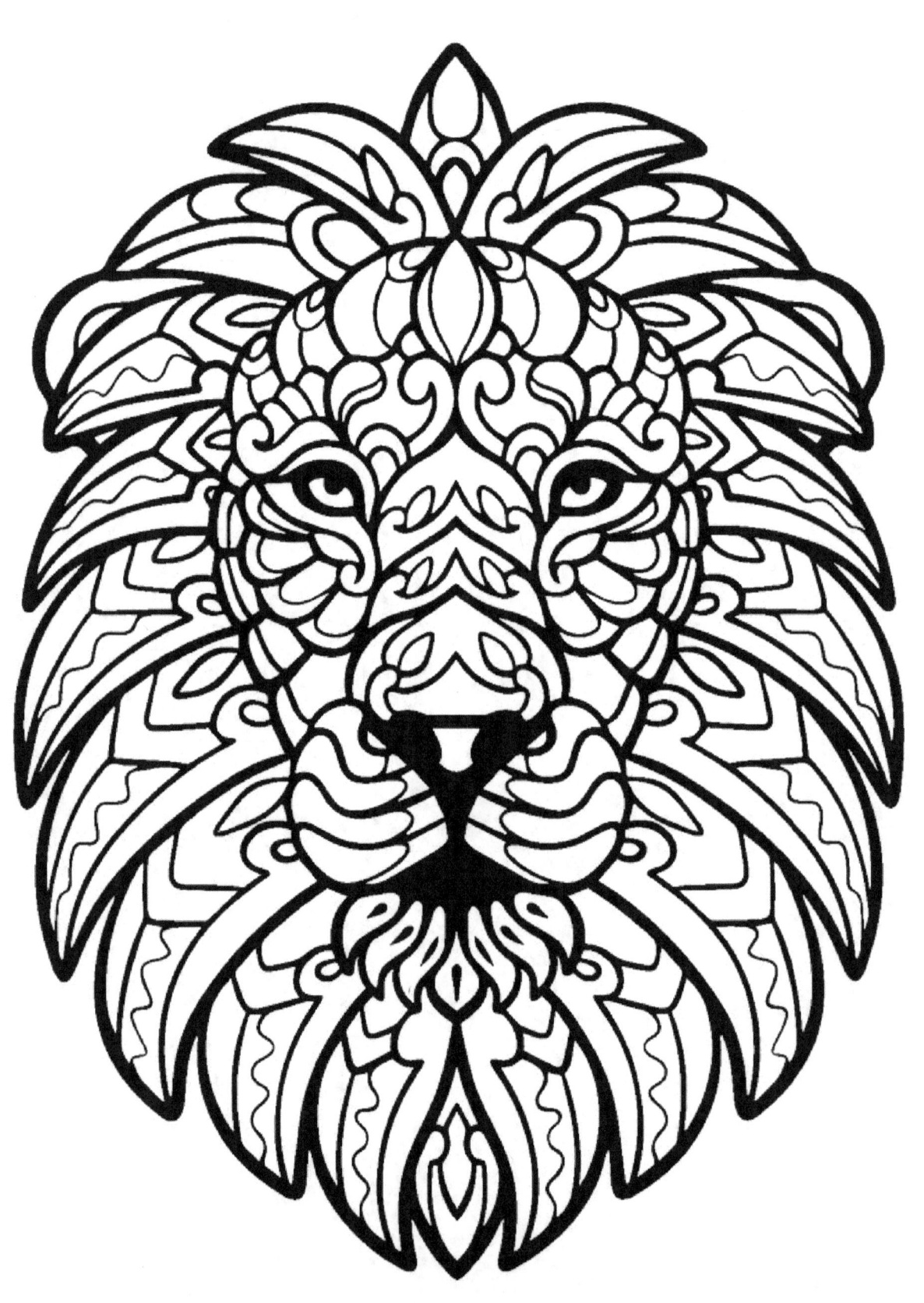

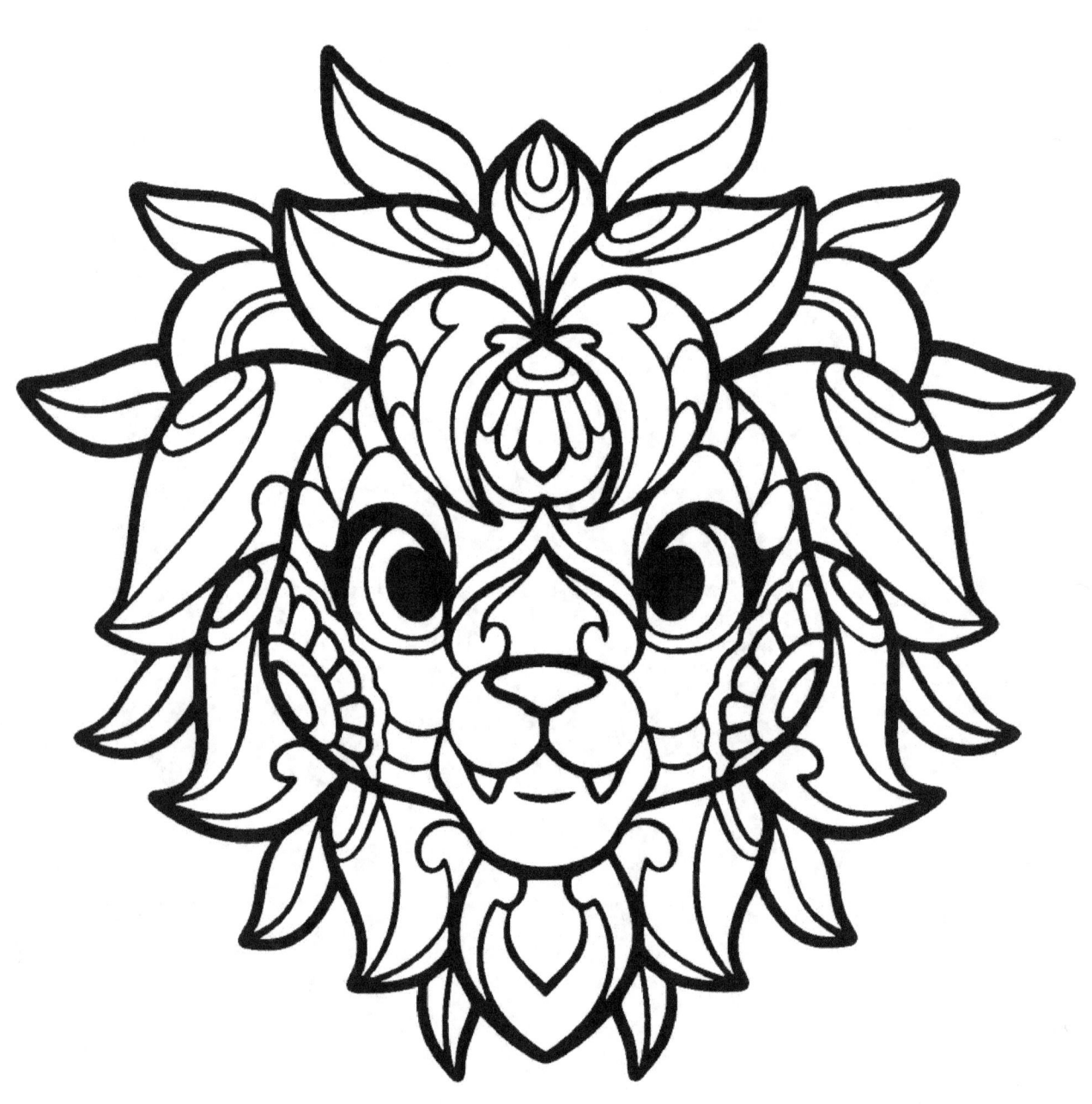

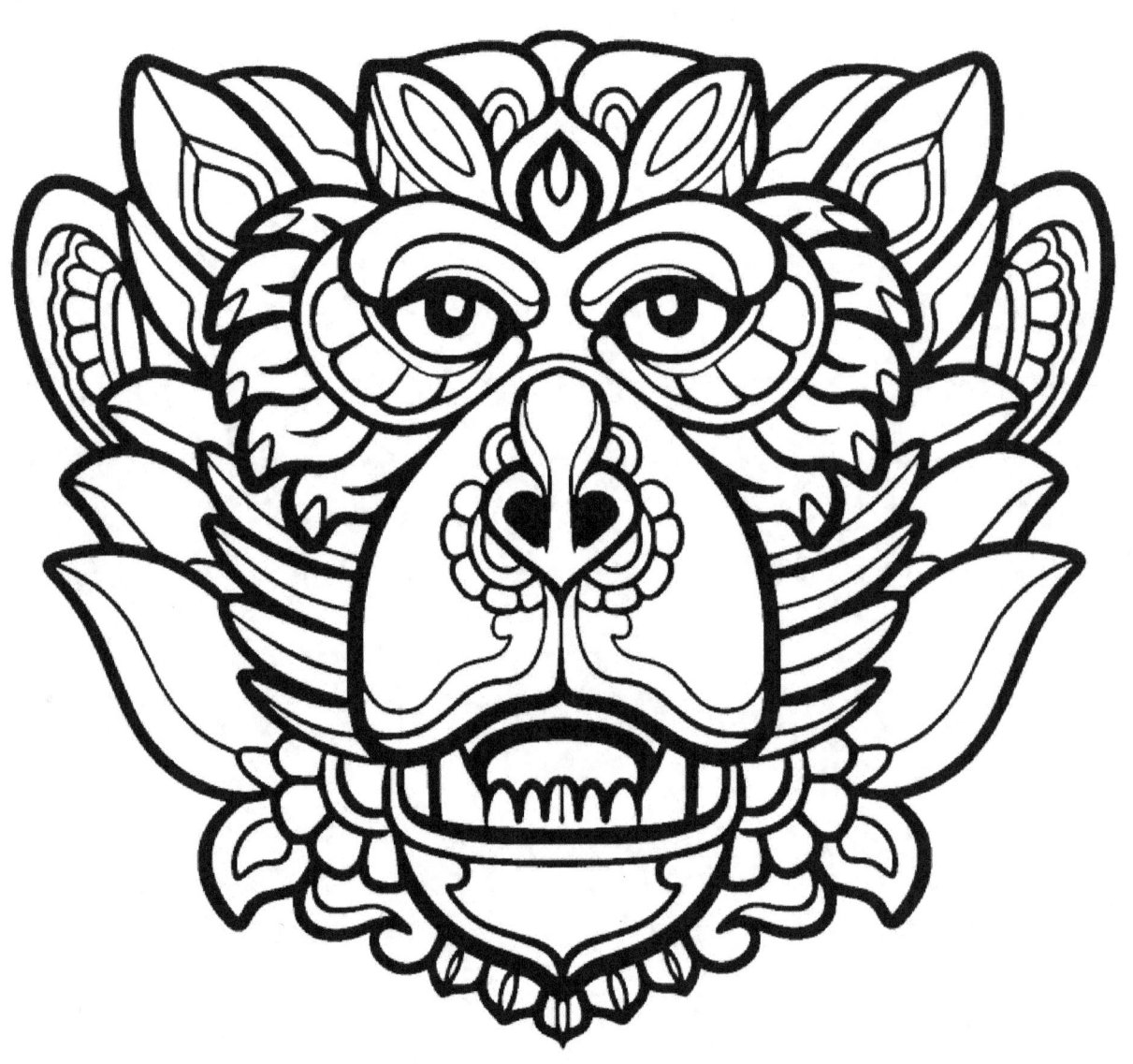

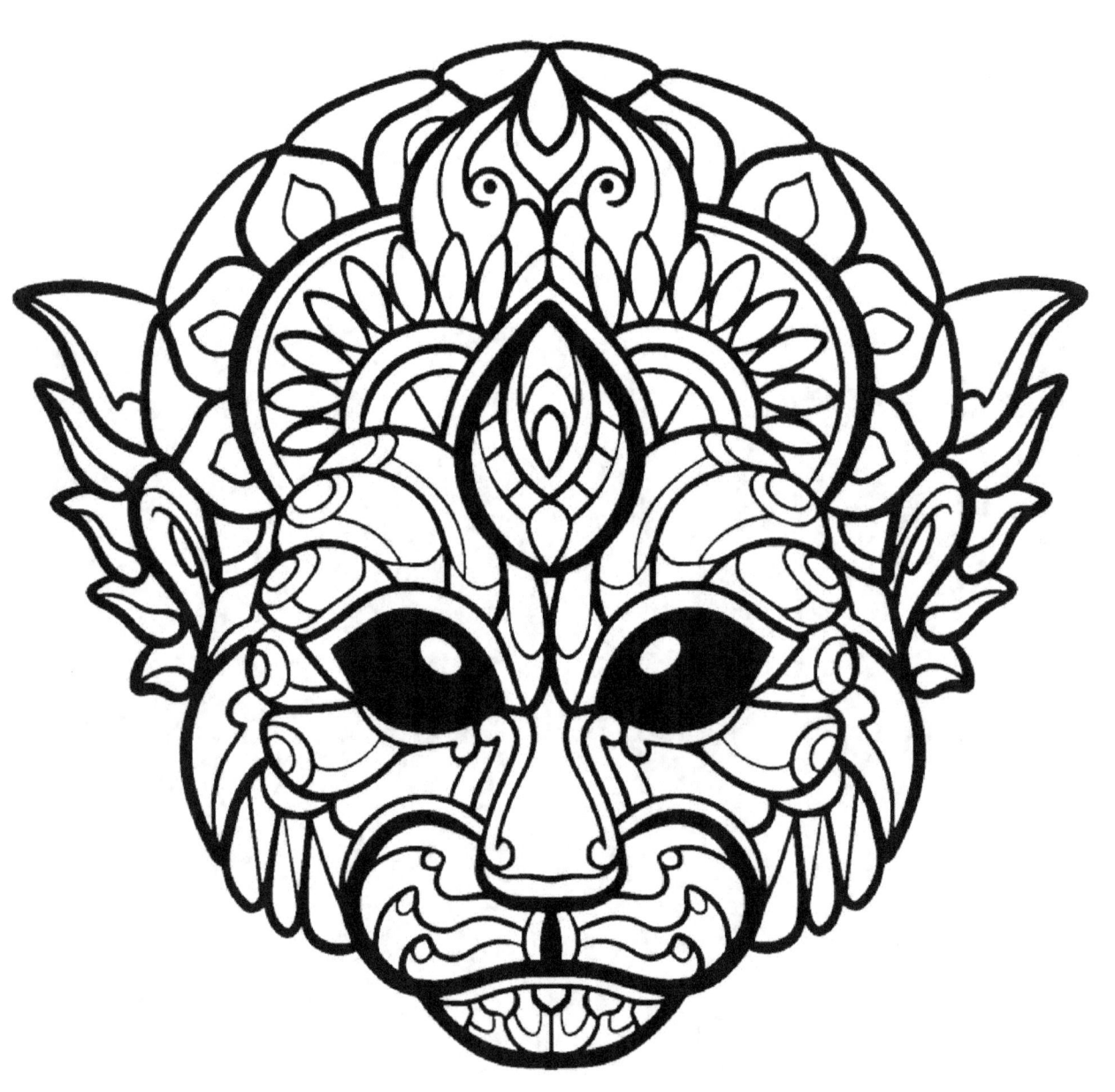

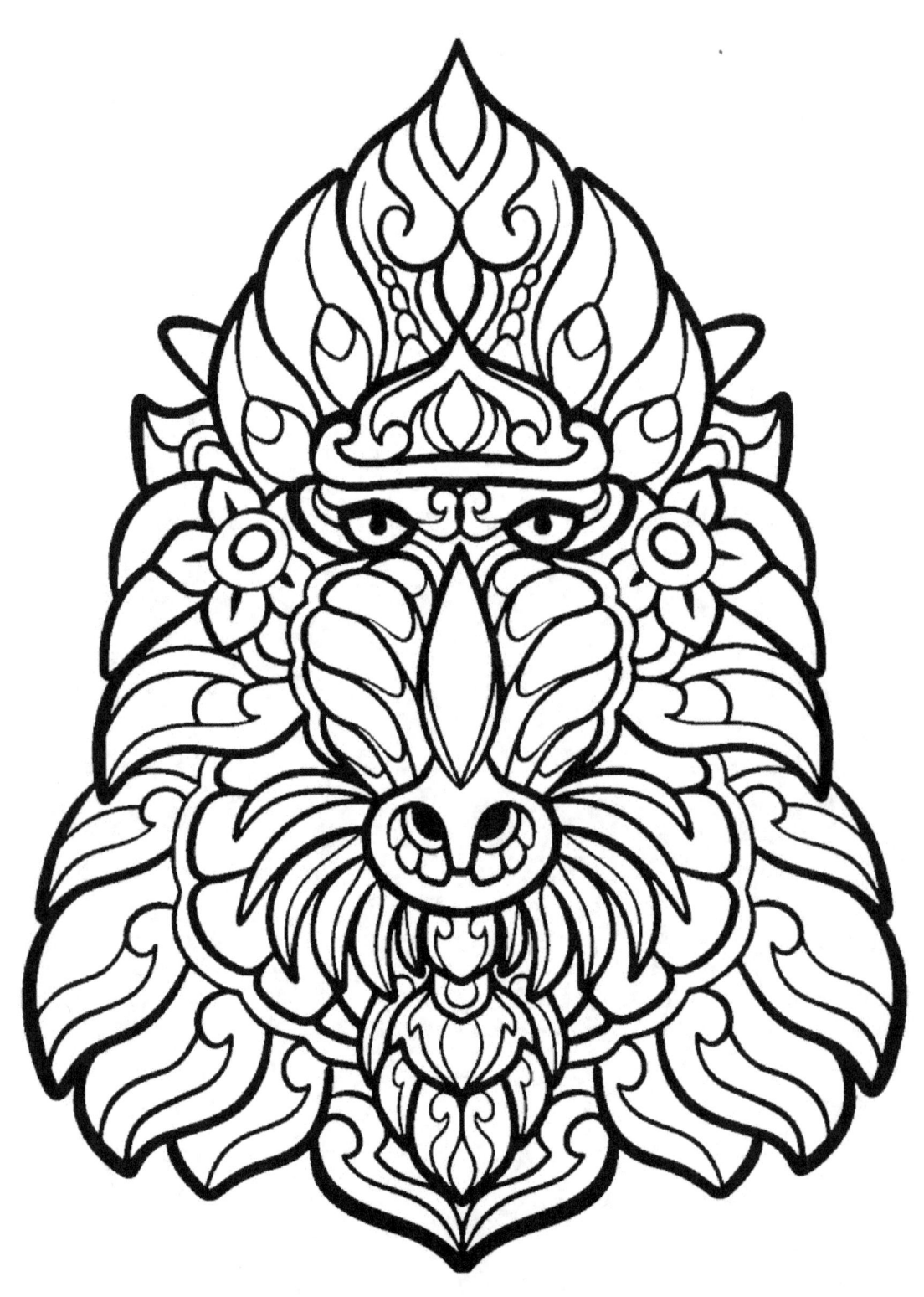

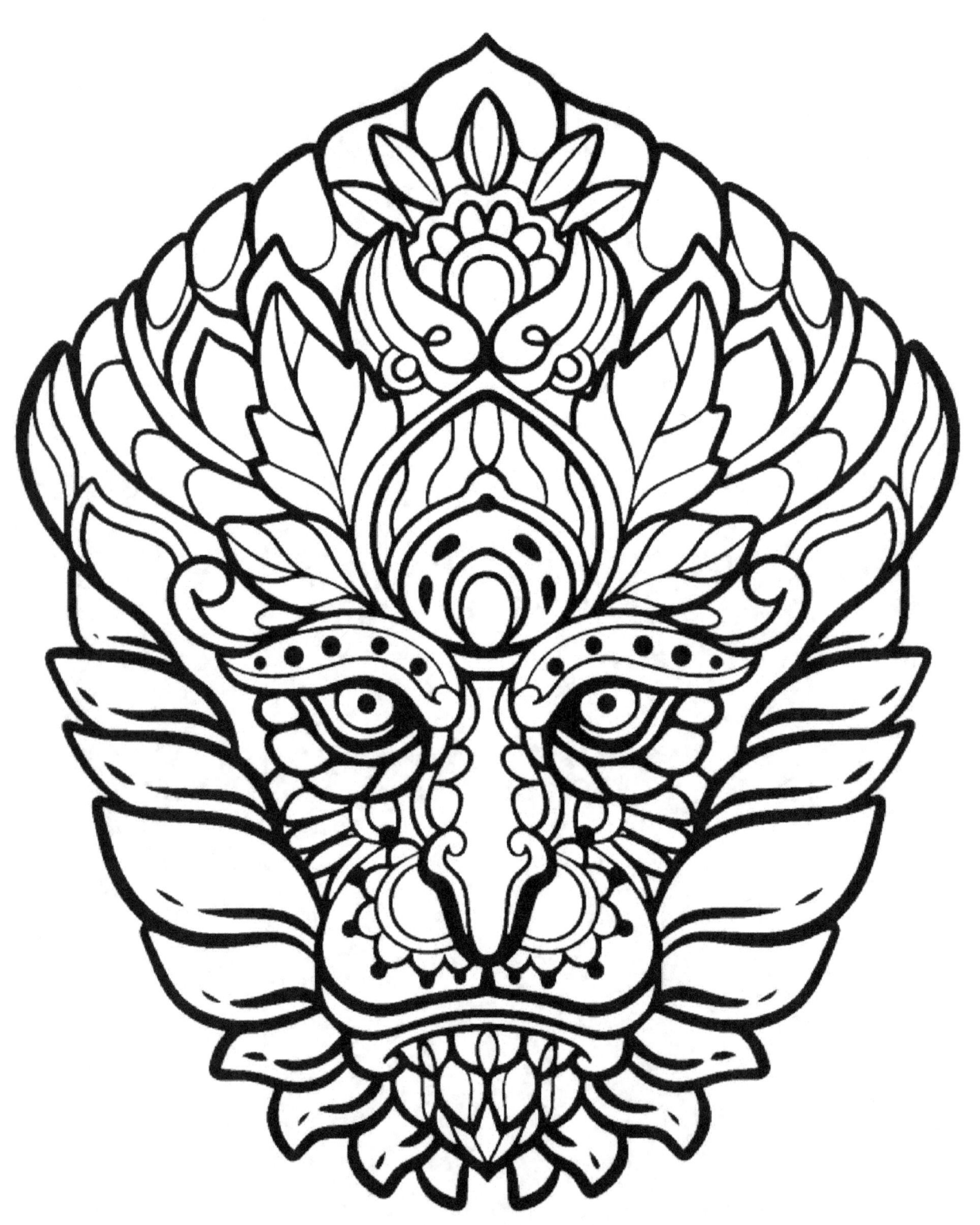

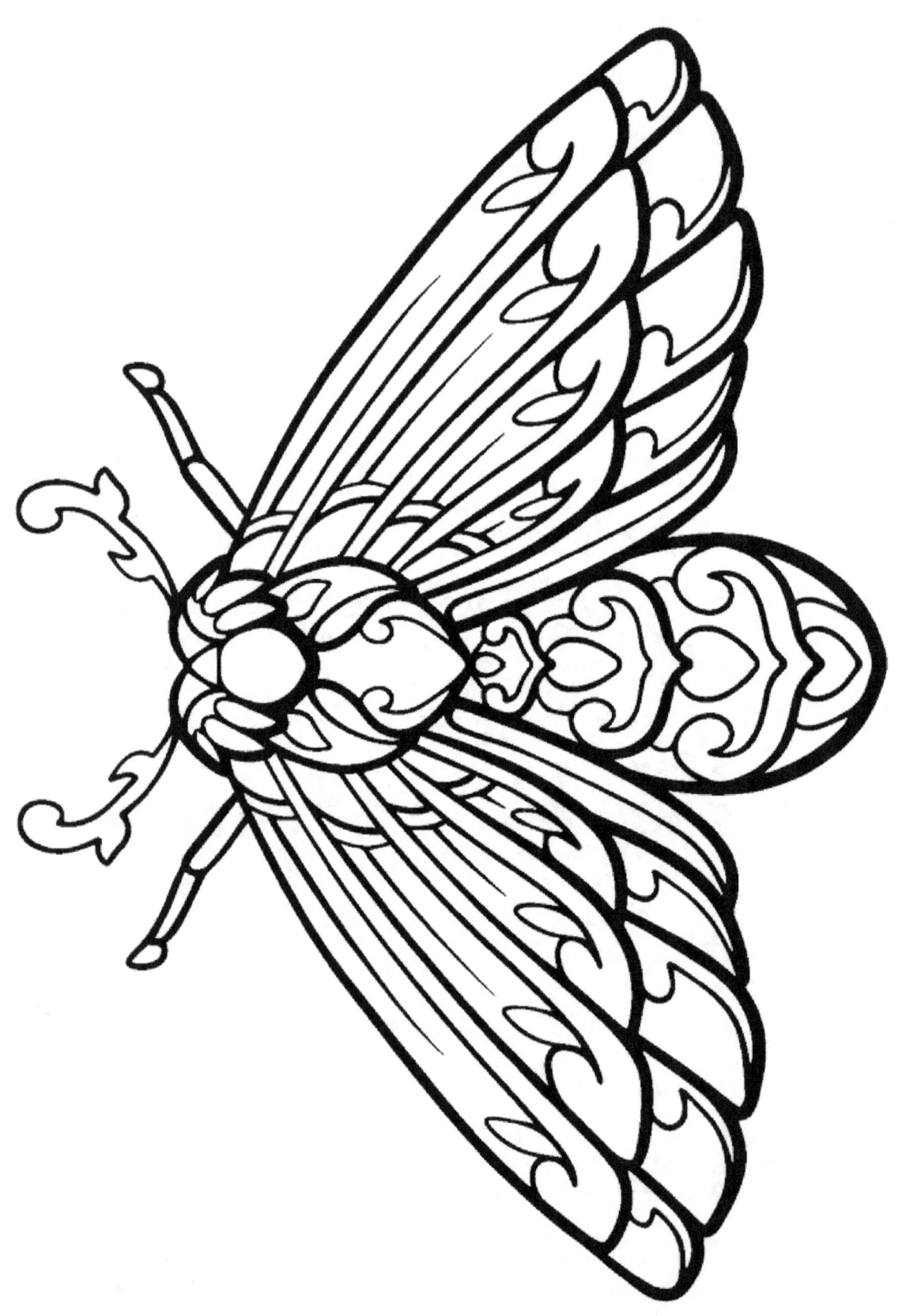

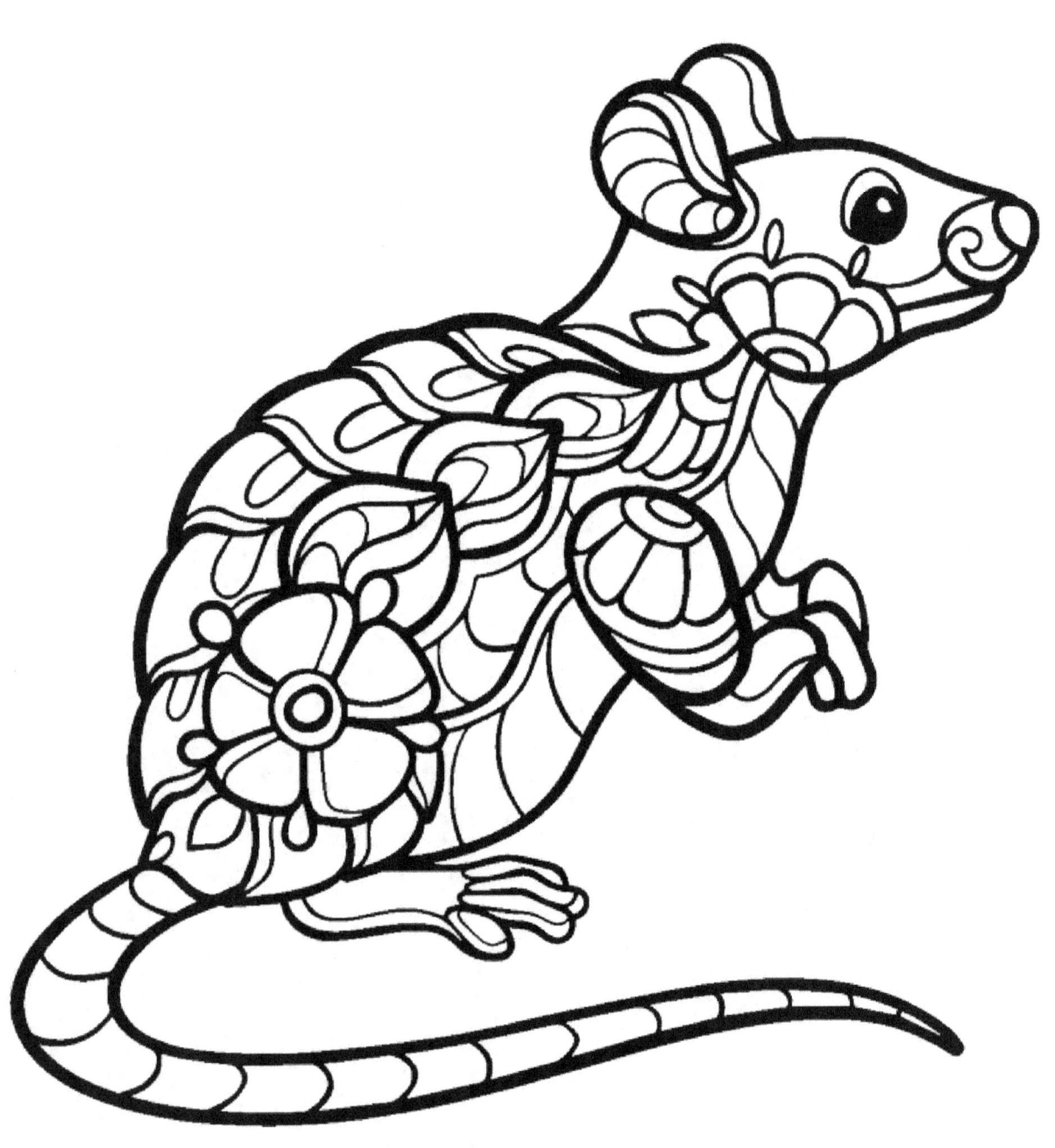

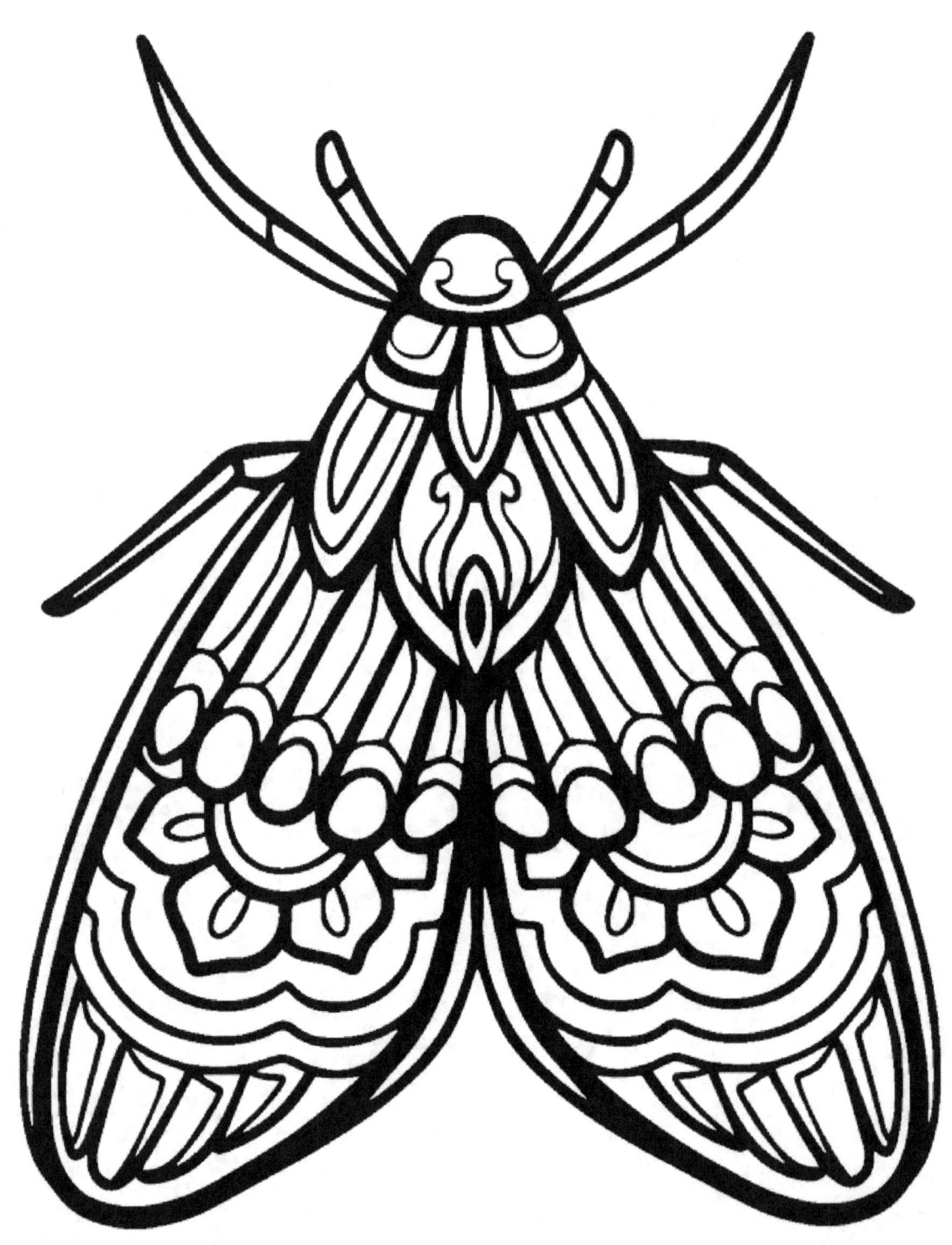

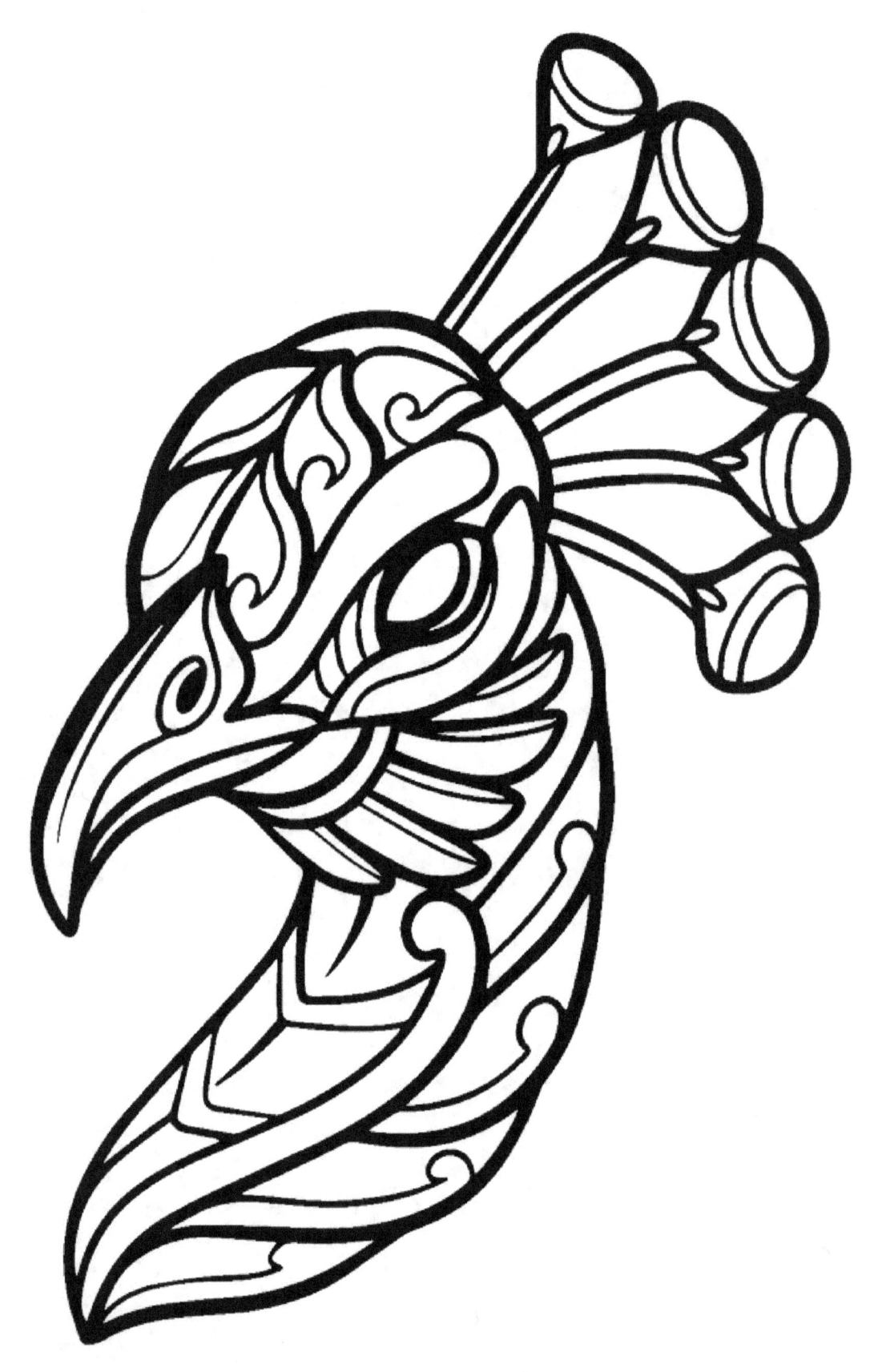

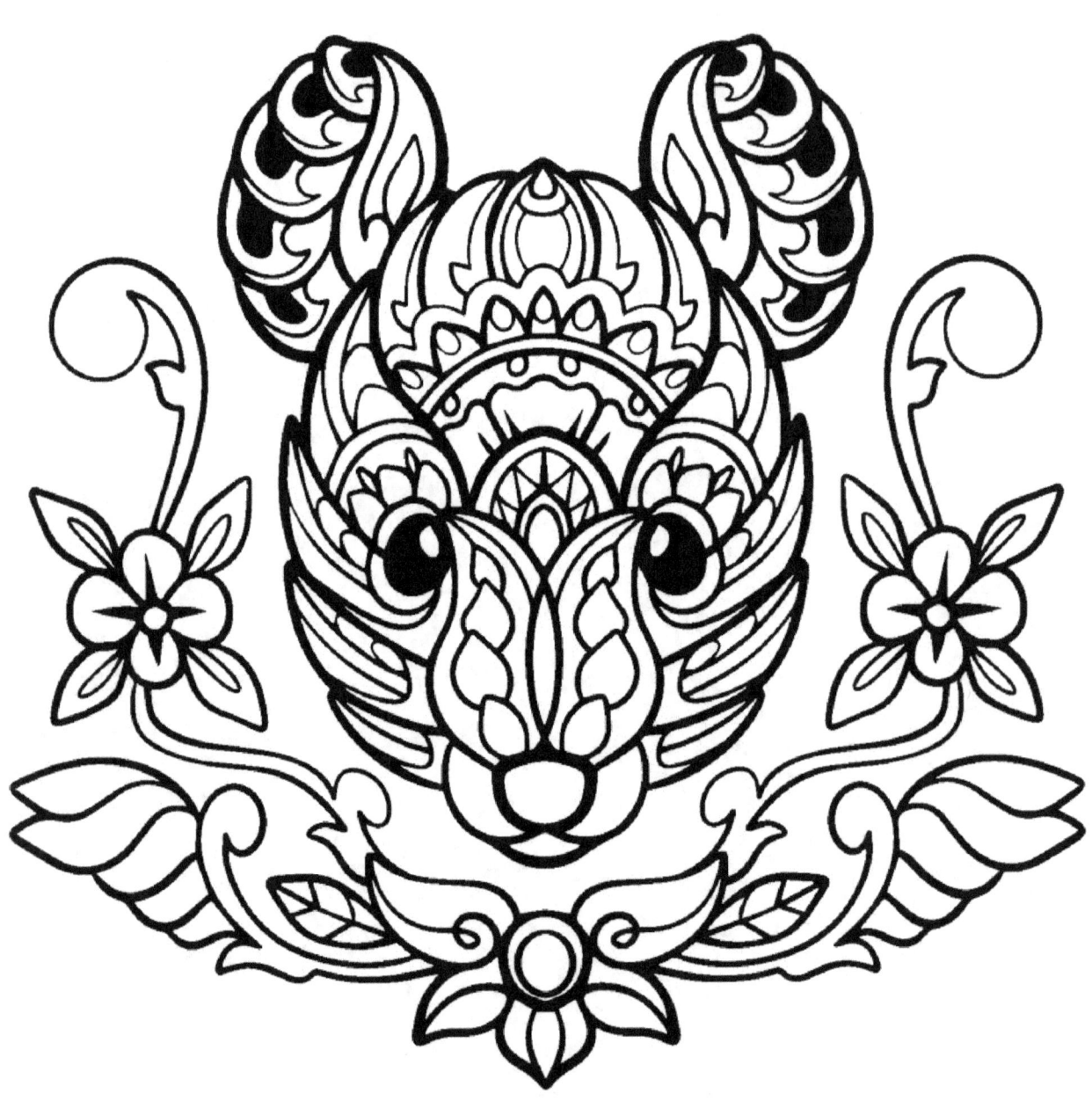

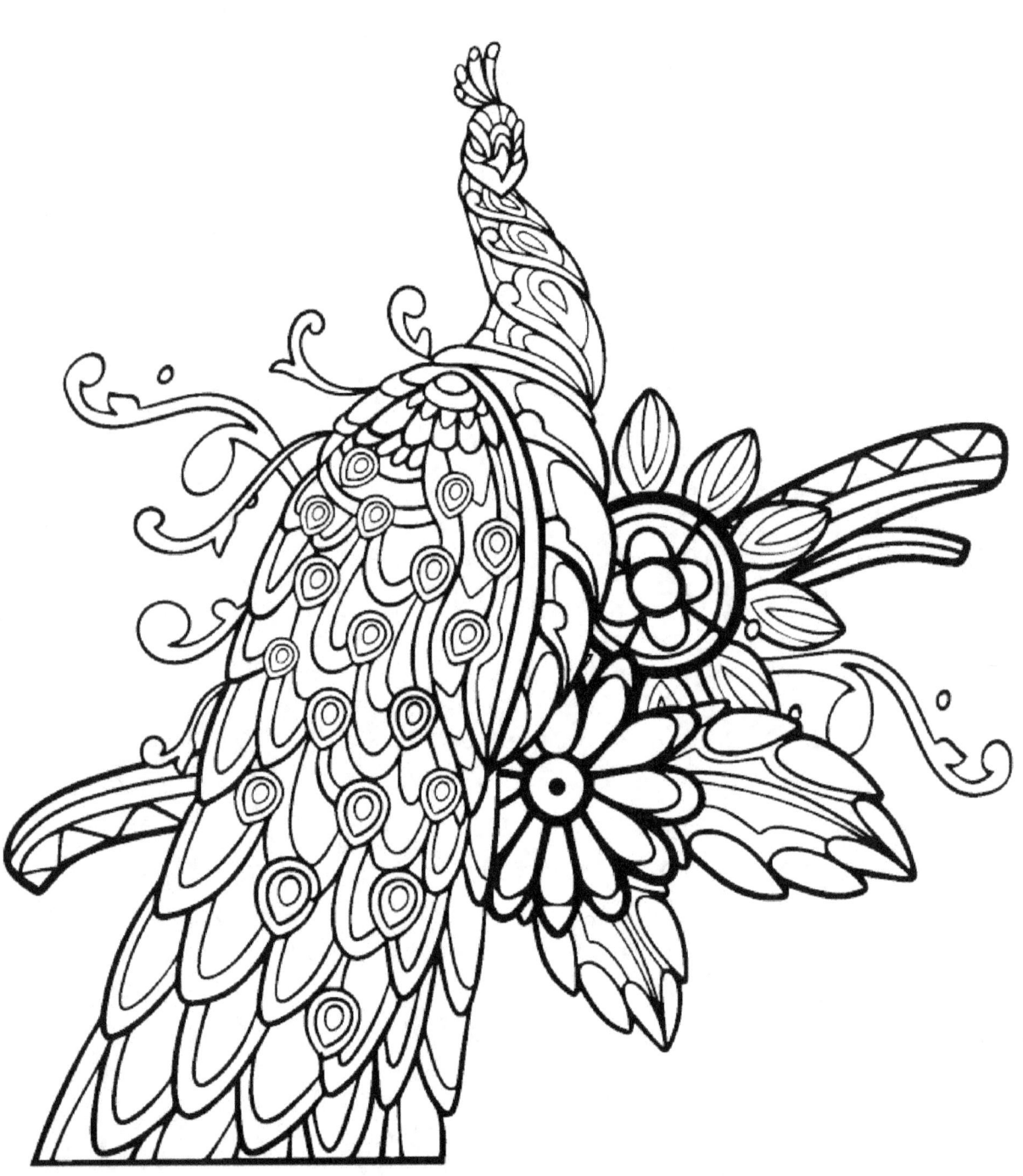

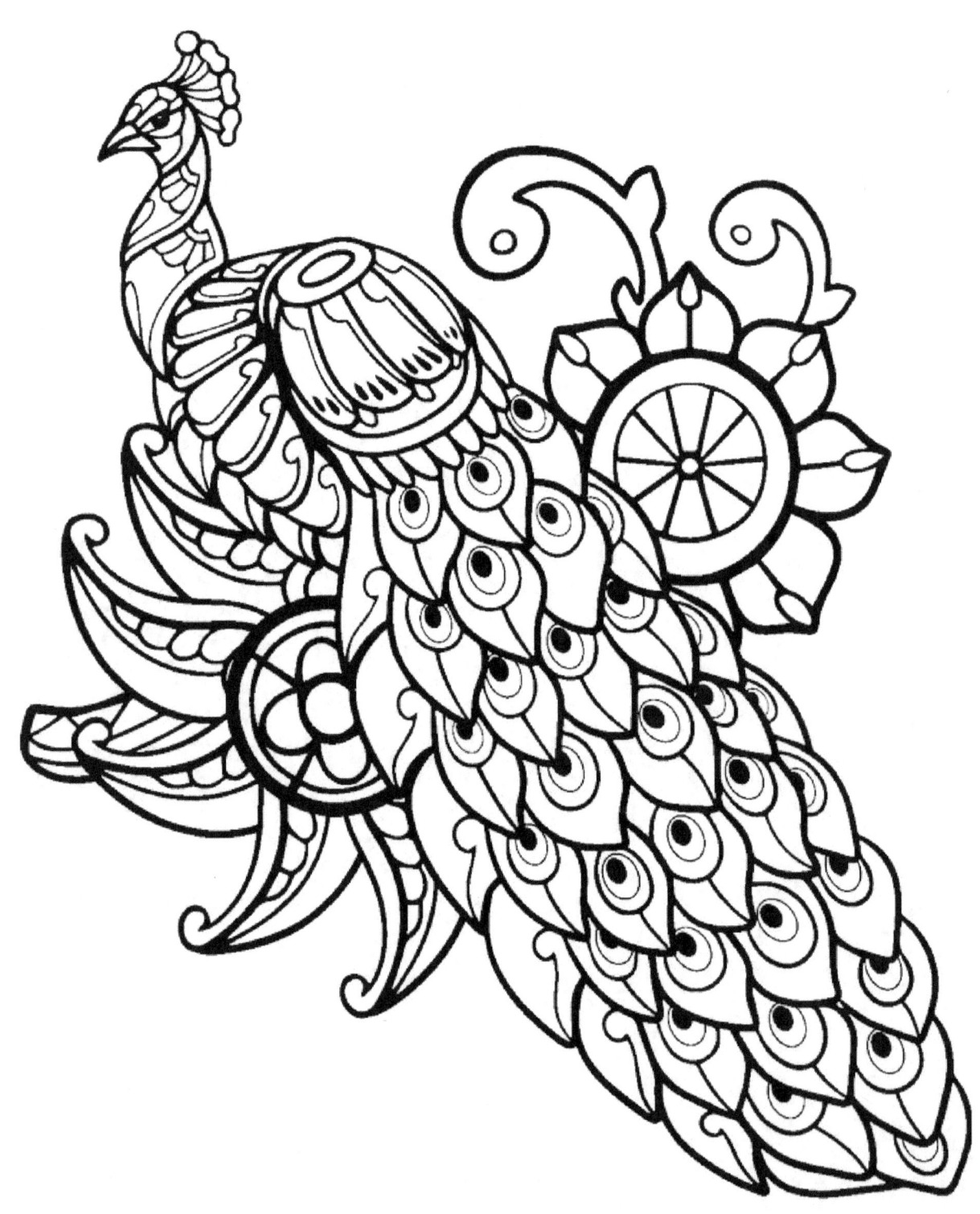

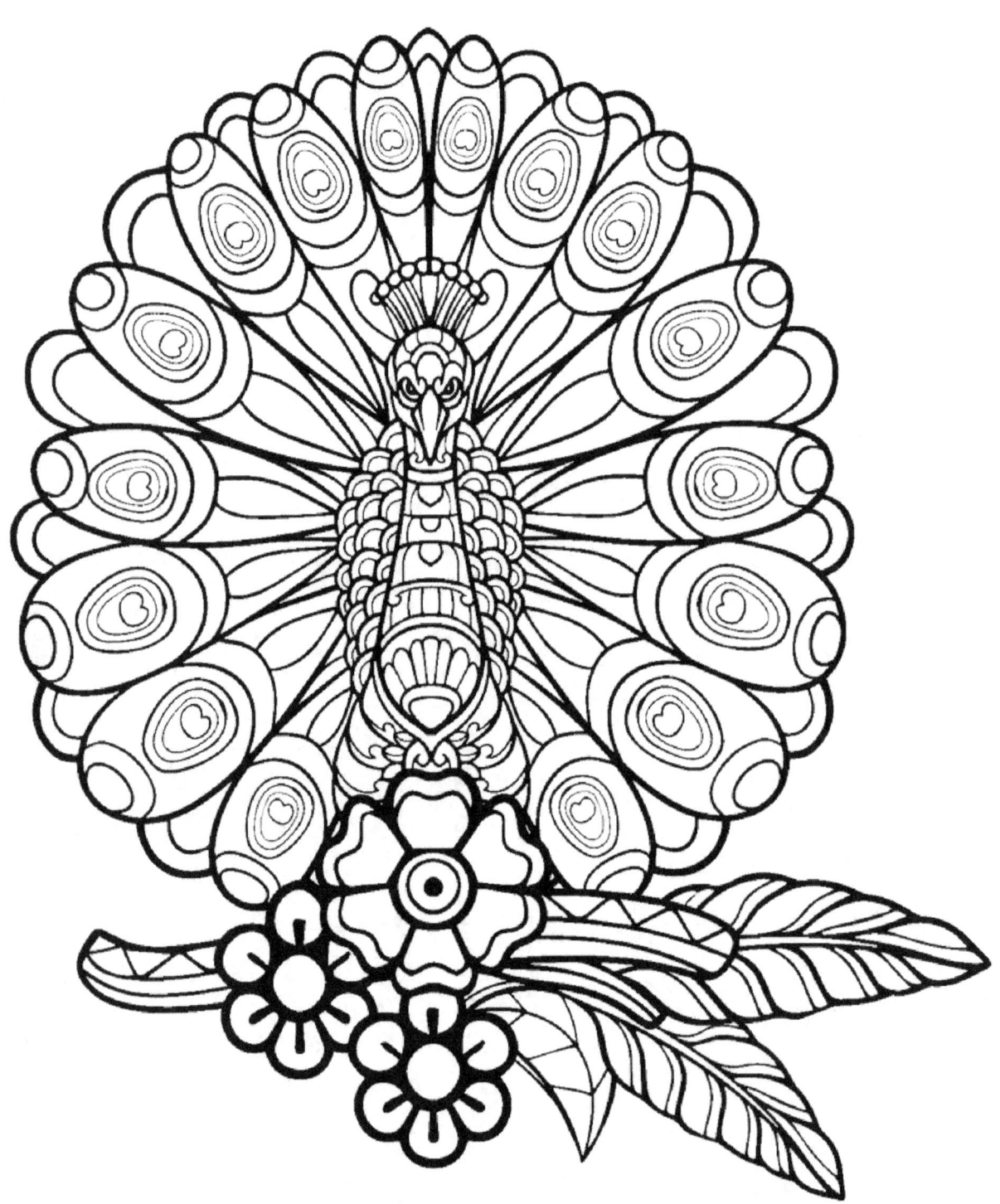

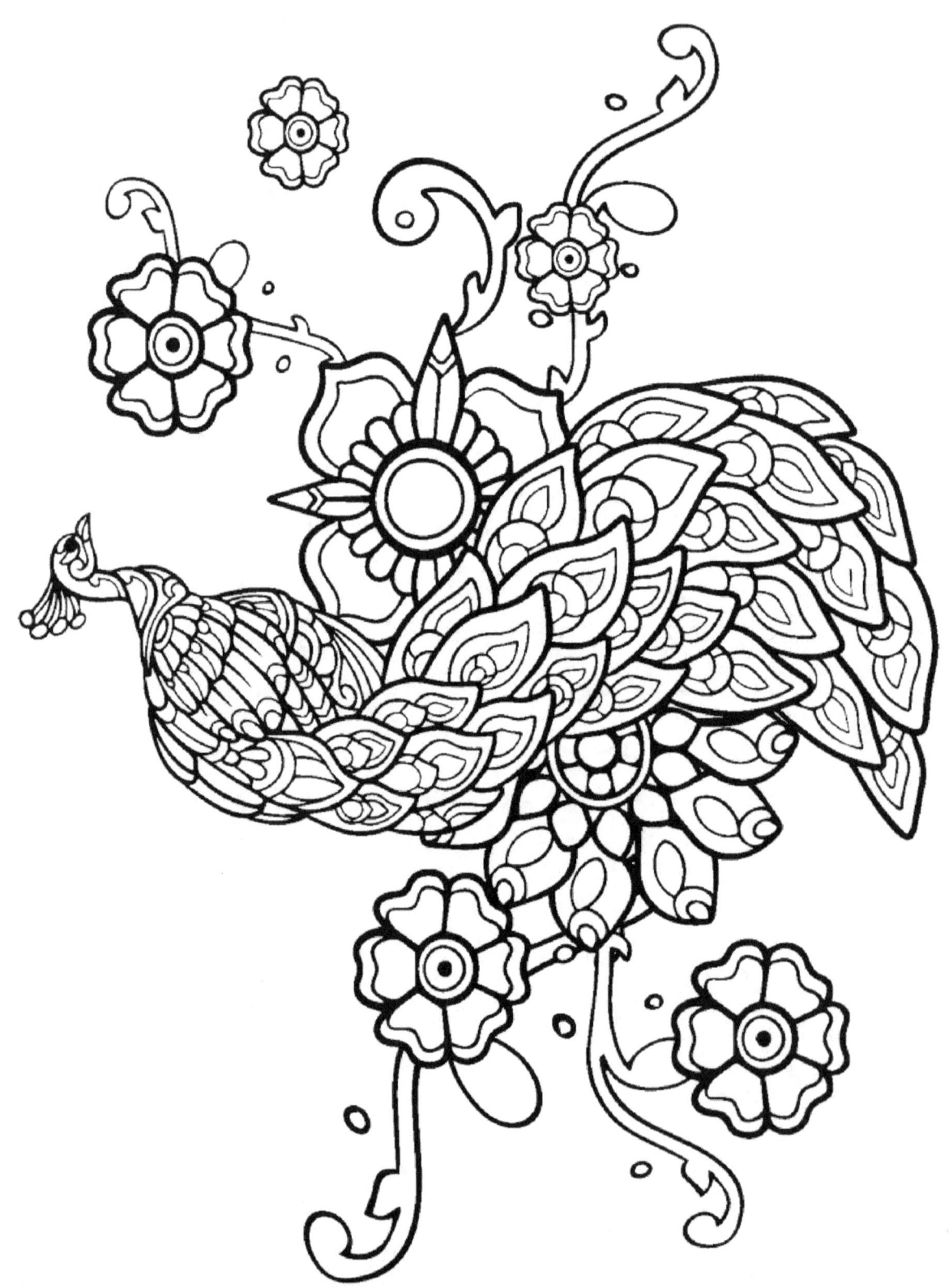

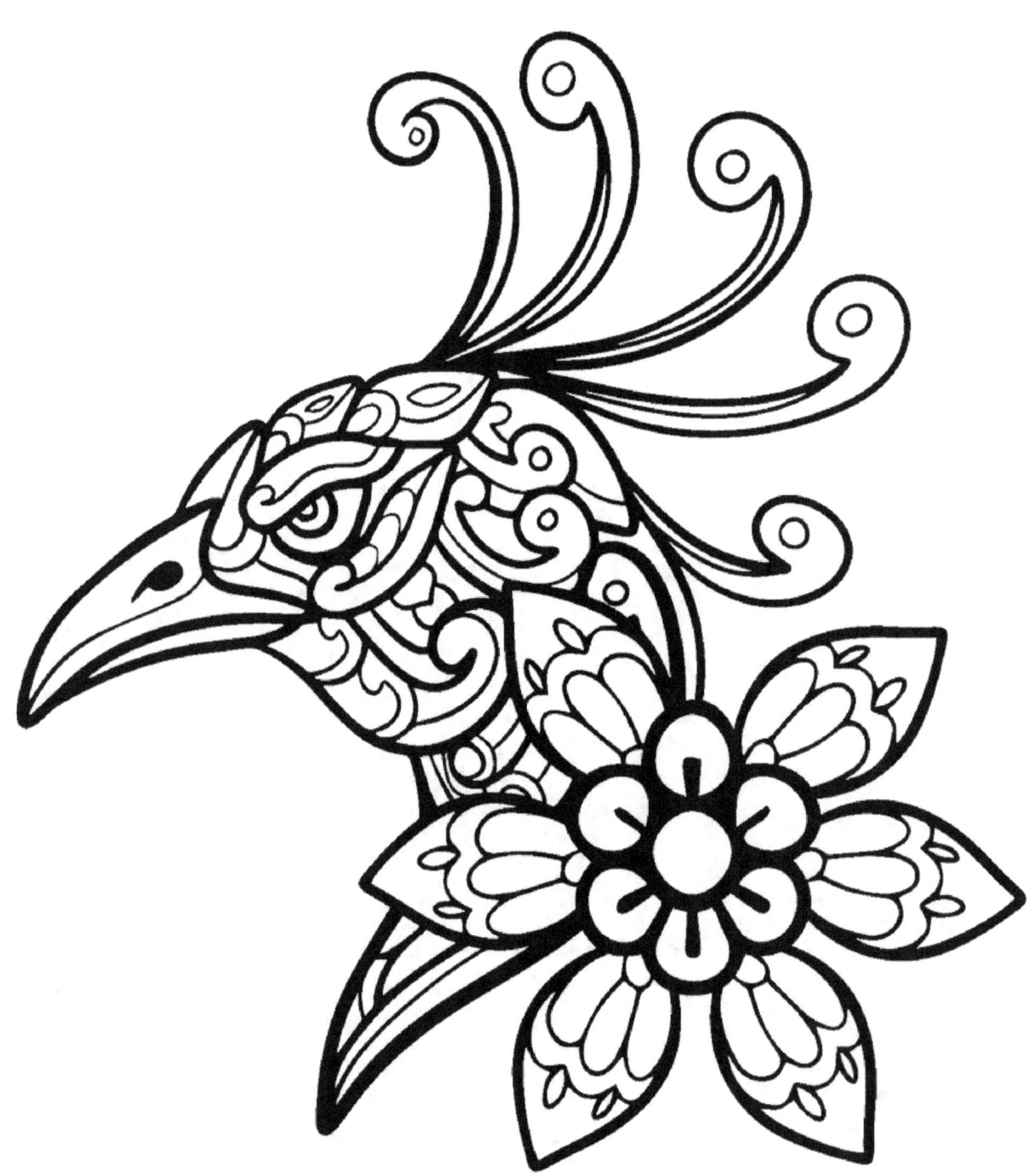

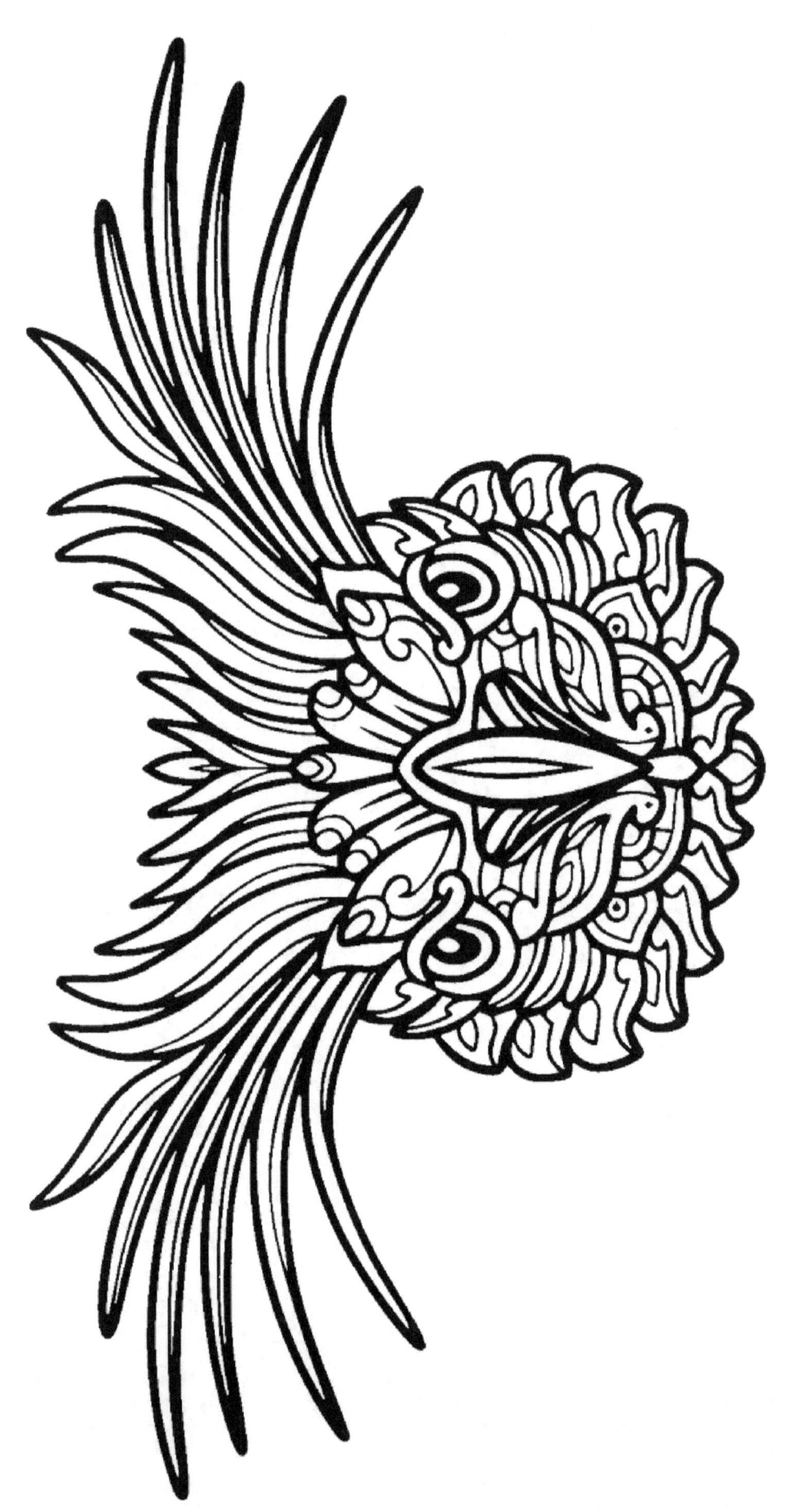

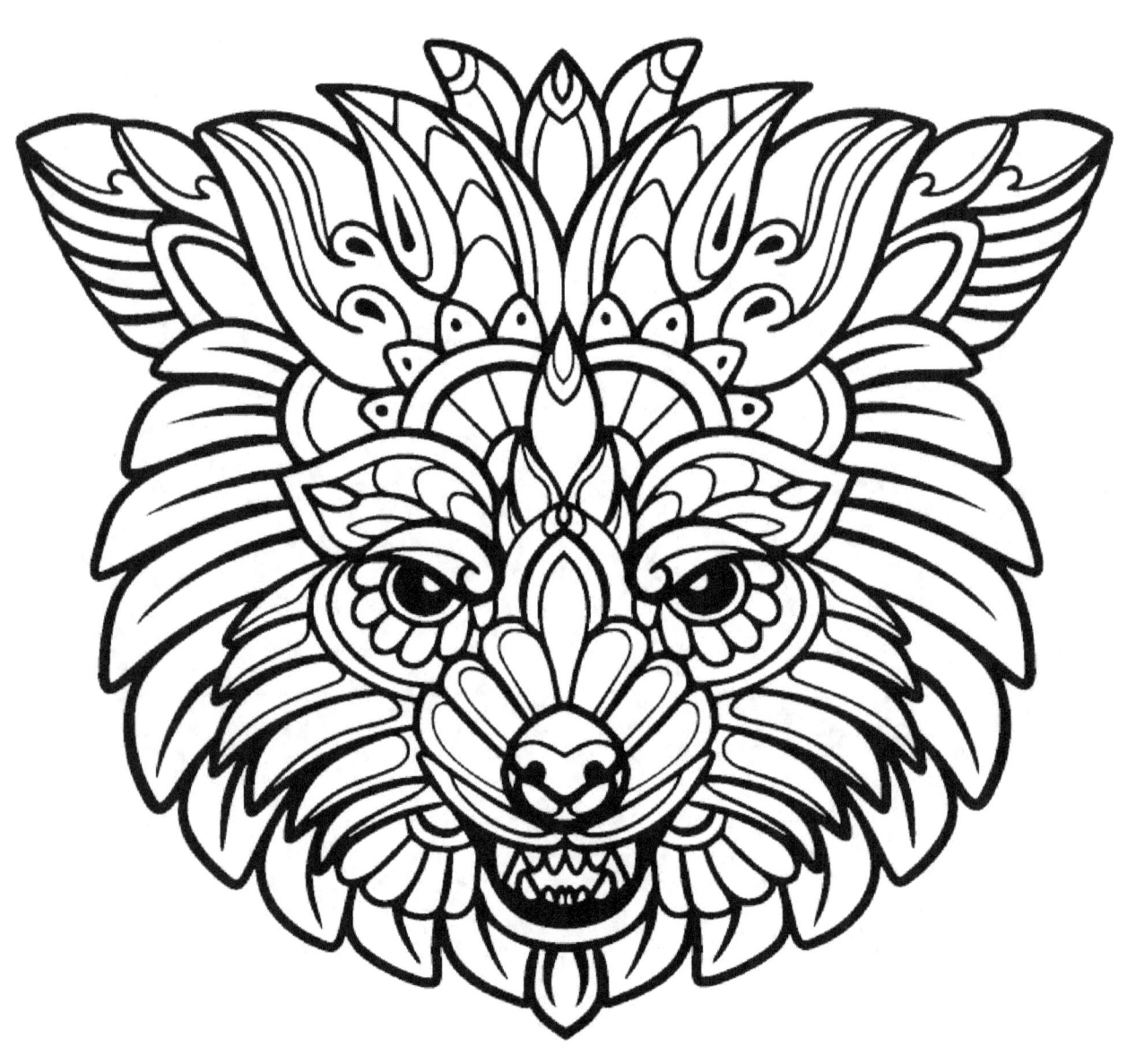

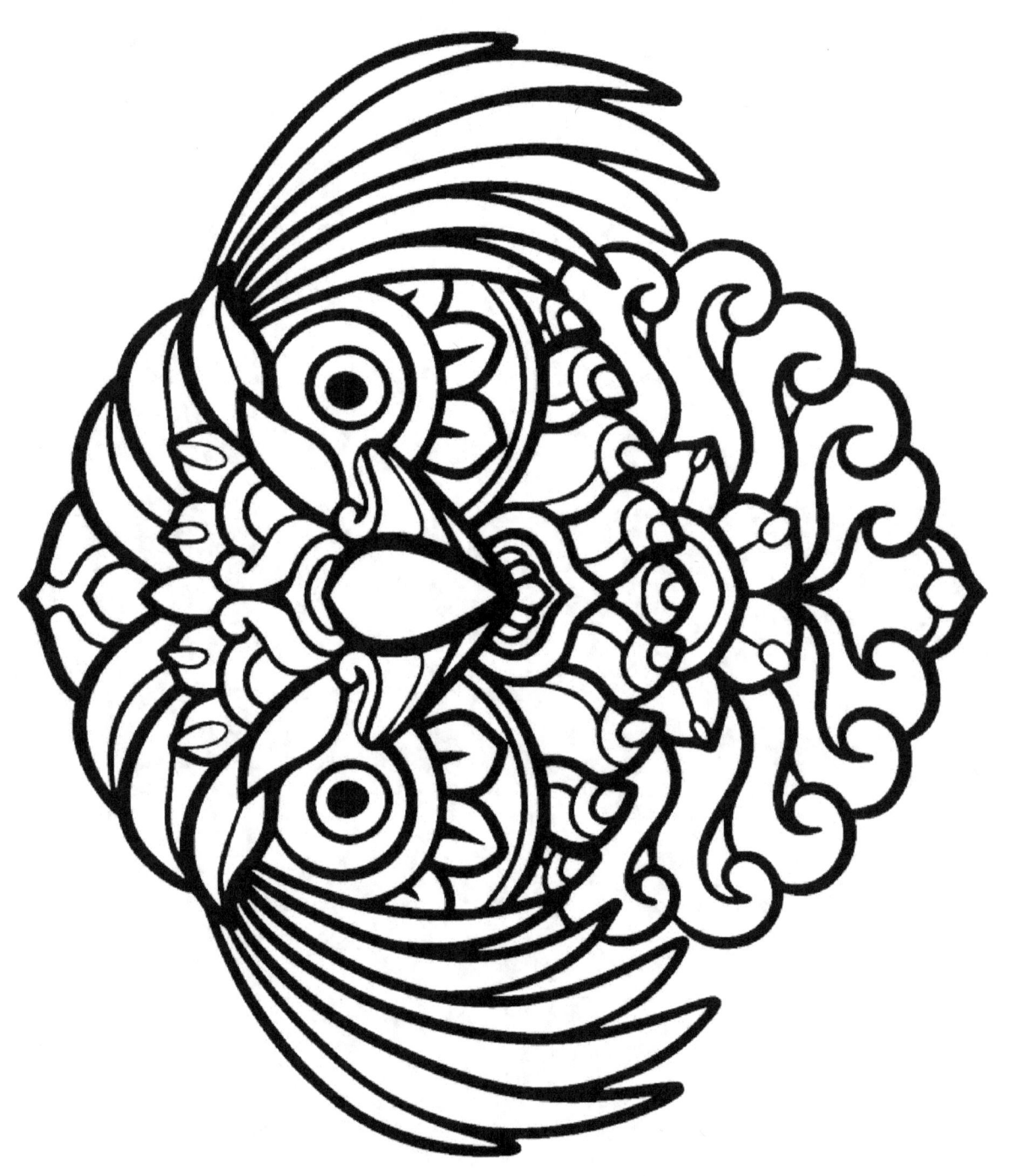

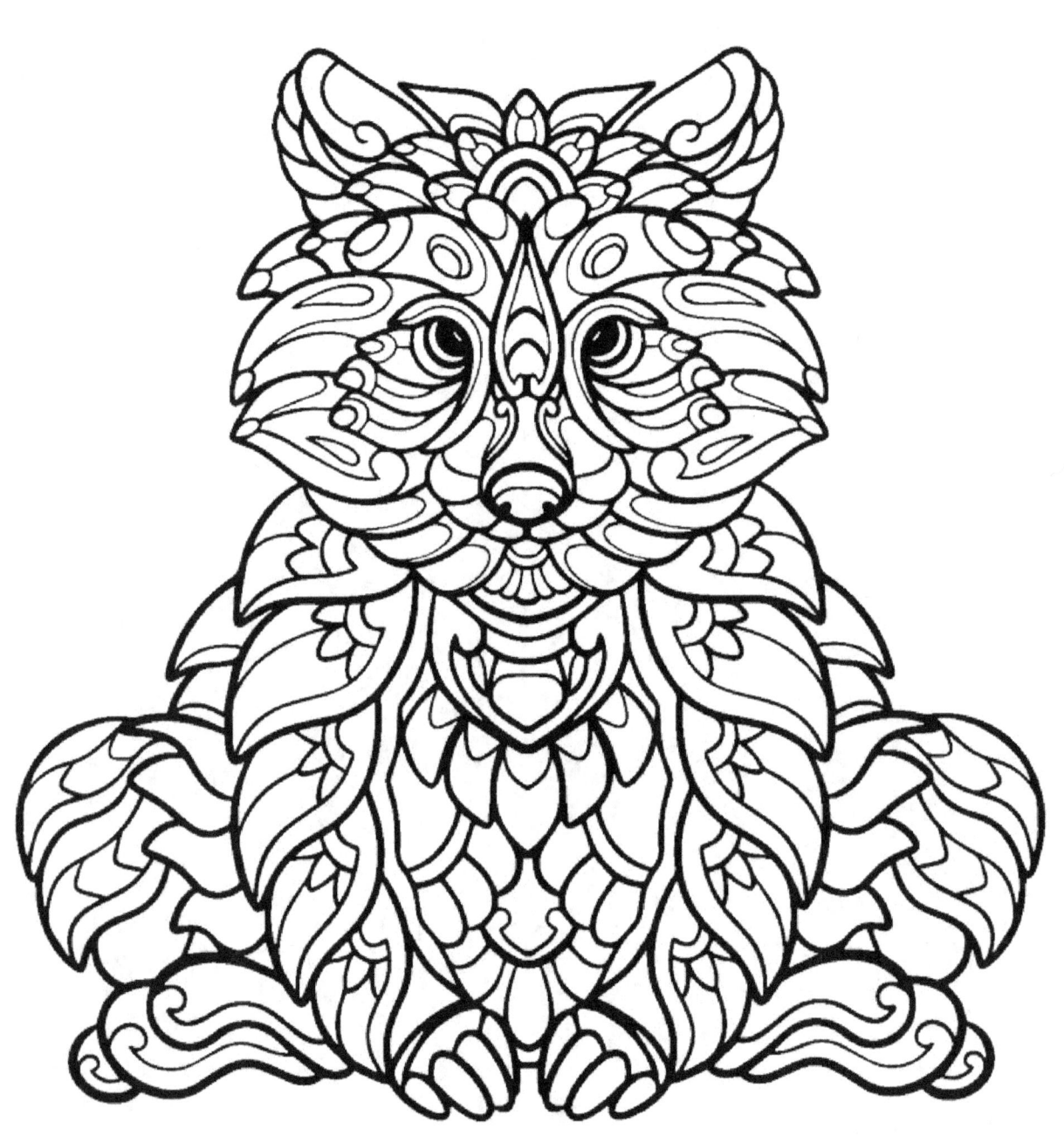

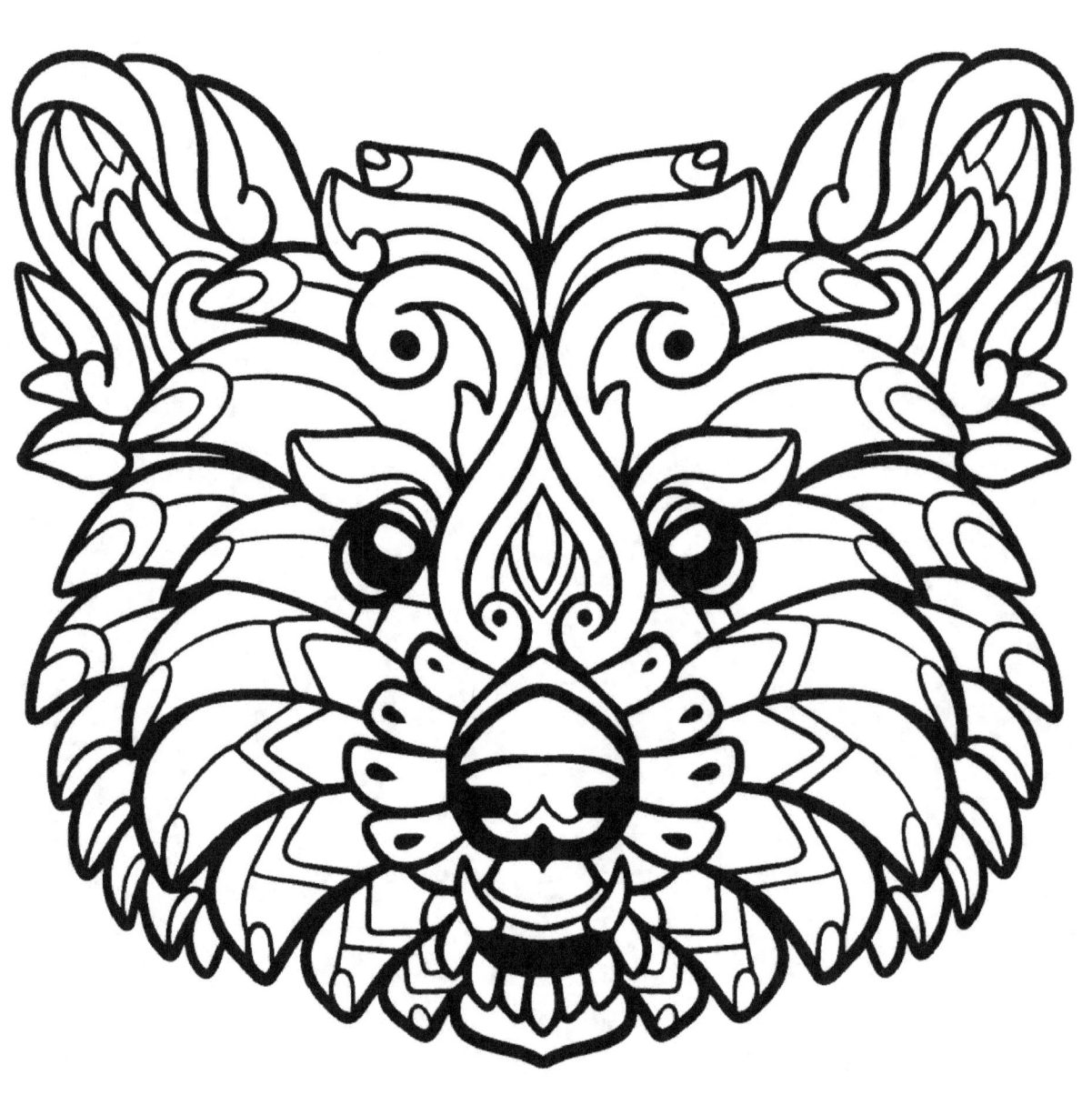

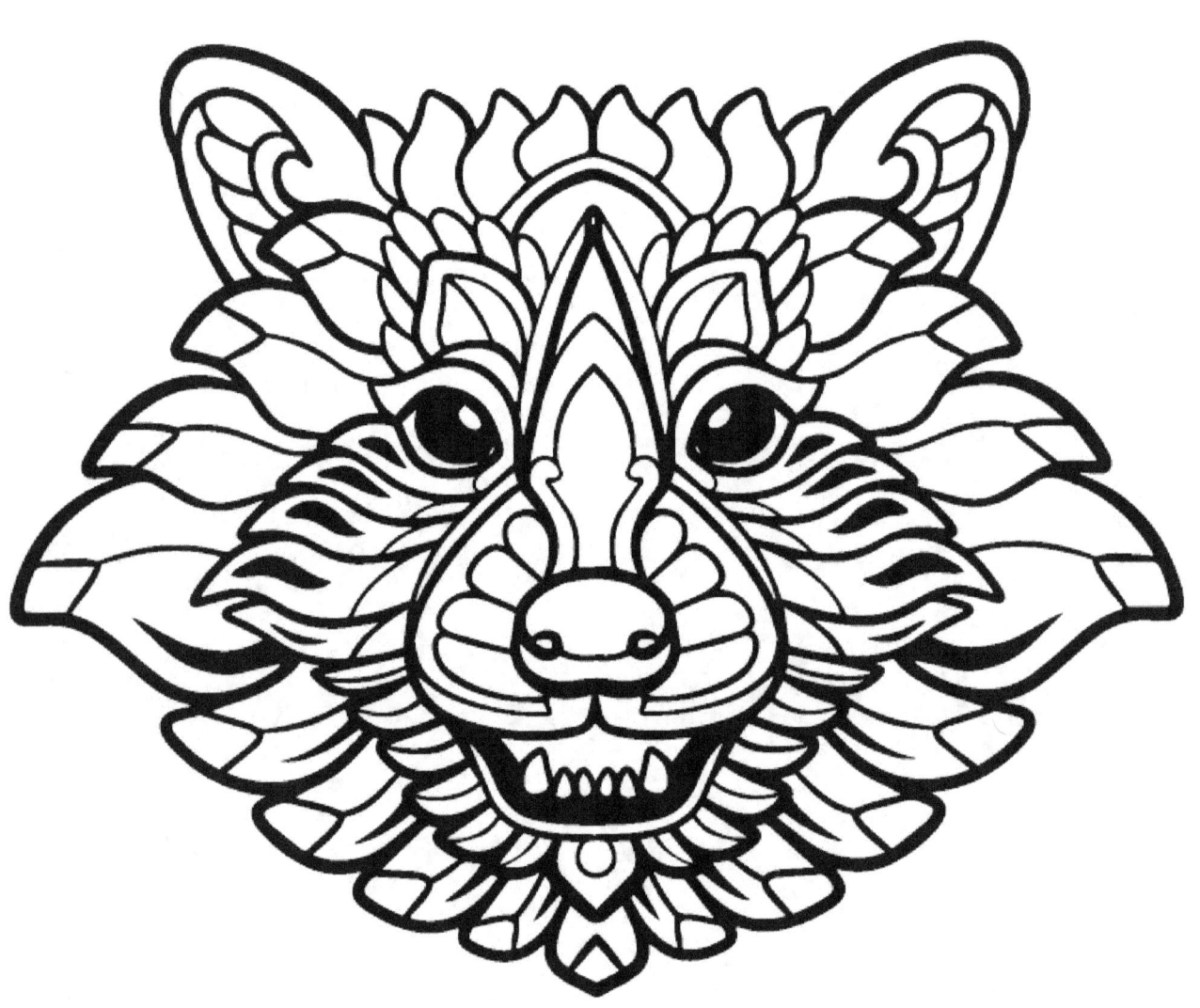

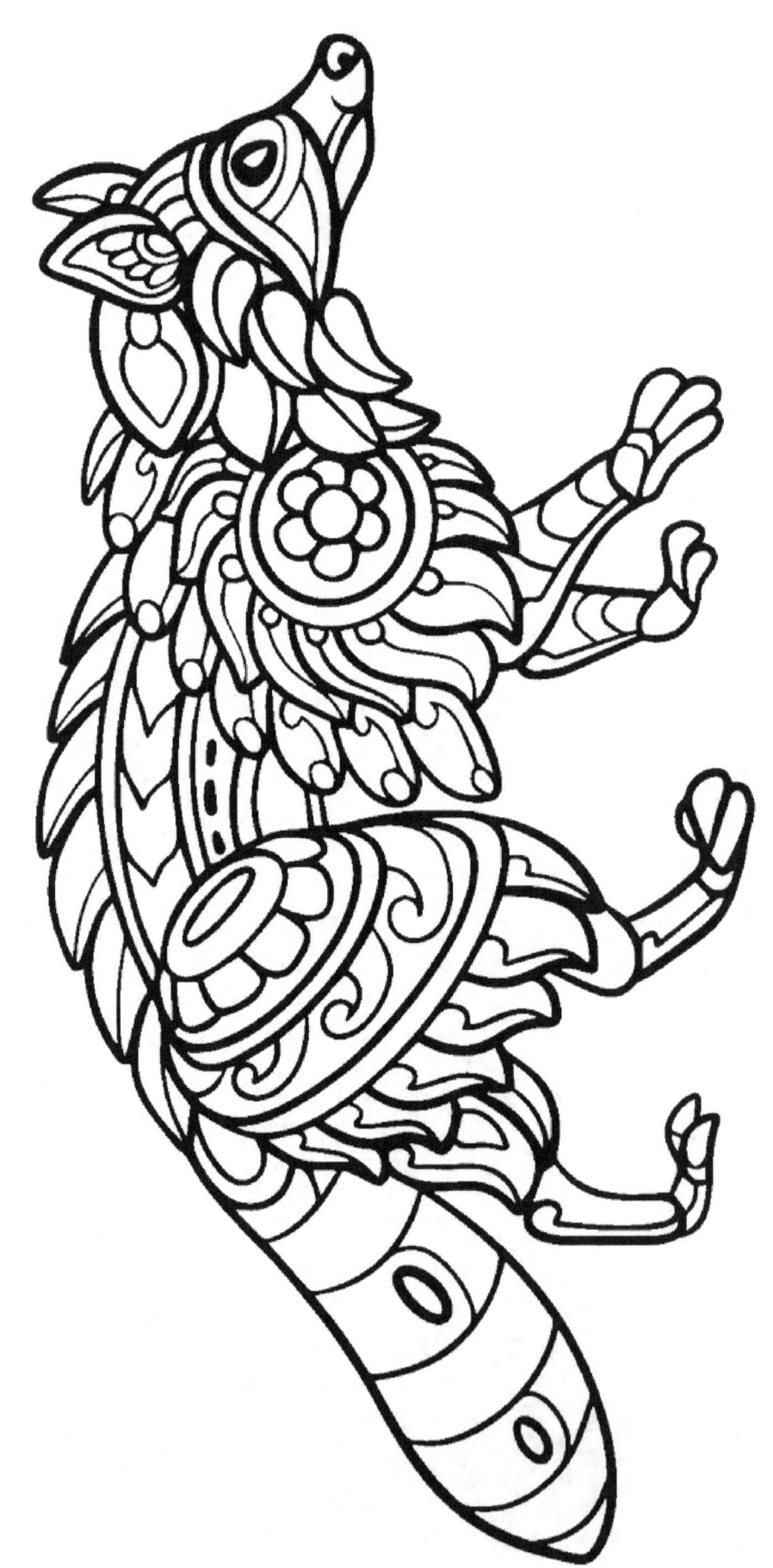

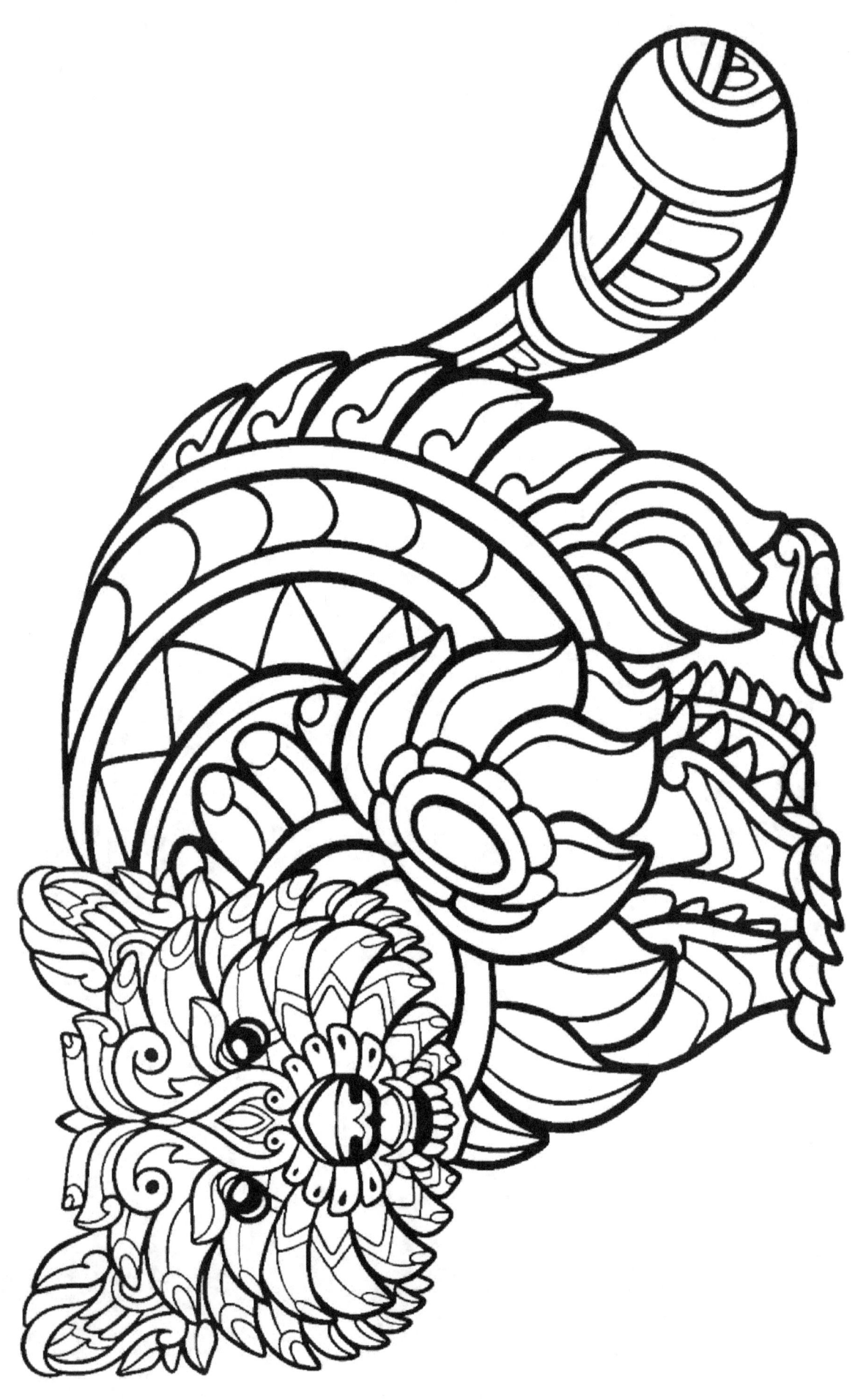

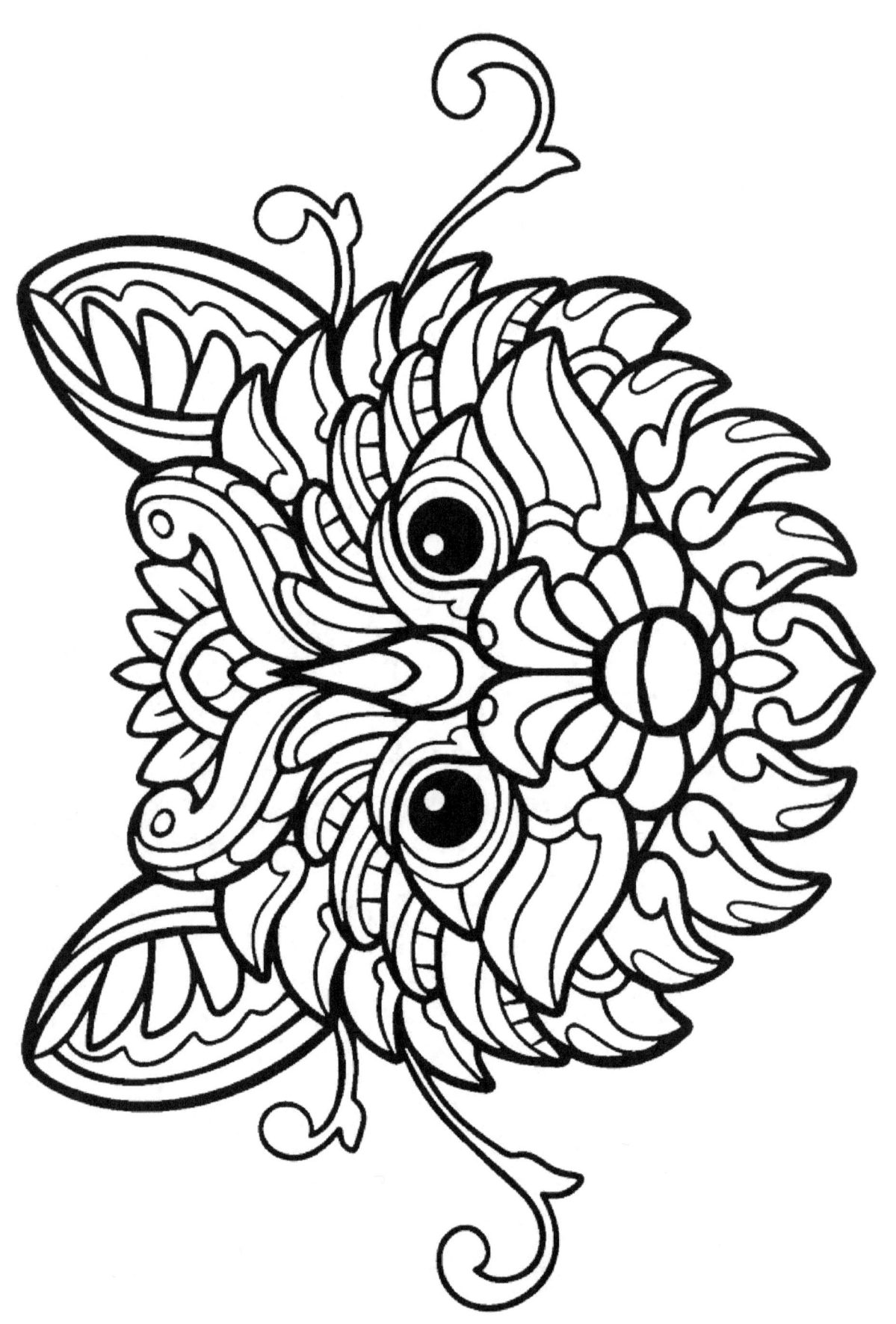

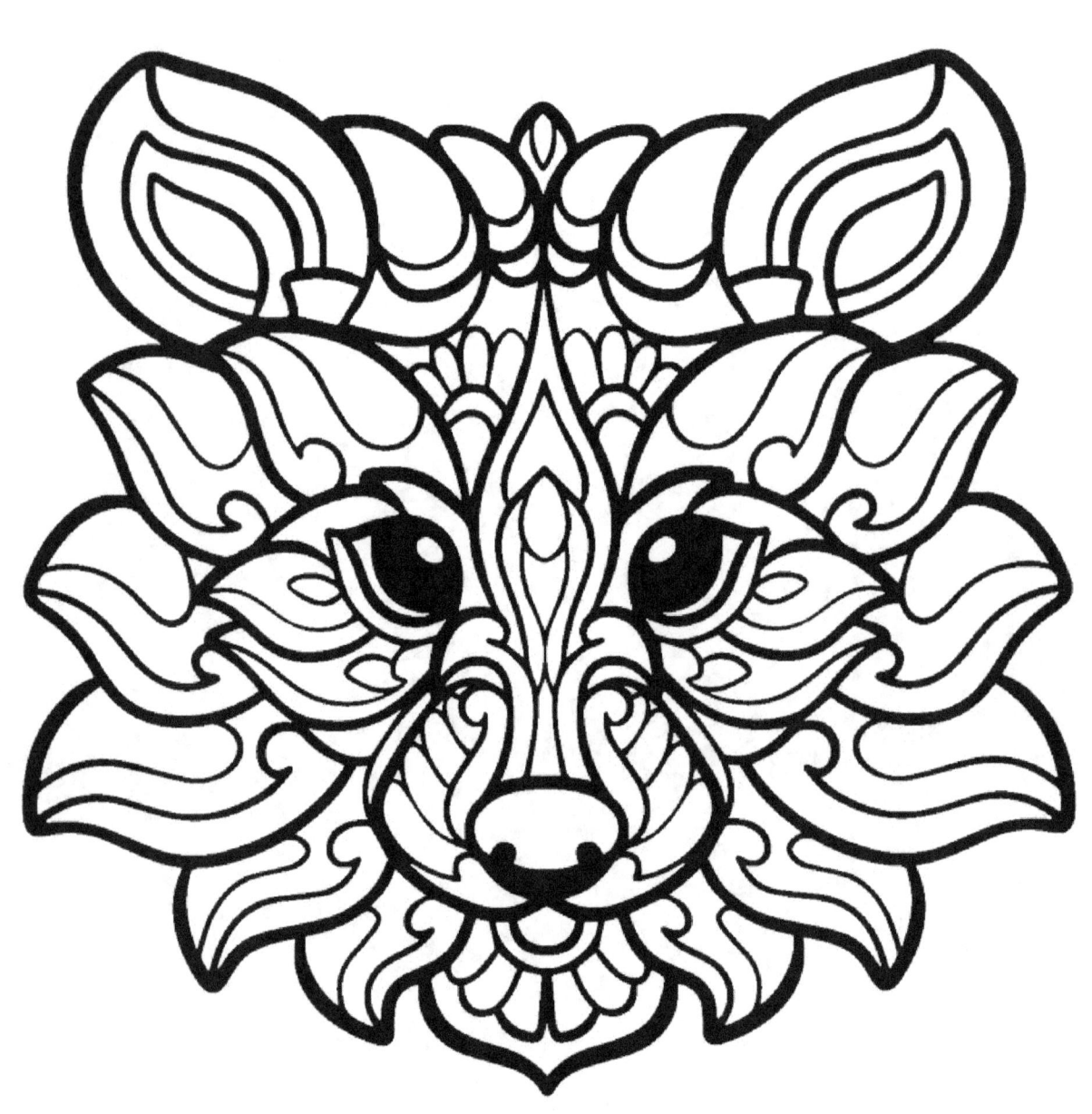

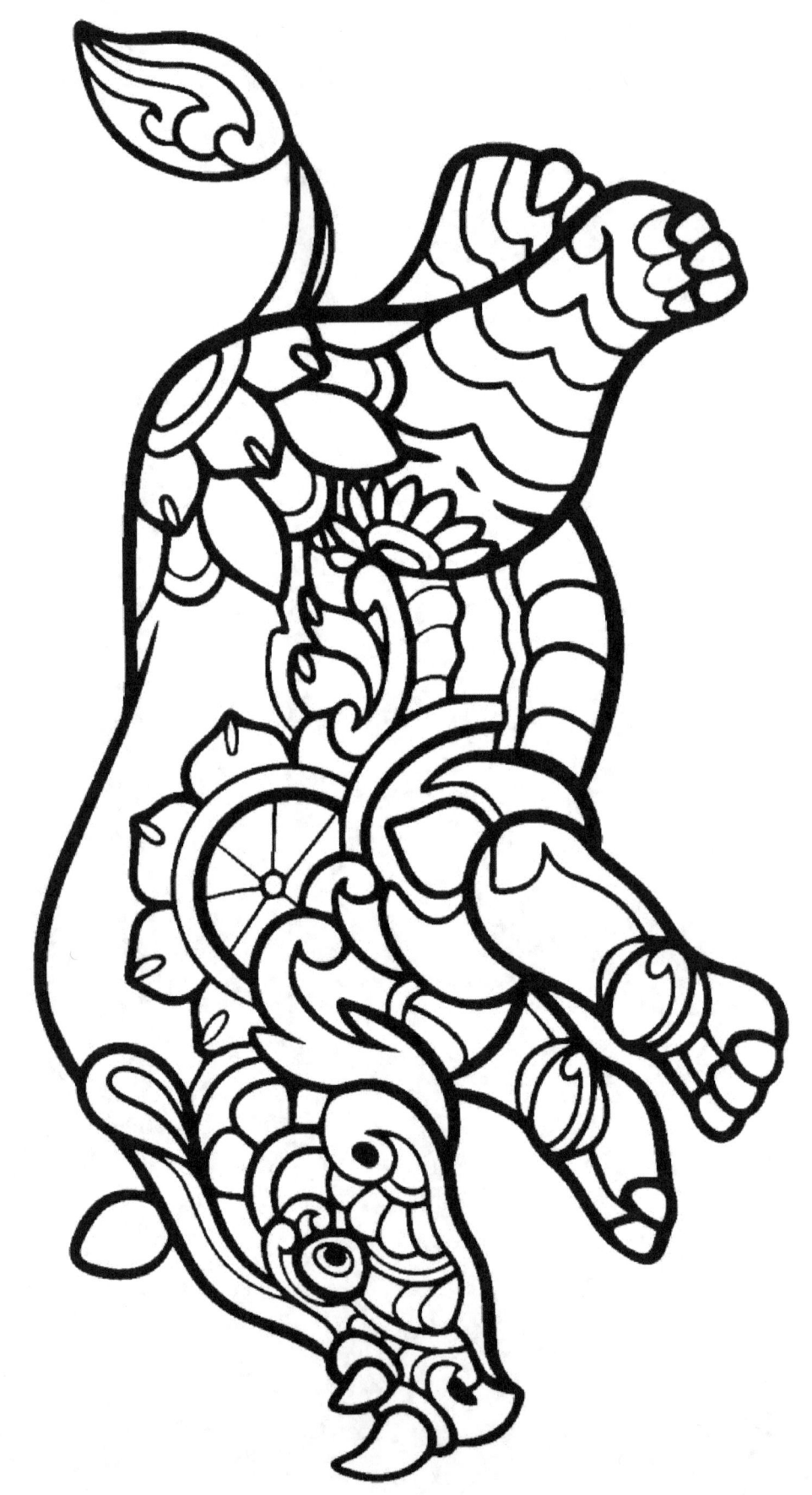

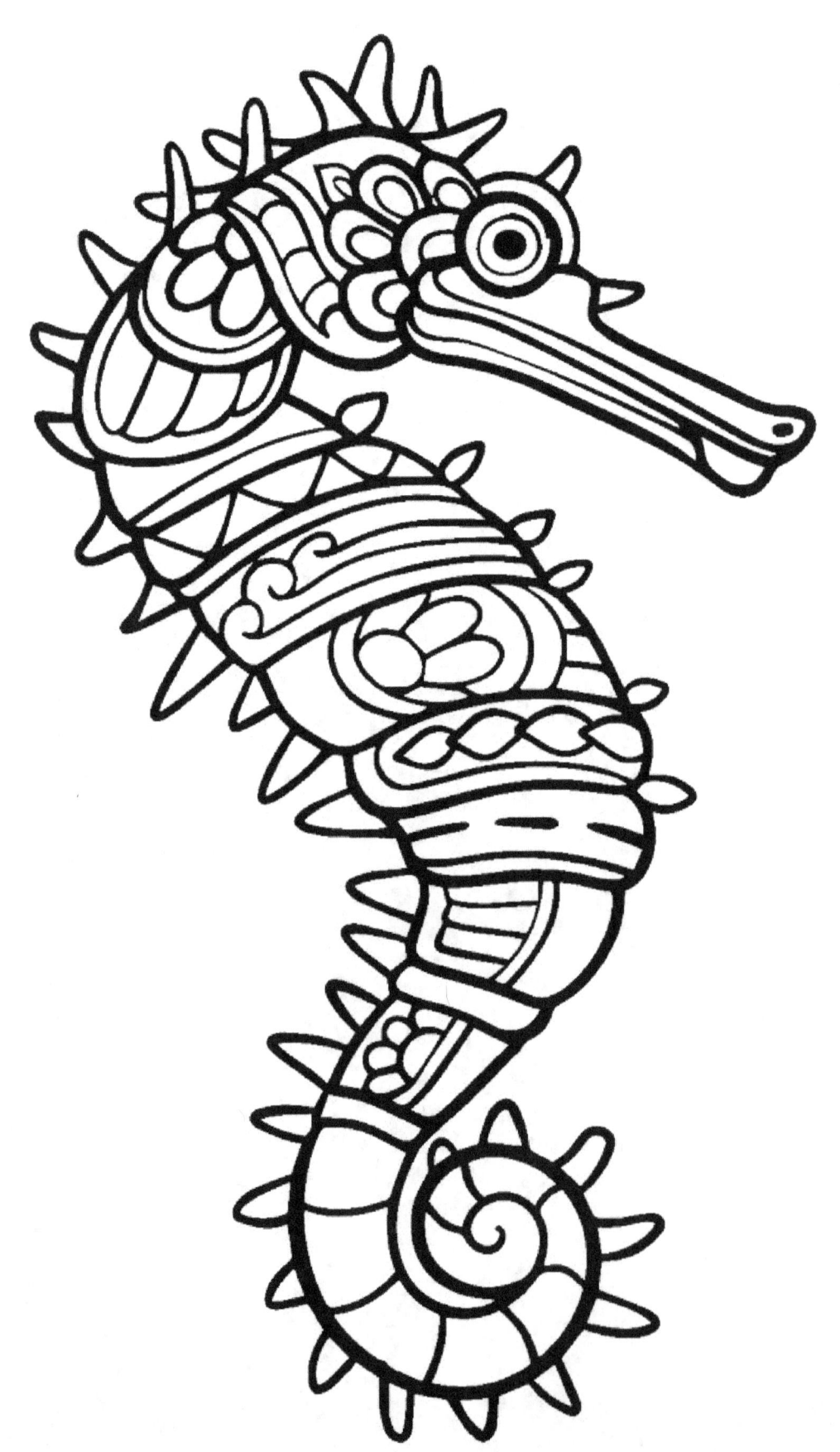

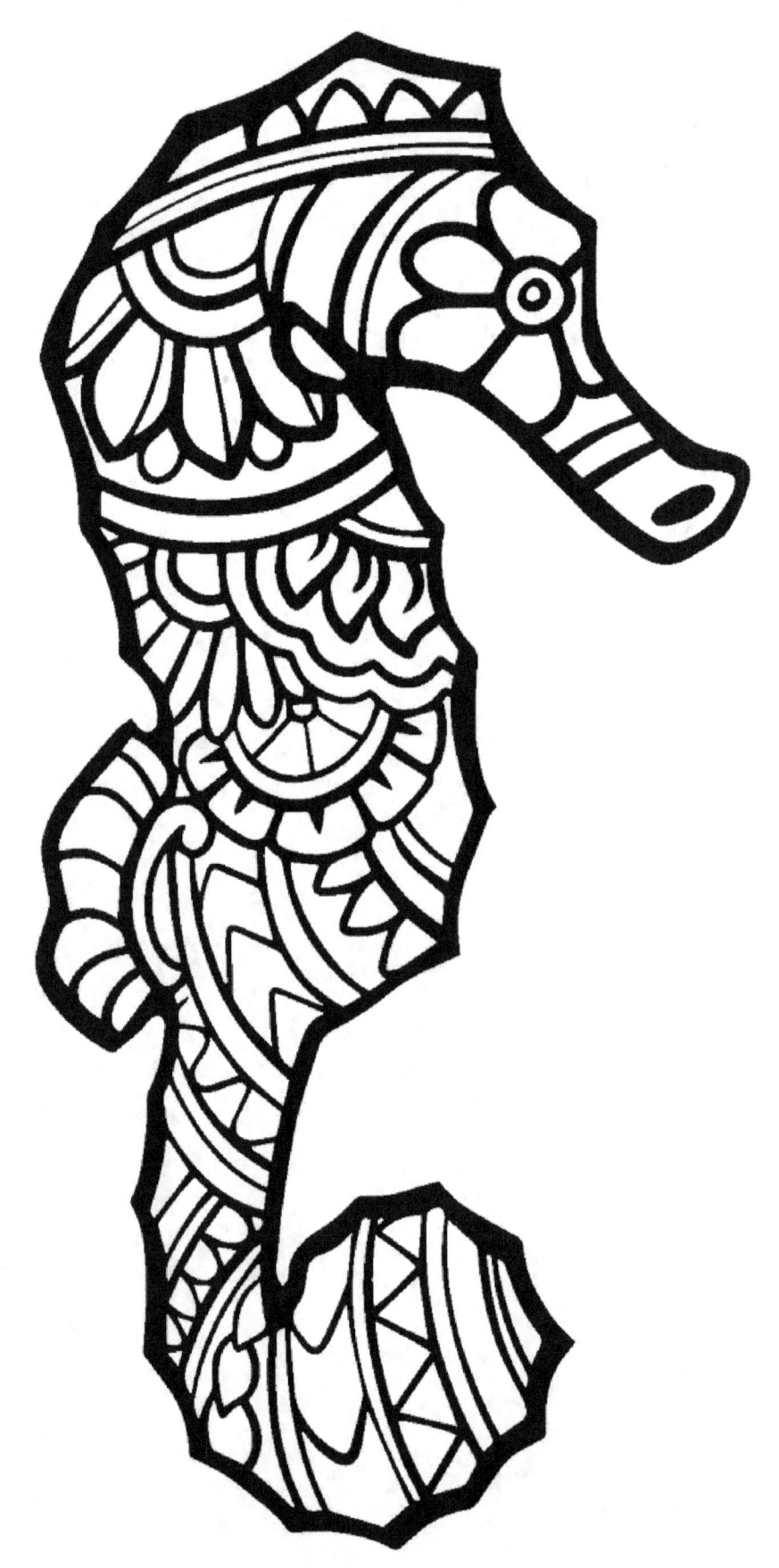

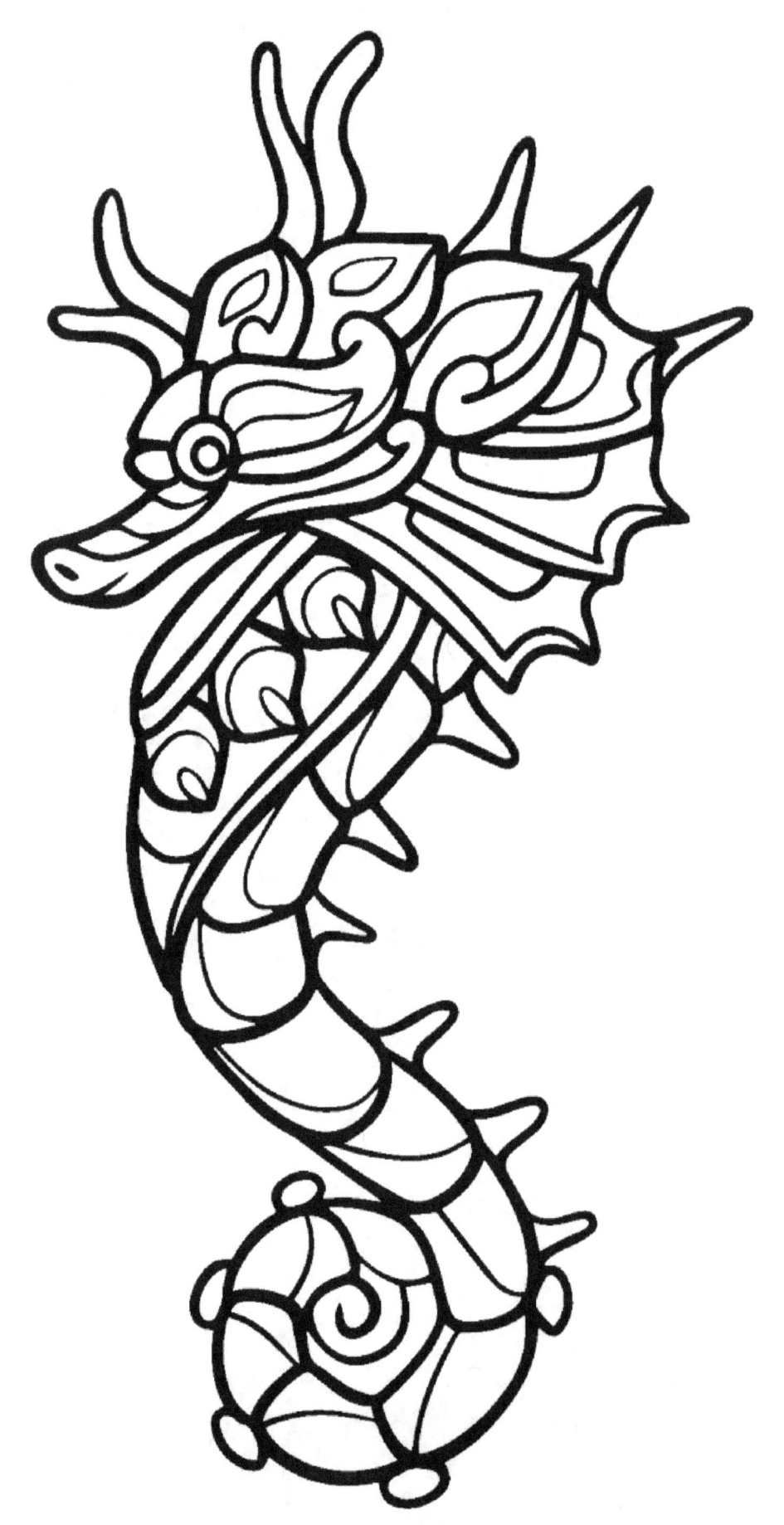

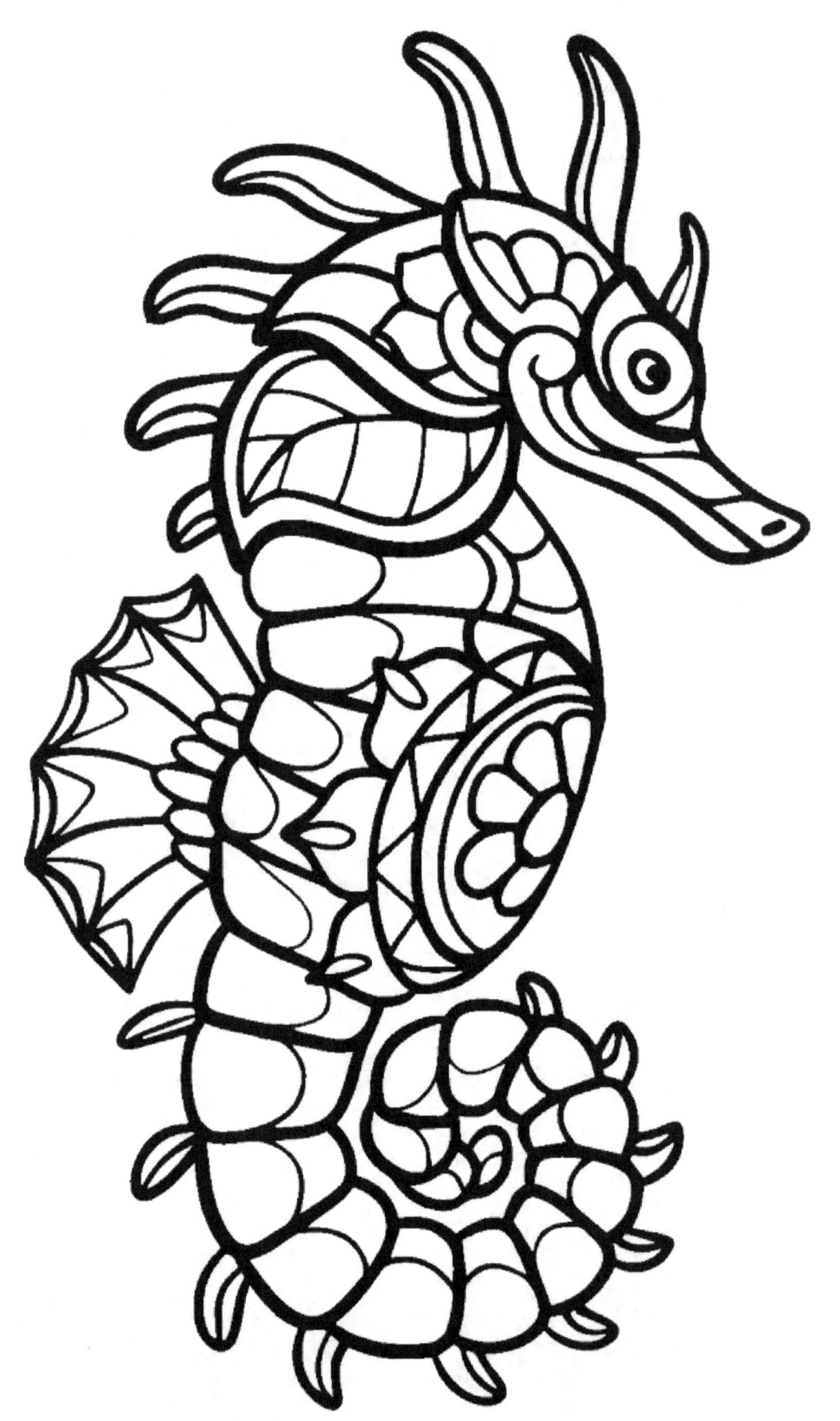

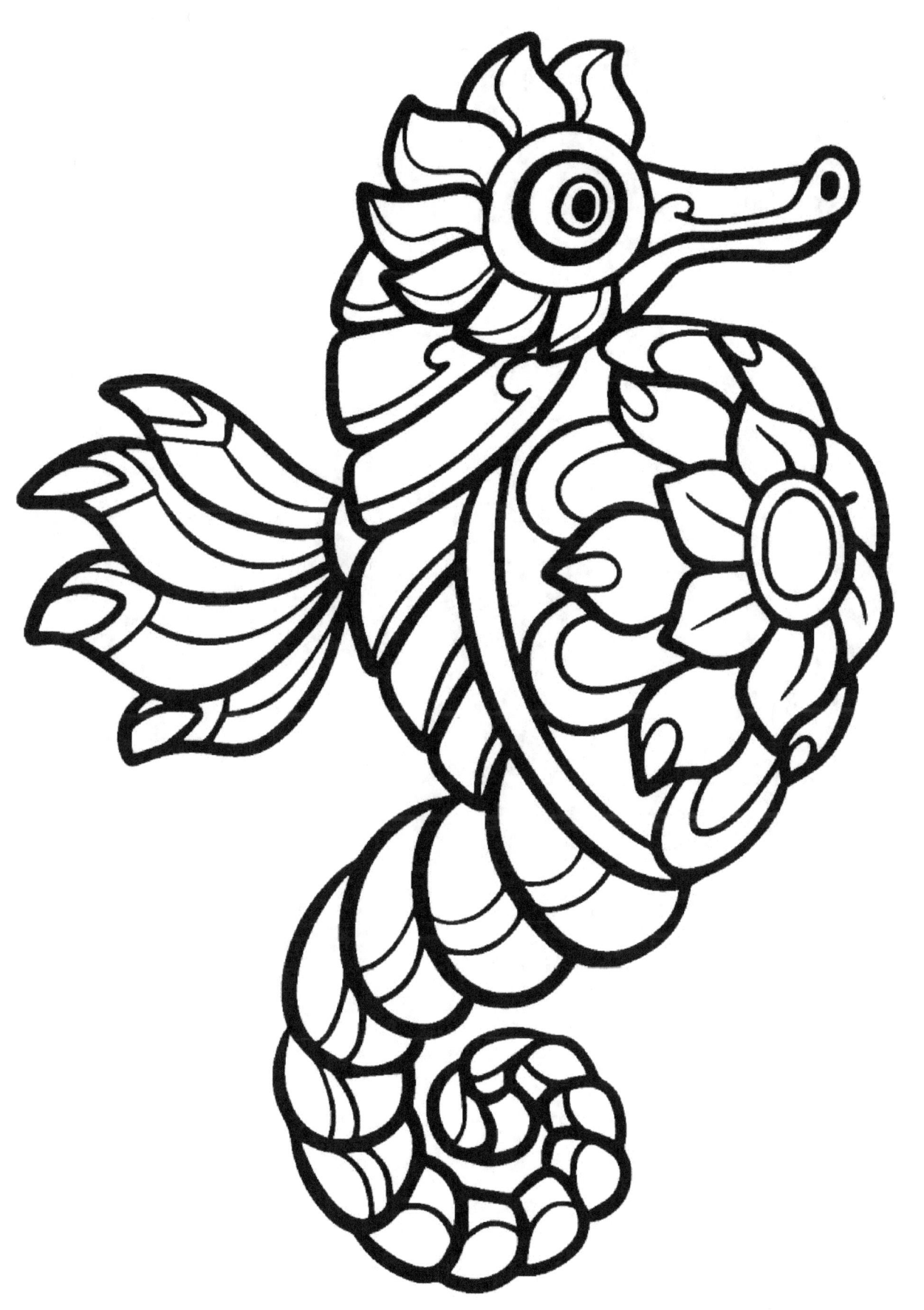

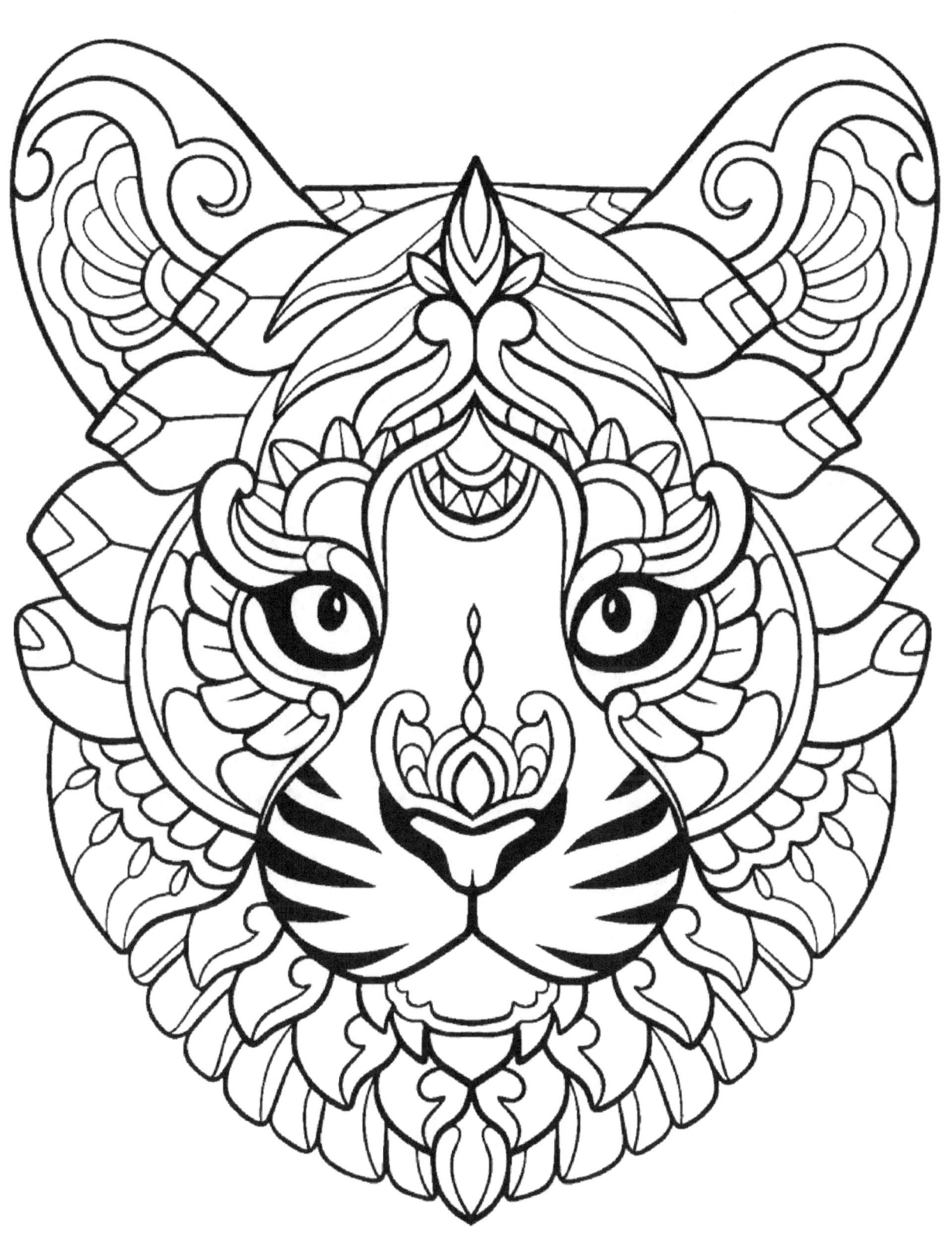

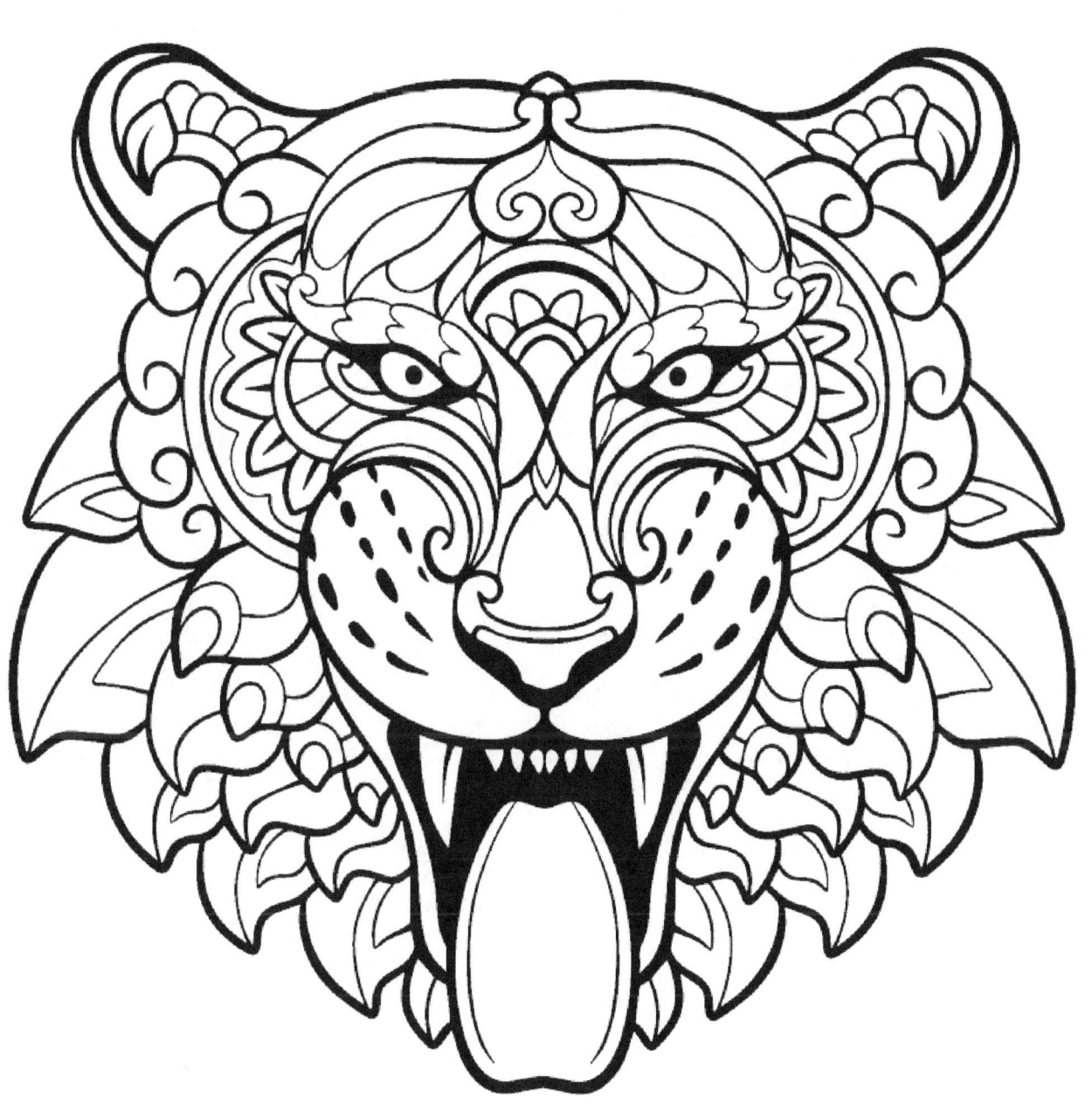

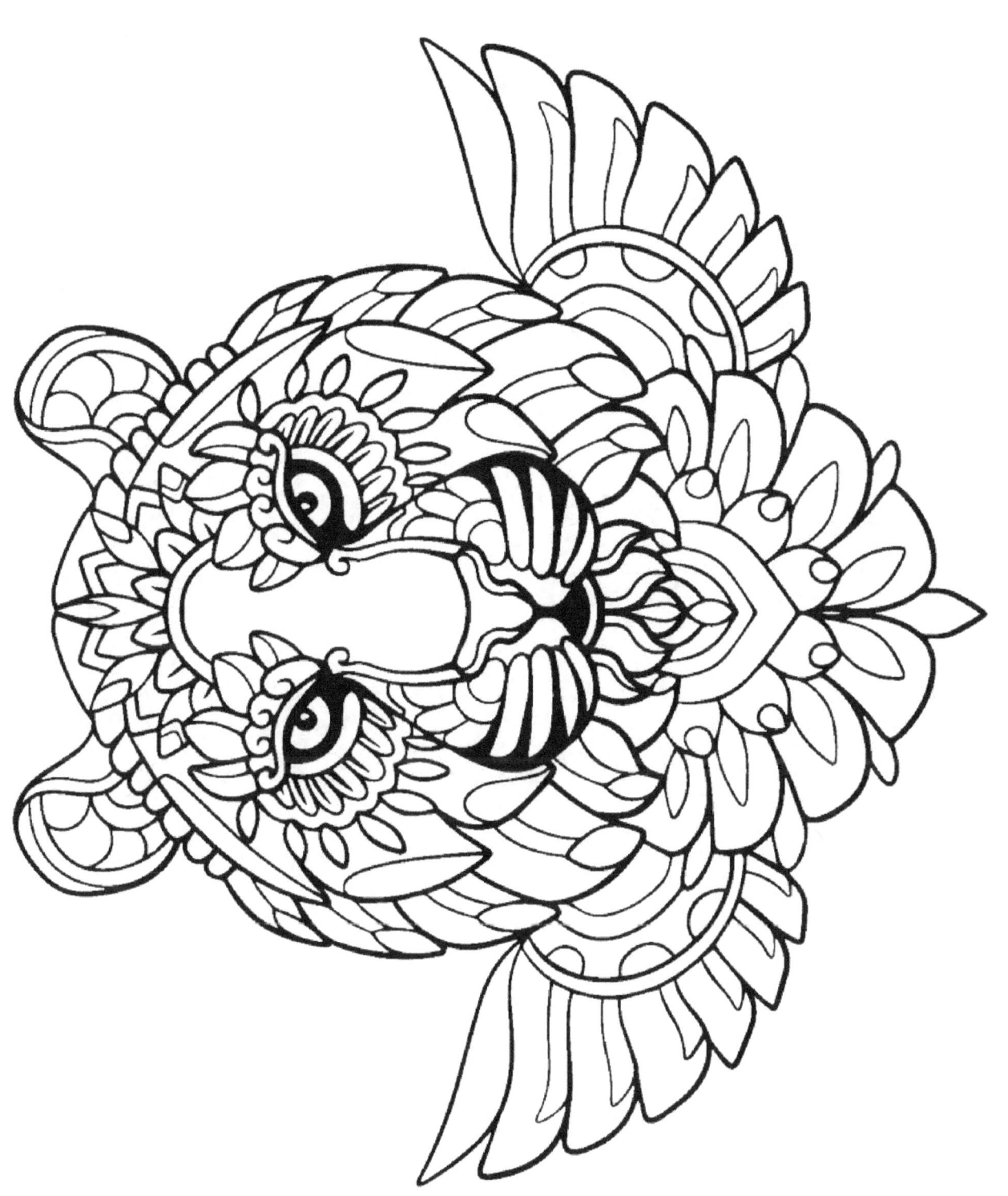

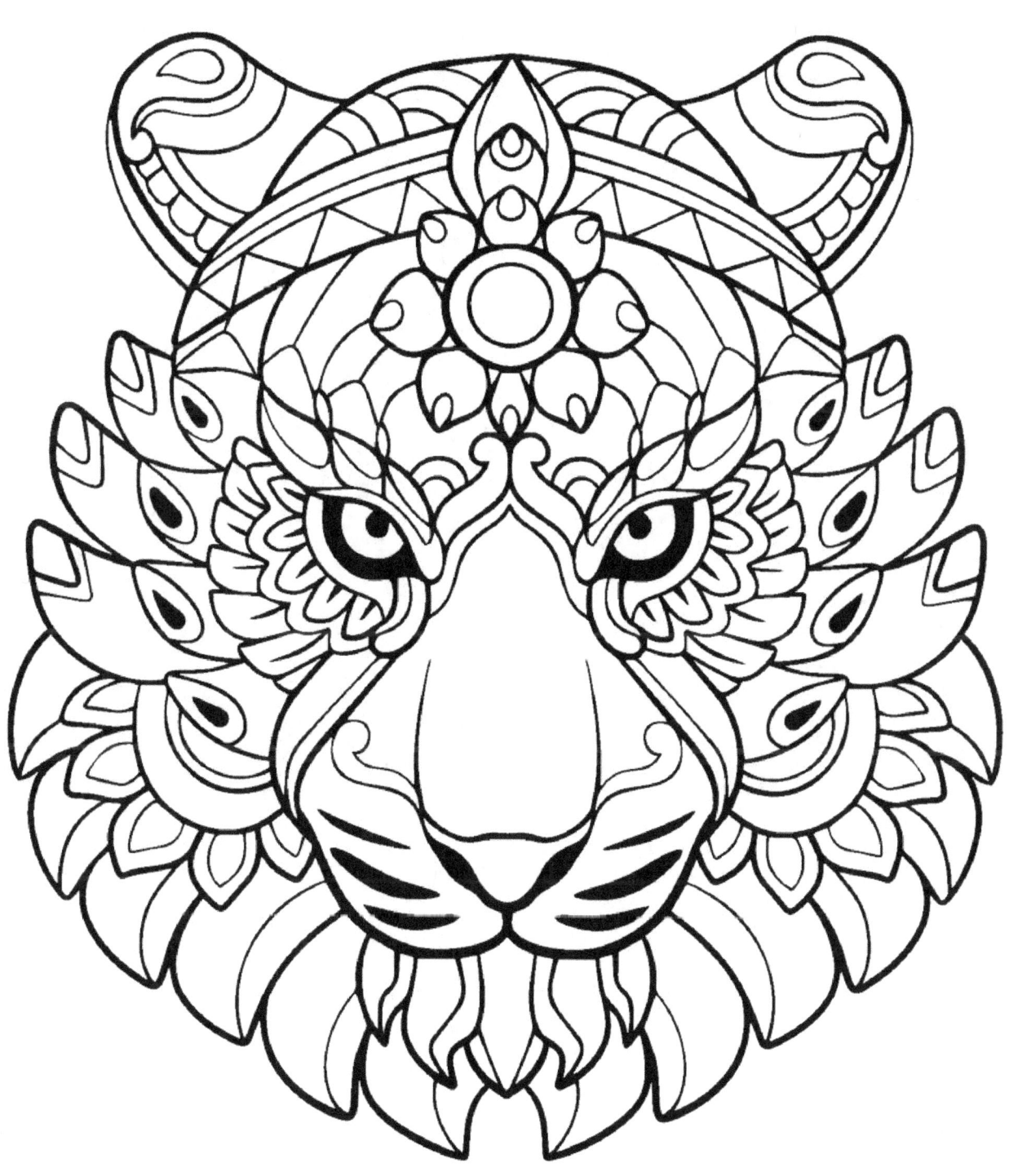

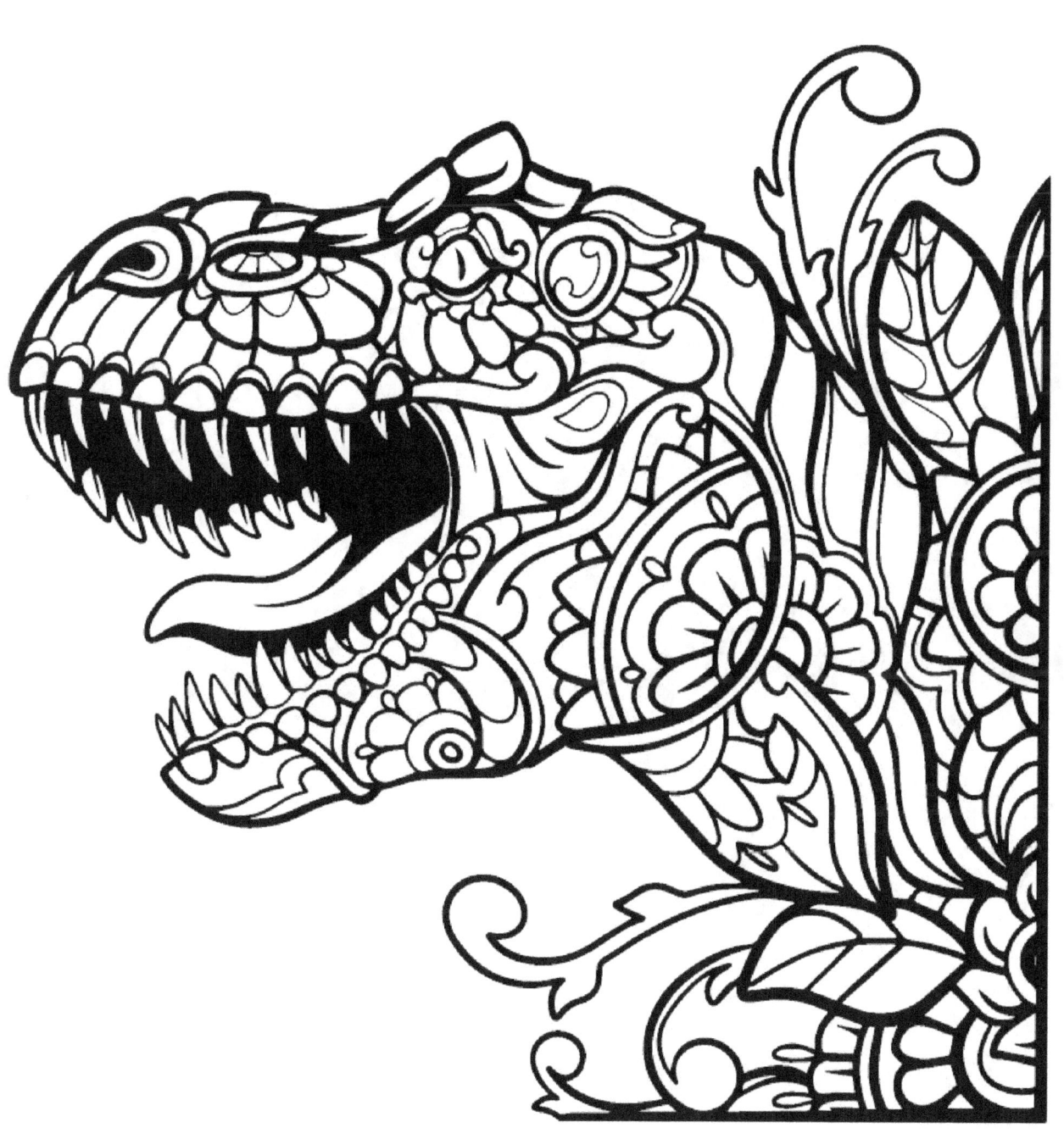